I0823046

POISONED IVIES

POISONED IVIES

THE INSIDE ACCOUNT OF THE ACADEMIC AND MORAL ROT AT AMERICA'S ELITE UNIVERSITIES

ELISE STEFANIK

THRESHOLD EDITIONS
New York Amsterdam/Antwerp London
Toronto Sydney/Melbourne New Delhi

Threshold Editions
An Imprint of Simon & Schuster, LLC
1230 Avenue of the Americas
New York, NY 10020

First Threshold Editions hardcover edition April 2026

THRESHOLD EDITIONS and colophon are registered trademarks of Simon & Schuster, LLC

Interior design by Silverglass

Manufactured in the United States of America

10 9 8 7 6 5 4 3 2 1

Library of Congress Control Number has been applied for.

ISBN 978-1-6680-8753-4
ISBN 978-1-6680-8755-8 (ebook)

To Sam, the light of my life

CONTENTS

INTRODUCTION

America's higher education system is in the midst of a historic reckoning. The compact that existed for generations between our republic, the American people, and our institutions of higher learning has irrevocably broken down. Universities once dedicated to the pursuit of truth and academic excellence have become centers of radical political indoctrination—all while being generously subsidized by hardworking American taxpayers.

Americans of both parties, college-educated and non-college-educated, have lost faith in our universities at a staggering pace. A September 2025 Gallup poll revealed an astonishing trend; only about one-third (35 percent) of Americans today think that a college education is "very important." That's a rapid drop from 2019, when 53 percent of Americans agreed with that proposition. In 2010, it was 75 percent.[1]

This hasn't happened in a vacuum. Colleges and universities across the country have actively undermined their standing in the public imagination. They have chosen to embolden the most radical members of their faculty and staff. They have forced the divisive and discriminatory "Diversity, Equity, and Inclusion" (DEI) regime as gospel. They have proactively silenced and canceled students and teachers who disagree with the groupthink progressive political agenda.

Just look at the data. Democrat faculty outnumber Republicans by at least eight-to-one at any major university. And political bias isn't the only troubling issue. More than one-third (34 percent) of college students now say "using violence to stop campus speech" is acceptable.[2] This is an absolutely stunning statistic and even more disturbing after the nation saw the horrific footage of Charlie Kirk's assassination on a university campus during one of his iconic college tours where the main purpose of the event was to engage in respectful discourse and peaceful debate. Many on the

Left, including some Democrat elected officials, viciously celebrated the loss of this young man's life, saying it was somehow justified and deserved. This is a deeply disturbing and dangerous turning point for our national fabric and political culture.

Activism has come at the cost of education. Students are not learning the skills in the classroom that once defined a college graduate. Not only are they showing up academically unprepared, but they are leaving uneducated, unemployable, radicalized, and deeply out of touch with American values. Approximately one-third of college students require remedial classes before they begin earning credits.[3] But once they start taking classes, grade inflation is worse than ever.[4] They know less, but get better grades, than previous generations. More than 60 percent of college students admit to cheating.[5]

Meanwhile, college tuition has increased at a preposterous rate as the value of a degree has declined. The average college student leaves school saddled with $40,000 of debt.[6] A mere 30 percent of 2025 college graduates found entry-level jobs in their chosen field, while nearly half felt unprepared even to apply for entry-level jobs.[7]

The American people are smart. We know that something has gone catastrophically wrong, and we are tired of being asked to foot the exorbitant bill on autopilot for a broken system that morphs students into anti-American zealots.

This didn't happen overnight. The tremors leading up to this earthquake have offered warning signs for decades. An education system that was the envy of the world is now facing questions of its importance, quality, and meaning. A course correction is long overdue—so overdue, in fact, that the questions are no longer about minor improvements and reform; they have become existential. Questions such as: Are American colleges educating or indoctrinating? Can higher education even be reformed, or do we need to completely rebuild it from scratch? What is being taught in the classrooms, and why? When colleges and universities lose their way, how do we hold them accountable? How much foreign money is funding American higher education? Is a traditional college education even remotely worth the absurdly out-of-reach tuition price tag? Are these "elite" colleges and universities even worth saving? Americans are right to ask these hard questions. And the toughest questions are being posed to the most "elite" schools.

The most prestigious colleges and universities in America make up what is known colloquially as the Ivy League. The Ivy League, nestled in the Northeast and scattered across New England, is made up of Harvard, Yale, Princeton, Columbia, University of Pennsylvania, Dartmouth, Brown, and Cornell. While each university has its own distinct character with unique qualities, these institutions taken as a group have historically been considered the bellwether and compass of American higher education. They set the standards and norms that other universities aspire to achieve, not just in the United States, but around the world.

Historically, Ivy League colleges were known for their institutional prestige, academic excellence, esteemed faculty, rigorous and extremely selective admissions processes, groundbreaking research, and extraordinarily successful alumni networks. Attending an Ivy League school was supposed to guarantee professional success for graduates. They were the crown jewels of the entire higher education system worldwide. For generations, admission to an Ivy League school meant winning a golden ticket to the American dream.

Today, that once-pristine reputation has been sullied. Most Americans understand the Ivy League schools as something different. Instead of bastions of knowledge and vibrant intellectual life, they are considered hotbeds of radical ideology, groundless elitism, intellectual laziness, and anti-American hatred. The reputation of these schools has declined dramatically. It has been poisoned.

This process of institutional decay, almost entirely self-inflicted, culminated in a once-in-a-generation congressional hearing on antisemitism with university presidents in December 2023. This was the moment Americans decided that enough was enough. Our universities were failing us and our next generation of leaders.

At that hearing, a single line of questioning revealed the depths of the moral and academic rot in higher education. The presidents of Harvard, University of Pennsylvania (UPenn), and Massachusetts Institute of Technology (MIT) were asked to testify before Congress on the wave of antisemitism on their campuses after Hamas's terrorist attack against Israel on October 7, 2023. One question went viral and quickly became the most viewed congressional testimony in United States history. It was truly the hearing heard around the world.

I know because I asked the question.

"Does calling for the genocide of Jews violate your university's code of conduct on bullying or harassment?"

This was not a political question. It was a moral one. I thought it would be the easiest, most straightforward question of the hearing.

I assumed their answers would be a resounding yes.

But to my shock, the presidents of MIT, UPenn, and Harvard, arguably the most prestigious universities in the world, answered one after another deadpan and nearly verbatim: "It depends on the context."

And the world heard.

Their morally bankrupt answers astonished everyone who heard them, including me. These university presidents were supposed to be some of the most learned, intelligent people in America, if not the entire world. They were the people responsible for teaching the next generation of leaders in every field imaginable. They were the leaders of the most prestigious universities in the world. My immediate reaction was apparent to everyone watching. I couldn't hide my shock. I questioned them further, asking them to elaborate on what they meant—giving them an opportunity to correct the record and state the obvious. And still, they refused to give a clear statement. They refused to state clearly that calling for the genocide of Jews violated their universities' codes of conduct.

I knew immediately that this was a significant hearing. I didn't realize in the moment, however, that it would become a historic earthquake that instantly reshaped the debate on higher education overnight. The hearing changed the trajectory of higher education. In the weeks and months that followed, campuses exploded into riotous antisemitic encampments. Subpoenas poured into campuses as Congress opened multiple investigations. Scandal-plagued university presidents and compromised trustees resigned. Campus chaos shaped a presidential election.

Today, as a result of this hearing, elite campuses are in the midst of a generational upheaval. Governance structures are in question. Faculty and curricula are under scrutiny. Billions of dollars in foreign funding have been exposed. The long-standing relationship between the federal government and universities is being revised. Matriculation trends are shifting. Nothing is the same.

Nor should it be. Our hearing reset the course of American higher education. It was a reset that I firmly believe was long overdue.

This book tells the inside story of what is happening on America's campuses and why. It goes in depth, with an insider's view, into the deep moral and intellectual rot in higher education. What began as a question about antisemitism triggered a watershed moment.

In the long term, the hearing lit the match for not only accountability, but a far-reaching educational reform movement that has only just begun. This very dark chapter for American colleges and universities can and must lead to light at the end of the tunnel. Our institutions of higher learning have fundamentally lost their way. They strayed far from their founding missions and grew nearly unrecognizable. But that does not mean that the American people have to settle for this rotted and poisoned status quo.

We can and must fix our higher education system and return our colleges and universities to their founding mission. It is within the American people's power to correct when these schools fundamentally lose their way. And it is our responsibility to ensure that we are educating and not indoctrinating our next generation of leaders. Our colleges and universities should promote academic excellence, intellectual inquiry, and our nation's highest ideals, not left-wing indoctrination, heinous antisemitism, and anti-Americanism. That's why it is important to look at what went wrong in this particular moment in history in painstaking detail. By seeing where and why our most elite schools failed, we can chart a better course for the future.

CHAPTER 1

The Hearing Heard Around the World

"It depends on the context."

—Claudine Gay, Former President of Harvard University, December 5, 2023

While the decay within elite higher education had long taken root for decades, the story leading directly to the congressional hearing itself began half a world away in Israel on the morning of October 7, 2023.

At sunrise that morning, over five thousand Hamas terrorists, the Iranian-backed terrorist group in Gaza, launched a highly disciplined and coordinated attack on Israel. They started with an artillery barrage, launching thousands of rockets over the border. Then they came by land—surging over the border with bulldozers and pickup trucks. They came by sea—landing in boats at the coastal kibbutz of Zikim. They came by air—descending in paragliders on young Israelis gathered to celebrate peace and love at a music festival. The carnage that followed on October 7th constituted the bloodiest day for the Jewish people since the Holocaust. Forty-six Americans were killed by Hamas terrorists.

In Kibbutz Be'eri, Hamas terrorists killed more than 130 people, or more than 10 percent of the total population. At the Nova music festival, an open-air event attended mainly by teenagers and young adults, nearly four hundred civilians, soldiers, and police officers were brutally murdered, many executed at point-blank range. At the kibbutz Kfar Aza, more than sixty residents were killed, including civilians tortured by dismemberment or decapitation.

The barbarity of the atrocities committed by Hamas terrorists is difficult to put into words. Women were raped and butchered. Babies and children were shot. Civilian women, children, and the elderly were ripped from their homes, raped, and massacred. Jewish families were bound together and burned alive. Israeli soldiers were brutally beheaded. Documents recovered from the bodies of dead terrorists included instructions to kill as many Jews as possible. These were atrocities against humanity committed by Hamas terrorists.

Many Hamas terrorists wore body cameras with the purpose of filming the bloody slaughter for use as depraved propaganda. Months later, as a member of Congress, I watched nearly an hour of this horrific body camera footage. Like many of my colleagues, I sobbed. As a mother, daughter, wife, fellow human, and an American, these were scenes of heinous carnage that I will never unsee.

The death toll of that day is well documented, despite the efforts of Hamas sympathizers in the Western Left and their media allies to downplay it or explain it away. More than two days later, by the time the last Hamas terrorist had been expelled from Israel, more than 1,200 innocent people had been killed, including dozens of Americans; approximately 3,400 were wounded, and over 250 had been abducted into Gaza as hostages, including a dozen Americans.

The vast majority of the victims were civilians. Young, old, men, women, children, and babies—the terrorists made no distinction in their slaughter. Some were raped, some were burned alive, some were beheaded. Some were dragged back across the border and into Hamas's hellish catacombs, dark tunnels where some hostages would be tortured in captivity for 738 days. In my many meetings with returned hostages and their families, I listened as the victims described the depths of inhumanity and torture. The pain of the hostages and the families awaiting their return was truly unfathomable.

When the rest of the world awoke to the shocking images and reports coming out of Israel immediately after October 7th, men and women of conscience were horrified by the savagery of the atrocities committed by Hamas terrorists. Yet on America's elite college campuses, arguably among the most "privileged" places in the world, thousands gleefully cheered.

In the days and weeks that followed Hamas's brutal attack—the single bloodiest day for the Jewish people since the Holocaust—colleges across the country played host to scenes reminiscent of Hitler's Germany leading up to World War II. Hamas terrorists were still inside Israel's borders when students and faculty at America's most prestigious institutions of higher learning exploded—not in condemnation, but in celebration.

At universities across the country, young people and their professors took to social media and poured onto campus quads to praise the terrorists. In a paroxysm of bloodlust, pro-Hamas apologists on these so-called elite campuses across America passionately cosplayed Hamas, calling for "intifada" and genocide, with signs saying "Final Solution," while chanting "Death to Israel" and "Death to America."

Students marched in "solidarity" with Hamas terrorists, chanting genocidal ravings about Israel and Jews. At George Washington University, one such genocidal slogan was projected onto the side of a campus building for all to see.[1] At New York University, there were calls to "gas the Jews" and proclamations that "Hitler was right."[2] Some 70 percent of Jews at MIT reported that they felt the need to conceal their religious identity for their safety.[3] At Cooper Union, a pro-Hamas mob surrounded a group of Jewish students, who were forced to barricade themselves in a room in the library while the pro-terrorist harassers violently pounded on the doors.[4]

Nowhere was the antisemitism targeted at American Jews worse than in the hallowed halls of some of the most esteemed universities in the world: the Ivy League. At Columbia, there were chants of "F*** the Jews" alongside those of "Free Palestine." University of Pennsylvania students huddled in fear in their rooms as pro-Hamas protesters threw smoke bombs and called for an "intifada"—violence against Jews.

Harvard University, my own alma mater, was the worst offender of them all and unfortunately set the standard for American higher education's morally bankrupt response, which would quickly unfold like wildfire. Harvard's Jewish students were subject to sustained antisemitic harassment, intimidation, and even violent physical assaults. Only at Harvard was the university's response to the attacks so meticulously well organized, and so sickeningly antisemitic.

The same day as Hamas's terrorist attacks, when the streets of Israeli towns and villages were still littered with pillaged bodies, including those of Americans, and burned and mutilated civilian corpses, more than thirty Harvard campus groups issued a letter titled "Joint Statement by Harvard Palestine Solidarity Groups on the Situation in Palestine" that declared, "We, the undersigned student organizations, hold the Israeli regime entirely responsible for all unfolding violence."[5] It was posted to Instagram the evening of Saturday, October 7, not even twenty-four hours after the Hamas terrorist attacks against Israel.

Some brave students and a handful of faculty condemned the letter, and some student groups later did the honorable thing and removed their signatures. But Harvard University, then led by President Claudine Gay, initially remained silent, refusing to denounce this blatant antisemitic and inhumane attack. Harvard's silence set a tone and stoked a campus environment for Harvard and across America where antisemitism exploded on college campuses, leaving American Jewish students and faculty under serious threat.

Statements like Harvard's, blaming Israel for Hamas's terrorist attack, appeared at colleges and universities across the country—at Rutgers in New Jersey, at UC San Diego, at the University of Minnesota, and at American University in Washington, D.C. In a social media post just hours after news of the attack broke, the Students for Justice of Palestine chapter at UC Berkeley praised "the resistance, the liberation movement," and declared that it "indisputably supports the Uprising." The student group later held a vigil for the "martyrs in Palestine" (i.e., dead Hamas terrorists).[6]

Amid still-incoming reports of the mass slaughter, rape, and kidnapping of American and Israeli Jews, many radical college students in America declared: they had it coming.

The students weren't the only ones. Members of the elite faculty were all too eager to join in. Russell Rickford, an associate professor of history at Cornell, called the Hamas terrorist attacks "energizing" and "exhilarating."[7] Joseph Massad, professor of modern Arab politics and intellectual history at Columbia, praised "the stunning victory of the Palestinian resistance" in an article published a day after the terrorist attack.[8] In response to a post on Bluesky condemning Hamas's attack on Israeli civilians, Zareena Grewal, an anthropologist at Yale, replied: "Settlers are not civilians." Later, she added: "Israel is a murderous, genocidal settler state and Palestinians have every right to resist through armed struggle."[9]

These were only the first expressions of support for Hamas. Faculty all over the country signaled, in ways large and small, that they were aligned with the terrorists. They signed open letters. They occupied buildings. They held classes in pro-Hamas encampments. Many violated their universities' policies and students' civil rights in their insatiable eagerness to show their blatant antisemitism and loyalty to the pro-Hamas cause.

If you're wondering what life was like for American Jewish students and faculty in the weeks that followed, consider the following.

At the University of North Carolina at Chapel Hill, an anti-Israel "Day of Resistance" sponsored by the university's Students for Justice in Palestine chapter was advertised with a flyer that featured the silhouette of a paraglider—a reference to the Hamas fighters who crossed Israel's border by air. The image circulated widely online and was adopted at other schools.[10]

Penn Against the Occupation hosted the "Collective Walk Out for Palestine," a rally on campus. One speaker demanded Jews "go back to Moscow, and Brooklyn and f**king Berlin where you came from." According to a lawsuit filed against the university, protesters harassed a Jewish student wearing a yarmulke and shouted profanities at other Jewish students wearing Star of David necklaces. Masked protesters at the edge of the rally told one Jewish student, "You're a dirty little Jew, you deserve to die."[11]

At New York University, students held a silent vigil in support of Israel on the perimeter of a SJP-sponsored "Rally for Palestine" in Manhattan's Washington Square Park. Pro-Palestinian protesters made throat-slitting gestures, shouted, "Hitler was right!" and "Gas the Jews!," and threatened to rape them.[12]

In Washington, D.C., several students returned to their dorms at American University to find swastikas drawn on their doors.[13]

At Cornell, messages posted to an online forum included a commenter who threatened to "bring an assault rifle to campus and shoot all you pig jews." The university's Center for Jewish Living issued urgent warnings to students to stay away from the building and the campus kosher dining hall.

At UPenn in early November, several staff members received an email threatening a mass shooting against UPenn's Jewish community, specifically its Hillel Center.[14]

That's only the first month after October 7, 2023, a small sample of countless instances of antisemitic intimidation, assault, vandalism, and more. Across the country, American Jewish students and faculty were threatened, harassed, bullied, assaulted, and worse.

For many American students, accessing basic university services became difficult, even dangerous.

At UCLA, pro-Hamas rioters encamped between the iconic Royce Hall and the Powell Library, the main undergraduate library, and established a "Jew Exclusion Zone." The encampers set up checkpoints and barriers, refusing to let students through unless they disavowed the State of Israel's right to exist. Those who agreed were given wristbands. Students who refused were prevented from walking through the encampment, effectively cutting off their access to the library and to certain classrooms.[15]

At Yale, protesters forcibly blocked Jewish students from crossing one of the campus's quads. When a Jewish student tried to document a pro-Hamas rally, she was stabbed in the eye with a Palestinian flag by a protester and had to be rushed to the hospital. Nearby police failed to intervene.[16]

Violently taking over university buildings and property became a dangerous and regular feature of the campus chaos.

Hundreds of protesters stormed the UCLA School of Law amid chants of "Death to Jews!" Earlier on the same day, a "UC Divest" rally featured an effigy of Israeli Prime Minister Benjamin Netanyahu that was used as a piñata. At least one protester was heard shouting, "Beat that f**ing Jew!"[17]

In late April 2024, pro-Hamas protesters, including some faculty, occupied Princeton's historic Clio Hall for several hours. Several of them were arrested, although charges were eventually dismissed.

At Columbia, the day after the Princeton incident, the pro-Hamas encampment occupied the historic Hamilton Hall for twenty-four hours, until the NYPD was finally allowed by the university to secure the building. During their destructive romp, the rioters caused extensive property damage and assaulted and abused a university janitor who was helplessly caught in the chaos when the mob invaded the building.

And, of course, there was the horror at Cooper Union in Manhattan. Jewish students were forced to barricade themselves inside the school's library for safety when masked protesters surrounded the building and began banging on the outside glass and shouting at them.

Imagine being an American Jewish student or faculty member trying to learn, teach, and participate in campus life under these circumstances. Imagine being any student trying to learn, teach, and participate in campus life under these circumstances. In the weeks and months after October 7th, students and faculty found themselves in the middle of a waking nightmare.

These episodes were attacks on fellow Americans solely because they were Jewish. These students and faculty were targeted not for anything they had said or done, but for who they were. The shocking reality was that the echoes of the horror of 1930s Germany were being felt in the 2020s in the United States of America.

How did university leaders respond?

They did not condemn the pro-Hamas encampments nor the riotous takeover of campus property. They did not condemn the sustained antisemitic attacks and physical assaults on Jewish students. They did not discipline the perpetrators of this vile antisemitism who had clearly broken university rules. Instead they responded with academically lazy moral bankruptcy.

Emails and text messages that our congressional committee subpoenaed showed that many university presidents engaged in tortured conversations with trustees, fellow administrators, and staff about the politically correct (i.e., morally bankrupt) way to react to the attacks and the emerging pro-Hamas riots.

Ivy League administrators, from presidents on down, did not want to confront the antisemitic protesters who were creating havoc on their campuses. Some were cowardly. Some supported and wanted to encourage the protesters. What they did not do, or want to do, was come to the defense of Jewish students. When American students became the targets of sustained antisemitic harassment and even violence—that is to say, when open antisemitism began parading around Ivy League campuses—university leaders silently looked the other way.

As members of Congress, we have the responsibility to hold universities and their leaders accountable when they violate federal law. It didn't take long for us to start hearing from students, faculty, and university employees about the scourge of antisemitism taking place on college campuses—a violation of civil rights and of the universities' obligation to safeguard those rights. It was crystal clear to me from the get-go that university leaders were failing to lead and needed to be held accountable. I knew we needed to haul these university presidents in front of Congress.

I encouraged my colleague Virginia Foxx from North Carolina, the highly revered chair of the House Education and the Workforce Committee, to host a hearing with presidents of the highest-profile universities who set the morally repugnant tone that ignited the scourge of antisemitism reverberating across higher education. There was no question in my mind that the unflappable Dr. Foxx would be up to this job.

A dear friend and a mentor, Virginia has a spine of steel and a heart of pure gold. Virginia Foxx is a no-nonsense, legendary member of Congress not just among Republicans, but across the aisle. One of Virginia's close friends and mentors is former Speaker John Boehner, who described her this way: "She's just a bull, and she just charges in every day, nonstop, from sun up until way after the sun goes down."[18] At age eighty-two, Virginia puts many fellow members of Congress to shame with her dogged work ethic and determination. She keeps a packed schedule that would tire out even the spriteliest Gen-Z movers and shakers.

Virginia's extraordinary personal story and path to Congress is one of American true grit and educational opportunity. Born to Italian

American parents in the Bronx, Virginia would share her memories with me of speaking fluent Italian with her grandmother who spoke no English. Virginia was raised by her parents in the mountains of Appalachia with no running water and no power. Her dedicated and loving parents had only ninth-grade educations. Virginia would go on to be the first in her family to graduate from high school, and she worked her way up to the highest halls of Congress by her bootstraps. She worked as a janitor, started a small business with her husband, earned her bachelor's, master's, and doctorate, taught in the classroom, and served as a president of a community college. Virginia ran unsuccessfully for school board, then was elected to the state senate and then Congress. She deeply understands the tremendous opportunity American higher education has to change the course of your life—she lived it herself.

Virginia was a kindred spirit in sharing my deep concern that American higher education had morally and academically lost its way and that the antisemitism exploding on elite college campuses was the canary in the coal mine exposing the intellectual and moral rot infecting American academia and in turn the students who would go on to be our next generation of leaders.

The hearing, titled "Holding Campus Leaders Accountable and Confronting Antisemitism," was booked by Chairwoman Virgina Foxx for December 5, 2023—less than two months after the Hamas terrorist attack on Israel. The witness list included the presidents of Harvard, UPenn, and MIT. Notably, one witness was not included because they were unavailable due to a scheduling conflict. That was Columbia's president. More on that later in this book.

Our three witnesses—Claudine Gay, then president of Harvard; Liz Magill, then president of UPenn; and Sally Kornbluth, president (then and now) of MIT—led three of the most prestigious universities in the world. And it was clear to me that they were directly responsible for the failure to address the college campus crisis of antisemitism. What was happening on their campuses was a travesty and a disgrace, and it unmasked how truly anti-American and out of touch these elite institutions had become. They had failed to lead these institutions, and they deserved tough questions from Congress.

I expected these university presidents to come armed with lawyers and lobbyists who had prepped them to oblivion. I expected them to have well-prepared and rehearsed answers to easily anticipated questions. I expected them to double down on their excuses for permitting and stoking the rise of antisemitism engulfing their institutions. I expected that the mainstream media would give them cover. After all, our elite chattering class had to protect their own and would continue to sugarcoat and insist that there was no antisemitism problem on American campuses.

What I did not expect was what actually happened at the hearing. Throughout my decade serving in Congress, I have been in some of the highest-profile hearings imaginable: Cabinet secretaries under oath, tech leaders sputtering, blockbuster hearings on election integrity and the Russia collusion hoax, and front and center in historic impeachment hearings. But I had never participated in a hearing quite like this one, where complete moral bankruptcy was on full, obvious display. And the truth is, I almost wasn't able to attend.

The night before the hearing, I had started to come down with a severe flu. Attempting to ignore it, after my two-year-old son Sam went to sleep, I stayed up late working through reams of research that I had worked with my staff to pull together. Hundreds of pages of insider accounts from students on what was happening on college campuses were supplemented by my own materials collected with close college friends and fellow alumni who were still deeply in touch with the goings-on at Harvard. I pre-drafted several rounds of questions based on this research and firsthand accounts. I called a few longtime key contacts and policy experts who I knew were following what was happening at these college campuses as closely as I was. They gave helpful suggestions and feedback. I went to sleep well past midnight hoping to feel better in the morning.

On the day of the hearing, I woke up at 5:30 a.m. with one of the worst flus that I've ever had. But I knew how important the day was for so many brave students who had come forward and shared their horrific experiences facing antisemitism on campus. Armed with Kleenex, cough drops, and doused with over-the-counter cold medicine, I was at the FOX News studio by 6:30 a.m. for a *Fox & Friends* interview to preview the importance of the hearing. After the media hit, I attended my weekly Republican members' House Intelligence Committee meeting in the classified SCIF (sensitive compartmented information facility). At 9 a.m., I chaired the weekly House Republican Conference meeting with all Republican members of Congress. When serving in top leadership as Conference chair, I was responsible for chairing this weekly meeting, which is the only time all Republican House members come together when Congress is in session. I was responsible for leading and developing the communications and messaging strategy for the House Republicans, working closely with the Speaker of the House, Majority Leader, and Majority Whip on a daily basis. After gaveling out the hour-long Conference meeting, I kicked off and led the weekly Republican leadership press conference at the Capitol. And then I had a few minutes to clear my head to prepare for the hearing, walking swiftly with my box of Kleenex, which you can see in the hearing footage, and taking my seat on the top dais in the Education Committee room.

Harvard, UPenn, and MIT's presidents were escorted in and sat at the witness table under oath. Students who had come forward to the committee recounting their horrific experiences on these campuses sat in the rows directly behind the witnesses. The room was packed to the brim. Members all took their assigned committee seats. The press was crawling and crouching down on the floor to take photos of the witnesses. Spectators in the audience were riveted. Millions of Americans tuned in live.

Chairwoman Foxx dropped the gavel to begin.

The hearing lasted the entire day.

Early in the hearing, I had focused my initial five minutes of questions on Harvard's President Claudine Gay, as I was the most invested and connected to what had been happening on Harvard's campus. I came at the hearing from the perspective not only as a congresswoman, but also as a Harvard graduate, the first in my immediate family to even have the opportunity to graduate from college.

What was happening at Harvard was unrecognizable to me from my experience as an undergraduate student nearly two decades earlier. I asked President Claudine Gay direct questions about Harvard's failure to combat antisemitism, the discriminatory double standard applied toward Jewish students, and Harvard's hypocrisy of hiding behind its sudden defense of free speech when they had consistently ranked at or near the dead bottom of free speech ratings for years. I think that because of the effectiveness of my initial questions, during the course of the hearing, other Republican members yielded me their remaining time so I could ask more rounds of questions. That happened organically and was not planned, and I am grateful to my colleagues for the opportunity.

Throughout the hearing, I felt that the university presidents were squirreling out of giving direct answers. The whole hearing felt like this. The three presidents were evasive and lawyerly. They leaned on canned prepared lines and bureaucrat-speak. They couldn't bring themselves to utter a real word condemning the antisemitism that was raging on their campuses.

The crucial moment came in the last three minutes of the hearing. I want to take you behind the scenes of that moment. After many hours, the hearing paused temporarily for House votes, which is when members leave the committee room and go to the House floor to cast legislative votes on behalf of our constituents. I happened to run into my Republican colleague Erin Houchin, a hardworking congresswoman from Indiana, during these votes on the House floor. At the time, Erin was a newly elected freshman and filled the most junior seat on the Education Committee. I have known Erin for many years and supported her when she first ran for Congress and lost nearly a decade ago. Eventually, Erin would win her seat in Congress and go on to serve as a great teammate and a very effective representative for her constituents. Erin asked me if I was going back to the hearing. She said that if I was, she would yield any of her extra time to me to close out the hearing.

I will be honest, I hesitated because at this point at the end of the day, I had already asked more questions than anyone else and I was uncertain what additional revelatory information I would be able to uncover. I hesitated because I had other scheduled meetings. I hesitated because I was so frustrated with the university presidents' vague and unacceptable answers. And I hesitated because I still had that horrible flu. I turned to my longtime loyal chief of staff Patrick, and we agreed and I said, "Yes, I think I might try one more round of questions." I share this because the question heard around the world almost didn't happen.

When I came back from voting on the House floor, the hearing room was almost completely empty. Everyone had seen enough. The press who had packed the room in the morning had all but disappeared. There were a few scattered people left in the audience along with Chairwoman Virginia Foxx, the ranking Democrat Congressman Bobby Scott, freshman Congresswoman Erin Houchin, the university presidents, a small handful of other members, and me.

Still unclear whether I would even have a chance to ask any questions, depending on whether Erin used her full five minutes, my mind remained on the exchanges from the morning.

I thought to myself, *How can I ask this in a very simple way, a moral way, that will force them to answer YES?*

I quickly scratched out a question in pencil on a scrap of paper, barely legible.

"Does calling for the genocide of Jews violate your university's code of conduct?"

Simple. Straightforward. Not political. I expected them each to say "Yes." In fact, I assumed they would say yes without hesitation. And my plan was to follow up with a question on what disciplinary action they had taken against those who violated the code of conduct.

Turns out, I wouldn't get the opportunity for the follow-up.

Not in a million years did I imagine their response.

MIT's president Sally Kornbluth admitted that she had heard chants that might be antisemitic "depending on the context." But she couldn't commit. UPenn's Liz Magill hedged and smiled when asked about genocide. It was, she said, a "context-dependent decision." Harvard President Claudine Gay said over and over again regarding calling for the genocide of Jews: "It depends on the context."

That was how the three university presidents responded.

Across all three campuses, terrorist-sympathizing students and faculty were calling for the eradication of Jews at home and abroad. That was the "context."

The leaders of America's most prestigious institutions of higher learning flunked the most basic moral test imaginable.

I was stunned. Truly astonished.

The question was not a political one, it was a moral one. And it was a question that if you asked everyday Americans, they would know how to answer correctly. I thought of my approximately seven hundred thousand constituents—take a mom, a farmer, and a small business worker from Upstate New York. All three would know without hesitation how to answer the question with an unequivocal yes. You don't need an Ivy League degree to know that calling for the genocide of Jews is wrong and does not depend on the context. Yet these three university presidents of the most elite colleges on Earth utterly failed the most basic test of humanity, intellectual fortitude, and moral compass. And in that moment, they exposed the deep rot in the fabric of American education that had been brewing for generations.

Their disgraceful attempt to contextualize genocide of Jews was a symptom of decades of moral decay, intellectual laziness, and dangerous radical groupthink at so-called elite institutions across society. The fact that they essentially mimicked one another to give nearly verbatim the same answer—"it depends on the context"—encapsulated to me the depth of academic indolence and lack of independent thinking that have perverted our college campuses.

It would later be revealed that all three university president witnesses were prepped by the same overpriced law firm: WilmerHale. Almost worse than their answers was the fact that they didn't even understand in the actual moment that what they had said was so morally wrong. Upon reflection, one of the most disturbing parts of the hearing was that after my final question and their unacceptably perverse answers, which concluded the hearing, the three university presidents stood up and went on their way acting certain that they had answered the question correctly.

Little did they know that the hearing would set off an unprecedented, gigantic earthquake.

As I walked back to my office, I called my longtime senior political advisor Alex and said: “I think I just asked an important question that led to a very important moment in that hearing.” My staff quickly scrambled to get up to speed. Other than my chief of staff, Patrick, most of my staff were busy doing constituent services or other legislative work, unaware that I had even gone back for additional questions, so they did not see the final moments of the hearing live. I knew it was a significant moment because I was so stunned, but I couldn’t fathom how big it would become, and how quickly.

Video of my exchange with the three university presidents went viral across all social media platforms at warp speed. By the end of one week, the video would rack up more than 1 billion views, shattering all records of congressional testimony in history. That number would climb to the multiple billions in short order.

Calls echoing my demand for the university presidents’ resignations were swift and overwhelming. The cacophony of condemnations went from the highest-ranking elected officials and candidates like President Trump who had watched the hearing closely, to corporate titans, prominent university board members and donors, and everyday people across the country and around the world. It ignited a flame across the political spectrum of real-world America. Republicans’ condemnation was near universal and immediate.

Of course, there were a handful of the usual apologists in the mainstream media doing cleanup for the Left, claiming it was a carefully laid “trap” or a gotcha question. It wasn’t even a prepared question. I specifically worded it to be an easy, straightforward moral question. Despite these efforts by some in the media, the pressure was immense to condemn the university presidents. Even the White House under President Joe Biden felt compelled to distance itself from the university presidents’ comments. “It’s unbelievable that this needs to be said: Calls for genocide are monstrous and antithetical to everything we represent as a country,” said a White House spokesman.

Democrat Governor Josh Shapiro of Pennsylvania, who is Jewish, declared UPenn President Liz Magill’s comments “unacceptable.” The day after the hearing he told reporters: "It should not be hard to condemn genocide, genocide against Jews, genocide against anyone else. I've said many times, leaders have a responsibility to speak and act with moral clarity, and Liz Magill failed to meet that simple test. There should be no nuance to that—she needed to give a one-word answer."

Even Harvard Law School Professor Laurence Tribe admitted that the hearing was alarming: "I'm no fan of @RepStefanik but I'm with her here," he wrote on X, the social media platform formerly known as Twitter. "Claudine Gay's hesitant, formulaic, and bizarrely evasive answers were deeply troubling to me and many of my colleagues, students, and friends."[19]

But it wasn't just politicians and academics. What was so astonishing was just how much the hearing permeated popular culture.

Dave Portnoy, a popular sports and politics commentator, entrepreneur, and the owner of the Barstool Sports franchise, called for the resignation of the university presidents and swore never to hire another Harvard graduate.[20] David Schwimmer, who famously played Ross on the hit sitcom *Friends*, posted footage of the exchange on his Instagram page.[21]

Billboards went up in Israel in Jerusalem. My chief of staff's email crashed daily for months as he received hundreds of thousands of emails in various languages referencing the hearing. I've been in plenty of high-profile hearings, but I had never experienced a hearing like this one. In a single moment, the moral bankruptcy of an entire educational system was exposed. And it caught the whole country's and the world's attention.

For the next few months, the hearing and its fallout saturated the news. There were endless headlines, op-eds, think pieces, essays, podcasts, television appearances, all on repeat analyzing the aftermath of the hearing and its repercussions. It even led to what would become known as *Saturday Night Live*'s (*SNL*) worst cold open ever (more later in the book). It was everywhere all the time.

The university presidents desperately tried to do damage control, but it was too little, too late. The world had heard their answers. They had been exposed.

Four days after the hearing, Liz Magill was forced to resign as president of UPenn after her floundering attempt to do damage control. The pressure had been intense. Just twenty-four hours after the hearing, more than three thousand people affiliated with the university had signed a petition calling for her resignation. Major donors had threatened to withhold further contributions—more than $100 million worth. Pennsylvania's Governor Shapiro urged university trustees to meet immediately to address the situation.

"One down, two to go," I tweeted.[22]

The writing was on the wall.

Harvard's President Claudine Gay held out a little longer. In the days following the hearing, faculty, alumni, and the Fellows of the Harvard Corporation rallied to Gay's defense. It was less than a week after the hearing when multiple sources uncovered an extensive history of alleged plagiarism by Gay across her academic career.

Less than one month later, on January 2, 2024, Gay was forced to resign.

Two down.

As for the third of our witnesses, Sally Kornbluth clung on to her post and is still the embattled president of MIT.

But the consequences of my exchange with university presidents at the hearing were far more than the subsequent resignations of these particular university presidents. Our hearing launched a reckoning in higher education that has only just begun. It led to an unprecedented congressional investigation with more university president hearings leading to even more resignations. This oversight revealed not only the systemic antisemitism, but the larger crisis within American higher education.

Within the week, I passed a resolution in Congress condemning the college presidents' testimony and calling for their resignations. It passed 303–126, an overwhelmingly bipartisan vote—a rarity in today's Washington.

The House Committee on Education and the Workforce hired dedicated investigators and allocated resources to help deliver transparency and accountability. The committee hired an exceptionally talented lead investigator, Ari Wisch, who did yeoman's work with our office to dig deep into these universities. Subpoenas started flying out the door. University faculty, staff, students, and board members sat for depositions. The universities were forced to turn over to the committee more than one hundred thousand documents. We uncovered foreign donations to universities, and how foreign donors were influencing university policy in ways that hurt American students. We examined the federal accreditation system, which helped enforce progressive ideology at universities under the guise of "accountability." We investigated universities' countless assaults on viewpoint diversity and free speech, especially under the DEI regime. We looked at the erosion of academic integrity. And, of course, we devoted significant resources to a fulsome assessment of the comprehensive failure to protect American Jewish students, faculty, and staff.

What was started in Congress went into hyperdrive with the second inauguration of President Donald J. Trump. I know firsthand that President Trump had been watching what was happening on American college campuses closely. He also followed the hearing in real time, as well as the news at each university. He and I spoke many times in depth about this particular subject, both in person and on the phone, about the hearing testimony and the situation at each school. He was typically one of the first calls or texts I would receive when another university president resigned or there was breaking news related to these hearings. People often forget and the media often tries to brush it under the rug that President Trump himself is a graduate of the prestigious Wharton Business School at the University of Pennsylvania. He knows the Ivy League very well, as do his children and many of his closest, longtime business friends, particularly those from New York. Some of them have experienced elite academia's prejudices firsthand. All were universally appalled at how far these once-great institutions had fallen.

Combatting antisemitism and digging out the rot in higher education became a mainstay of President Trump's messaging and rallies on the campaign trail. It became an incredibly important part of his platform of promises to the American people. This hearing resonated in such an intense way that to this day, whether it is in my district in rural Upstate

New York or delivering a keynote speech at the Republican National Convention in Milwaukee, consistently the loudest applause line from voters comes when I reference my important questions from the hearing. It struck a chord that continues to reverberate around the world.

With the stroke of his pen on Day One of his second term, President Trump kept good on his promise to combat antisemitism and began establishing policies that have already transformed the landscape of higher education. Building on my questions and our congressional investigation, the Trump administration launched major investigations of universities that failed to protect American Jewish students and were out of compliance with federal policies. Some, like Harvard and Columbia, had lawsuits filed against them. Many more have had billions of dollars of federal contracts, including research dollars, frozen or ended. The Trump Department of Justice established a multiagency Task Force to Combat Anti-Semitism. "Anti-Semitism in any environment is repugnant to this Nation's ideals," declared Senior Counsel to the Assistant Attorney General for Civil Rights Leo Terrell. "The Department takes seriously our responsibility to eradicate this hatred wherever it is found. The Task Force to Combat Anti-Semitism is the first step in giving life to President Trump's renewed commitment to ending anti-Semitism in our schools."[23]

In less than one year, because of the higher education oversight work of Congress, the Trump administration has reached or is in talks to reach many multi-hundred-million-dollar settlements with universities in the Ivy League and beyond.

Parents and college students are also voting with their feet and their wallets. They're abandoning the poisoned Ivies and so-called elite academia for sunnier, politically friendlier, and more affordable destinations. What's happening right now is the most important moment in American higher education in generations. These schools proved incapable of fixing themselves. But under pressure from the federal government and from the self-inflicted mistakes of a forced radical ideology, American higher education, especially elite academia, is being transformed.

Why did the hearing garner so much attention—not just from politicians and academics, but everyone from pop culture icons to everyday Americans? Why did so many people—people who had never watched a second of congressional testimony before—watch this, post it, share it?

I believe it's because the university presidents' answers summed up something ordinary Americans have known for a long time. Our elite higher educational institutions, founded on timeless academic aspirations, are now fundamentally broken. They have fundamentally lost their way. They've succumbed to decades of moral decay, academic laziness, and radical groupthink. They've become hollow, empty, soulless. And so have their leaders. When the opportunity came to speak truth clearly and courageously, the leaders of some of our most coveted institutions failed. They acted like a brainwashed herd, all trotting out the same lawyerly verbiage and bureaucratic talking points. They exposed the moral bankruptcy that has rotted these institutions from the inside out. These once-great institutions, many of which predate the founding of our nation, have fallen so far from their founding missions.

This book is a deep dive into what happened on the most storied American campuses in the aftermath of October 7th. These elite schools, revered for their rich history and important contributions to our nation's identity, were among the worst offenders propelling the scourge of antisemitism. The events in question were a seminal turning point in higher education. This book investigates how we got here and charts the path ahead to save American higher education.

Americans want, and deserve, better. Americans want clear moral leadership. They want institutions that embody and strive for academic excellence, prize independent thinking, value basic decency, prioritize American students, and that are not anti-American and anti-West. Americans want academic exceptionalism, not indoctrination.

This was never about a few presidents or a few universities. It's not just about antisemitism.

It's about saving American higher education, because it has proven incapable of saving itself.

CHAPTER 2

Harvard

Founded 1636
Veritas
"Truth"

"The Ivory Tower is often used to dismiss academia, and the metaphor is rarely examined for its virtue. Ivory is a natural substance that is rare, precious, and pure. It's also fragile: An ivory tower probably wouldn't stand without a mix of steel and concrete. It signifies a university that is indeed in society but towers above it because it seeks to find truth out of what society takes for granted. A university doesn't possess truth as much as it honors it. Society's interest above all is justice—the Declaration of Independence states "self-evident" truths that serve justice—and society surely wants its justice to be true, but it doesn't honor truth as Harvard does by having 'Veritas' as its motto."

—Harvey Mansfield, Professor of Government, Harvard University, *Wall Street Journal,* **January 11, 2024**[1]

Founded in the seventeenth century by Puritan leaders of the Massachusetts Bay Colony, Harvard's original mission was to educate and train a literate clergy to lead the Puritan ministry for future generations. These religious underpinnings were etched in the first known Harvard seal, adorned with the Latin words *In Christi Gloriam*, meaning "to the glory of Christ." Additional historic documents reflect Harvard's original intent, demonstrating the explicitly moral and spiritual founding principles of the university. Even two hundred years later, when Harvard updated its seal, the university introduced the motto *Veritas Christo et Ecclesiae*, which translates to "Truth in Christ and the Church." The motto was shortened to *Veritas* or "Truth," which is what it is today. To me, this etymological genealogy shows that at Harvard, the meaning of *Veritas* is "moral truth."

After Harvard's founding in 1636, other universities quickly followed. These pre–Revolutionary War colonial colleges scattered across New England mostly shared Harvard's explicitly evangelical religious beginning. In New Haven, Connecticut, Yale was founded by conservative Congregationalists. The first Princetonians were New Jersey Presbyterians. Brown was started in Providence, Rhode Island, by pious Baptists, and in Hanover, New Hampshire, evangelicals commissioned Dartmouth.

During the Revolutionary War, most of America's Ivy League colleges served as pillars of academic excellence and bastions of moral clarity fueling the people's quest for independence. Leveraging the teachings of John Locke and Jean-Jacques Rousseau, Harvard's curricula bolstered America's fight for freedom and democracy. Harvard's early founding years were so quintessential to America's founding story that the British feared the colonial colleges had fomented a spirit of rebellion among American patriots. Founding Fathers like John Adams and John Hancock were educated at Harvard, and General George Washington's Continental Army troops were quartered in the historic Massachusetts Hall, which remains a mainstay of the university today, hosting the Office of the President of Harvard right in the heart of Harvard Yard.

The first time I ever set eyes on Harvard was in 2001. I was on the Charles River, seated in an eight-person crew boat with an oar in my hands. I was seventeen years old. It was the fall of my senior year in high school, and I was a novice member of the Albany Rowing Club team, in one of the least experienced shells competing in an amateur boat in the famed Head of the Charles rowing regatta. While I had played varsity lacrosse for a number of years in high school, I started rowing because I had wanted to try a new sport in my senior year. The crack-of-dawn crew practices on the Hudson River, under the looming gray highways of "787" in downtown Albany, were a new and challenging experience.

But make no mistake, while I always enjoyed sports as a kid, I was not recruited by colleges for athletics. Growing up in Upstate New York, I was an extremely dedicated and academically focused student with a bursting extracurricular calendar and a part-time job. My educational journey began at a nursery school affiliated with a local Catholic church. My elementary school years were an early mix of parochial and public school before my parents transferred me to an all-girls private school in the middle of fourth grade. After months of relentless physical bullying from classmates, my parents were adamant that they would find a school that was a better fit for me academically and socially. They enrolled me in Albany Academy for Girls, a historic and academically rigorous independent day school founded in 1814 that was the oldest continuous all-girls school in the country. At the time when I transferred, the private school tuition for Girls Academy was a significant financial stretch for my hard-working parents, who were also just starting a small business. But they were determined to make it work.

I remember my mother taking me in for a midyear school tour and an initial visit with the admissions officer. I took the admissions test, and the school administrators discussed how they were concerned that I would likely be behind other students in the class, and they wanted to wait to see the results of the standardized test. Determined to remove me from my current school's bullying environment, my mother informed Albany Academy for Girls that even if I was behind academically, I was a hard worker, a quick learner, and that I would be in the proper uniform and starting in the classroom on Monday. Whether I would be admitted or not wasn't even up for discussion to my parents, who were set on putting me in a better environment. To this day, their decision remains one of the most important moments in my life.

Both my parents were raised in large, mostly working-class, Catholic families in Upstate New York—my mom is Italian American, and my dad is Polish American. My dad is the youngest of eight kids, and my mom is the middle of nine. My maternal grandfather was a stonemason whose work I can still identify, by his unique artistry, in buildings in

Upstate New York. My paternal grandfather was a truck driver and a mover. My grandmothers were primarily what were then called "housewives"; however, both worked at various times. My maternal grandmother would go on to work in clerical roles at a university, and my paternal grandmother was a practical nurse—i.e., a nurse's aide. Both my parents were working nearly full-time before they were even old enough to consider college. They both graduated from high school and entered the workforce.

My father, Ken, is an extremely hard worker who excelled at sales and understanding products and materials, developing strong and loyal professional relationships with customers over many decades. My mom, Melanie, is extremely smart, driven, intellectually curious, and is one of the most well-read people I know. When I was growing up, my mom took college classes at night when my parents could afford them. She squeezed in courses between running a small business, raising a family, and shuttling my brother and me to our extracurriculars. I remember my father would take my brother and me to a weekly pizza night when my mom had class. To this day, I do not know how or when my mother was able to complete her reading and homework assignments. Years later I asked her, and she said she made time after my brother and I went to bed at night.

Ultimately, neither of my parents had the opportunity to earn a college degree. They are two of the smartest people I know and certainly the most hardworking. As parents, they showed us unconditional love coupled with endless encouragement and opportunity. I consider it among my greatest blessings in life to have been born to them. Taking a massive risk to start a small business when I was growing up, my parents would go on to build a very successful business from scratch, growing it into one of the largest wholesale distributors of plywood and veneer panel products in the Northeast, selling to millworkers, cabinetmakers, furniture manufacturers, and specialty customers. In their entire thirty-five-plus years of business, there was not a single weekday that the trucks were not on the road delivering materials to customers and that the phone calls were not always answered. Over the weekends, my mom cleaned the office and my dad would reload the trucks if they weren't loaded properly. They both did this into their seventies. My younger brother and I both grew up innately understanding the challenges of running a small business. We knew the importance of answering phones, keeping a clean warehouse, dealing with customers, making deliveries, maintaining inventory, and understanding different types of wood products—plywood, hardwood, edge tape, panel, hinges, melamine, MDF, and veneer. Over the years growing up, my brother helped sweep the warehouse, and I helped my mom file invoices, send faxes, and design and send sale coupons to customers. It is only because of our parents' extraordinary hard work that I had the opportunity to even attend a private school and dream of applying to the top universities in the country, let alone go on to make history serving in Congress.

Because of my encouraging parents, coupled with exceptionally dedicated teachers, a strong school administrative leadership, and a vibrant school life, I absolutely thrived at Albany Academy for Girls. I was actively involved in school clubs, sports, and the arts, in many cases taking on leadership positions as I progressed from lower to middle to upper school. From leading student council to competing in mock trial, volunteering as a school tour guide, singing in the chorus, taking dance classes, playing sports, acting in school plays, and working part-time, I was what prospective colleges then referred to as a well-rounded student.

I truly loved all my classes, and I was supported by the school with a challenging academic course load that, by the time I was a junior and a senior, consisted of numerous Advanced Placement classes, multiple languages, and independent studies. Over the summers, when I wasn't at home playing with my younger brother, which was a lot of the time, I worked part-time in retail at Old Navy, took local community college courses, and participated in academic, athletics, and art camps ranging in theme from dance and lacrosse to robotics and astronomy. To this day, I am incredibly grateful to my teachers for encouraging and cultivating my intellectual curiosity. By far, I am most thankful to my parents, for working so hard to provide any and all opportunities no matter what the barriers. I am a true believer in the life-changing power of high-quality education and the centrally important role of parents in determining the best school and academic opportunities for their children. It is a gift I am determined to give to my son. And it has fueled my passion as a legislator for education reform.

During the fall of my senior year at Girls Academy, I applied to four colleges for what was then known as "Early Action" admission: Harvard, Georgetown, University of Chicago, and MIT. Incredible to think now, I actually handwrote the entirety of my applications except the long essay, which I typed on our family's one central desktop computer. There was no professional admissions consultant who seems to be de rigueur today. I worked with my school and teachers and had all the materials spread out along our family's dining room table at home for weeks. I thought that I might get accepted into Georgetown and the University of Chicago. Early acceptance to Harvard and MIT seemed incredibly daunting, and I assumed that I would be deferred to regular admission to try again.

I was stunned when I was admitted early to all of them.

Years later, after I was first elected to Congress, I would read a book by a left-leaning "journalist" who was teeteringly close to suffering from full-blown stalker syndrome, and whose book purported to be an insider's look at my young life. It definitively stated how I got into Harvard, where I applied, and when I found out I was admitted. It was factually totally wrong, and when my office was given the opportunity to weigh in on the publication fact-checking process, we were actually denied the edits to make it factually correct, because this obsessive hack was apparently more of an expert in my life and childhood than I was—you know, the one who actually lived it. One of the lessons here is to guard the precious memories and stories of your own life, my dear reader!

Here's the truth, and it's interesting in part because it shows a technological snapshot in time of the generation that bridged analog and digital. My senior year of high school was in the early days of email notification for initial college admissions decisions rather than having to wait for letters in the physical mail. High school students typically had their own free Hotmail email account, AOL Instant Messenger (AIM), and Napster accounts, but this was pre-Facebook, pre-Gmail, and well before the social media explosion. My senior year of high school was the first year that Harvard sent out their Early Action admissions decisions via email. On the day that we were supposed to hear the admissions decision from Harvard, I had promised myself that I wasn't going to check my email until I was home after school. But when I talked during lunch period with some classmates who had also applied early, they told me they had received emails and asked if I had heard yet, so I quietly went by myself to the school library computer lab to see. I didn't have anything in my inbox. With a great deal of uncertainty and confusion, I finished the school day wondering why there was no email and then went home. I was by myself when I logged onto the family computer at home, saw the email, and opened it to read the news that I had been accepted Early Action to Harvard. I was stunned, ecstatic, and overwhelmed. I immediately called my parents at their office, my closest high school friend, and my dance teacher Miss Barb at my dance studio whom I had known since I was three years old. This was a life-changing email.

It turned out that this first year that Harvard used email to notify applicants, there were a few glitches. First, they batched the emails by Denied, Deferred, and Accepted, causing delays, so they did not arrive at the same time. Second, and this made the national news, some Harvard admissions decisions were tagged as "junk mail" by all AOL accounts that year. Can you imagine a college acceptance from Harvard going into junk mail? A time capsule anecdote of college admissions at the turn of the millennium.

....

By the late spring of my senior year in high school, in 2002, I was attending what is known as "Pre-Frosh Weekend," when accepted students spend the weekend on Harvard's campus in Cambridge, Massachusetts. I knew a few incoming freshmen from my school, region, and scholarship programs, whom I hung out with, but otherwise I met new friends and attended information sessions learning about classes, concentrations (what

Harvard calls majors), housing, and the extracurricular clubs and organizations, of which there were more than I could have possibly imagined.

In the fall of that year, one year after the September 11th terrorist attacks, I started college as a freshman at Harvard. I arrived on campus one week early to participate in a program called Freshman Fall Clean Up. For the week before school there were a number of pre-freshman orientation programs that you could pay to enroll in: a program for the arts, an outdoor hiking and camping program, and others that cost an additional fee. The Freshman Fall Clean Up was part of Dorm Crew and was the only program where you worked to earn money. For one week before my freshman year, I was part of Dorm Crew, learning my way around campus and making new friends as we literally mopped the floors, scrubbed the toilets, dusted the shelves, and cleaned the dorms to prepare for move-in. I earned enough money doing Freshman Fall Clean Up to pay for my textbooks for the entire year. I loved it, and it was a great way to get acclimated to the campus and meet new classmates.

Overall, my four-year undergraduate experience at Harvard was an overwhelmingly positive one. I concentrated (majored) in government but took elective classes in lots of different departments that suited my broad interests. Looking back, I wish I had taken even more classes outside my major. I had a handful of exceptional professors, like Harvey Mansfield, Stephen Rosen, and Roger Porter, but to be honest, many professors were disconnected from undergraduates and seemed happy to fluff off the bulk of the actual teaching to graduate student teaching fellows ("TFs"). I was also highly involved in Harvard's bipartisan Institute of Politics as an elected undergraduate student leader and participated in other student organizations.

I had lots of friends from all walks of life and was consistently blown away by their creativity, intellectual capacity, drive, accomplishments, and dreams. Fellow Harvard undergrads during my time there ranged from Olympic and world-class athletes to future crypto-kings, entrepreneurs, tech titans, authors, screenwriters, scientists, doctors, and actors. I was friends with several up-and-coming political figures, from Peter Buttigieg and Vivek Ramaswamy to Ruben Gallego and Kevin Kiley, both of whom I served with in the House of Representatives. One keepsake that I still have is the "Freshman Facebook," which is the actual facebook that looks and feels like a yearbook and is issued to freshmen, with a photo in it of each classmate. My freshman facebook includes a photo of the student who would go on to be our most famous classmate by far, Mark Zuckerberg. Mark roomed his freshman year with a close friend of mine and got the name for his website, which he launched on campus our sophomore year, from our actual freshman "facebook." I still vividly remember Facebook's launch during our sophomore year, but that is another story for another book (and another movie). I hope Mark himself writes the real book someday to tell his story on his terms.

While it was obvious that the overwhelming student population of the Harvard community skewed way left politically, there was still a vibrant Harvard Republican Club, a handful of prominent conservative tenured professors, various conservative publications and columnists featured in student papers, and a number of culturally right-leaning organizations. In fact, still today many of my closest friends from college are from the small, but mighty, conservative network of undergraduate students from Harvard. Because we were so outnumbered, young conservatives learned to strengthen our arguments and stand up for our values even when they went against the grain. Little did I know how useful that particular skill set would become in the years and decades ahead.

And yet, during my time at Harvard, it is worth noting that there were three distinct harbingers of what was to become of the school over the next two decades. Two happened while I was an undergraduate; the third happened years later when I was a Harvard alumna serving in Congress.

The first was during my senior spring in college. As I was preparing to enter the workforce like many of my fellow classmates, I attended a national security career panel hosted by Harvard's Office of Career Services. It was sponsored by the university and featured various government agencies, like the CIA and the Department of Homeland Security, as well as think tanks that work with the government in the defense and intelligence sectors. While some of my classmates were pursuing finance or consulting jobs, where you are offered positions in the fall of your senior year, I was interested in public policy, a less straightforward job search without a set timeline for recruitment.

The audience was probably a few dozen students who were listening and taking notes as the panelists outlined various career opportunities. It was an informational event, not a political event. Midway through the presentation, it was disrupted by campus Far Left activists who took over the event with heinous disruptions to silence the panel. They coughed continuously and clapped loudly to drown out the speakers. They asked ludicrous questions, such as "Isn't it true you train your employees to torture?" They staged a mock deportation of a protester midway through the discussion. One protester sitting three rows behind me physically made himself vomit. These activists did not seek to engage in robust debate. Their goal was to stop the panel discussion from happening. It was my first introduction to the tactics of disruption that would only become more entrenched on elite college campuses in the following years.

I was so disgusted that as soon as I left, I went back to my dorm room and wrote an op-ed called "Political Vomit" that was published the following morning in *The Harvard Crimson*, the widely read student-run daily newspaper. I recounted the revolting episode, and I rejected the anti-intellectual strategies of my radical peers. I knew that there were many other students, like me, who wanted mutually beneficial dialogue and rigorous discussion, not juvenile stunts. The episode, I wrote, was an embarrassment to an institution that stood for free thought and free speech. And, I added, what a horrible irony that these self-proclaimed socialists, supposedly standing up for workers' rights, forced Harvard's custodial staff to clean up their literal vomit.

The op-ed was widely read on campus and was discussed in dining halls at lunch the next day. Many student Democrats, knowing full well that I was a conservative, came up to me and said they agreed with the sentiment of the piece and were concerned that the university had let the panel get overrun and out of hand. To my surprise, my op-ed in the

Crimson was linked by *The Wall Street Journal*, and I was contacted by a number of conservative radio shows to do national interviews about what happened. Harvard's official administrative response was to have staff sit down with the radical disruptors and force "all sides" to have a moderated discussion, which meant listening to self-righteous pleas for radical socialism. It struck me as an extremely weak response from the university. The socialist protesters never did answer my question in the op-ed as to who literally cleaned up their disgusting vomit.

The second occurrence was covered widely by the press. My senior year was the last year that Larry Summers served as Harvard University's president before he was arguably pushed out by the faculty. I agree with many in the Harvard alumni community who believe now that the seemingly forced resignation of Larry Summers in 2006 was a real turning point for Harvard that led directly to the rot exposed at our congressional hearing nearly two decades later. My assessment, both then as an undergraduate and now as a congresswoman looking back with more life experience and perspective, is that Larry Summers was a reasonably effective Harvard president.

My recollection from when I was a student was that as Harvard president, Larry Summers tried to focus the faculty on actually teaching undergraduate students and improving the academic rigor in the classroom; he refused to be beholden to the Harvard faculty's increasingly radical groupthink, and he expanded Harvard's commitment to sciences and scientific research. While I did not agree with all of Summers's decisions at Harvard, overall I believe that Larry prioritized students over faculty and academics over indoctrination—a rarity for university presidents even then.

And that became the crux of the problem for Larry's university presidency. He refused to bow to the tenured faculty.

In 2005, President Summers participated in a conference on women and science hosted by the National Bureau of Economic Research, with the intention of "reinforcing his strong commitment to the advancement of women in science, and offering some informal observations on possible fruitful avenues for further research." Larry's remarks were purposefully focused on increasing women's representation in tenured positions in science and engineering at top universities and research institutions. In his extensive remarks, he made very straightforward commonsense statements such as: "There is reasonably strong evidence of taste differences between little girls and little boys that are not easy to attribute to socialization. . . . So, I think, while I would prefer to believe otherwise, I guess my experience with my two-and-a-half-year-old twin daughters who were not given dolls and who were given trucks, and found themselves saying to each other, 'Look, daddy truck is carrying the baby truck,' tells me something."[2] He also stated that one of the reasons for so few women in these positions was because of "intrinsic aptitude, and particularly of the variability of aptitude." The Harvard faculty cacophony of outrage was swift and unforgiving. Within days, Larry issued a public apology to the Harvard community. In less than two months, the Harvard faculty passed a vote of no confidence in Larry Summers. He resigned in 2006.

We know now that Larry Summers should have been removed for an altogether different reason: his despicable association with sexual predator Jeffrey Epstein, which was recently uncovered as part of my vote in Congress to release the Epstein Files.

The 2005 Summers episode was an early instance of what we now sometimes call "cancel culture." The professors who disagreed with his arguments didn't try to engage him, debate him, prove him wrong. They tried to destroy him. Their purpose wasn't truth; it was power. So when, years later, some of the very same Harvard faculty who ran out Larry Summers defended antisemitic protesters by crying, "Free speech!"—well, let's just say it was hard to take them at their word.

In 2006, I was proud to graduate with honors from Harvard, especially as the first member of my immediate family to even have the opportunity to earn an undergraduate degree. I did not have a confirmed job until the week of graduation, when I was offered a position in the West Wing of the White House. I found out the day before my graduation, after having done numerous rounds of interviews in Washington and an extensive months-long FBI background check. I was excited for the next chapter of my life and the once-in-a lifetime opportunity to work in public policy in our nation's capital. I truly never imagined that in less than ten years after graduating, I would be serving as an elected representative in the United States Congress.

At Harvard, I had a very meaningful and fulfilling experience as an undergraduate that challenged me in so many ways. To this day, I deeply admire Harvard's founding principles and believe strongly that academic excellence is a cornerstone of American exceptionalism. But today, I, like so many alumni and millions of Americans, am deeply concerned that Harvard has fundamentally lost its way. It no longer strives for academic rigor and excellence, but instead is focused on radical anti-American indoctrination fueled by the groupthink of a Far Left monolithic faculty and staff who are propped up by significant funding from foreign adversaries.

The third incident that unmasked what Harvard would become occurred years later after I was already serving in Congress. In truth, it was less of an "incident" and more of a turning point for the university that was widely publicized. It was a minor news item for my congressional office that deals with a deluge of high-priority issues, but it was clearly a real ideological and public relations priority for Harvard.

After I was first elected to Congress, I was invited to serve on the Senior Advisory Committee for Harvard's Institute of Politics (IOP). I was honored to serve on this historically bipartisan board because I had been so heavily involved in the institute's programming as an undergraduate, starting the Women's Leadership Initiative and serving as a leader on the Student Advisory Committee. Despite my demanding congressional workload and calendar, I actively participated as an IOP Senior Advisory Board member and worked well and respectfully with my colleagues, ranging from prominent Democrats Caroline Kennedy and David Axelrod to well-known Republicans Olympia Snowe and Ken Duberstein.

It became increasingly clear during the first Trump term that I was the only board member who supported President Trump. The other Republicans on the board were all publicly anti-Trump. In fact, I would go so far as to say that I am near certain that I was the only person on the IOP's board who voted for Trump in 2016 or 2020 or 2024—let alone all three. The rest of the board publicly endorsed and voted for Hillary Clinton in 2016, Joe Biden in 2020, and Kamala Harris in 2024. So much for a balanced, bipartisan organization.

In the days following the contested 2020 election, I, like tens of millions of my fellow Americans, raised concerns related to constitutional election integrity. On January 6, 2021, as a member of Congress representing New York's 21st District, I delivered a speech on the floor of the House of Representatives. I reminded my fellow members that the People's House was precisely where the Founding Fathers wanted our fiercest, most contentious debates to take place. The Framers recognized that the American people would face unprecedented challenges, and they established the Congress as the place where the people's concerns could be aired, discussed, and resolved.

I stand by this speech today. It outlined constitutional issues and did so in a respectful, rigorous manner. I also vigorously condemned the violence that occurred that day. We settle our disagreements through open debate and at the ballot box. Political violence in any form is absolutely unacceptable.

Despite Democrat members of Congress objecting to the election certification of every Republican president in my lifetime, the cancel culture perpetrated from the Left and the media against Trump supporters during that particular political chapter was lightning-swift and venomous.

A petition was started by Far Left Harvard students and alumni to remove me from Harvard's allegedly "bipartisan" board of the Institute of Politics and finally purge the only Trumper. Over email with me cc'ed, fellow Senior Advisory Board colleagues swiftly bowed to the anti-Trump petitioner mob and said that I must resign. Harvard's dean of the Kennedy School, Doug Elmendorf, called to inform me that he'd had multiple left-leaning law professors analyze and assess my speech delivered on the House floor, and they did not agree with its premise, therefore I must resign.

I told the dean of Harvard's Kennedy School that I would not resign and that he would have to remove me. I informed him that as an elected member of Congress who actually represented seven hundred thousand people, unlike any of the left-wing mob of professors or most of the board members, I had a constitutional right to say whatever I wanted on behalf of my constituents on the floor of the House of Representatives.

I also reminded him that when I was an undergraduate student, a Harvard IOP board member serving at the time was Democrat Congressman Jesse Jackson Jr., who objected to certifying President George W. Bush's re-election. Harvard apparently had no problems with that because it was objecting to a Republican president. By the way, Jesse Jackson Jr. would end up serving time in prison for election finance corruption. I also warned Doug Elmendorf that this would have a significant chilling effect on conservative students, who would feel even more silenced in the classroom and on campus than they already were. He insinuated that the university didn't care about conservative students or professors feeling silenced. At least he was being honest in describing Harvard's attempt to purge conservative thought.

Harvard, with Dean Elmendorf in the lead, seemed to be launching a coordinated campaign to scheme my removal with Harvard's President Larry Bacow. Throughout this time period, Harvard became so Trump-deranged that under pressure they even considered revoking degrees and diplomas that were earned by prominent conservative alumni such as Ted Cruz, Ron DeSantis, and myself. A month later, President Bacow would give a lengthy speech to the entire Harvard faculty going into great detail defending his decision, which was heavily criticized, to remove me from the Institute of Politics board. He did begrudgingly admit that I would keep my degree despite what he described as "bad behavior" (by the way, my degree that was earned and tuition paid!). Bacow declared, "A Harvard degree is not conferred on the condition of future good behavior. We should expect that our alumni will be as intellectually rigorous in their careers as they were in their studies. Those who fail to meet this standard will be judged in the court of public opinion, not by Harvard." He said this in the same breath as he clutched his pearls, stating that the university was more committed than ever to free speech and freedom of inquiry. You don't need a Harvard degree to see the irony, hypocrisy, and intellectual dishonesty in that.

President Bacow was right, but only partially. I would in fact be judged in the court of public opinion: I was resoundingly re-elected by my constituents and elected to top House leadership. But in the years to come, he had failed to understand that Harvard would be judged, too.

My final comment to Harvard's Dean Elmendorf during this episode was a reminder that he was purging the only Trump Republican on the supposedly bipartisan board. Clearly Harvard had made a decision to double down on radical Far Left groupthink, totally belittling and condescending to more than half of America. It didn't matter to my life and political career in Congress one bit—personally or professionally. But it was a clear sign of Harvard's ideological derangement. I also reminded him that I served on the House Education Committee, where we had subpoena power.

It wasn't a threat. It was a fact.

CHAPTER 3

Harvard Exposed

"I am obliged to confess that I should sooner live in a society governed by the first two thousand names in the Boston telephone directory than in a society governed by the two thousand faculty members of Harvard University."

—William F. Buckley

The next communication I would have with Harvard was nearly three years later when Harvard's president was seated in front of me in Congress testifying under oath. Amazingly, almost three years to the day from when Harvard publicly removed me from the board of the Institute of Politics, Harvard President Claudine Gay was forced to resign because of her answers to my questions at the congressional hearing of the House Education Committee.

In those intervening three years, the situation at Harvard had grown even worse. A campus bereft of freedom of thought, an obsession with politically correct DEI, and a purging and silencing of conservative voices and viewpoints—Harvard had fully embraced the woke resistance. It no longer pursued critical thinking for the pursuit of "truth" of its motto, *Veritas*; sadly, it pursued monolithic radical progressivism trending toward anti-Americanism.

A 2022 survey of the Faculty of Arts and Sciences by *The Harvard Crimson* found that more than 80 percent of faculty self-identified as "liberal" while a mere 1 percent self-identified as "conservative." The rest claimed they were "moderates."[1] No surprise, this political bias impacted the classroom. As Niall Ferguson has pointed out, by 2024, in a survey conducted of Harvard's graduating class, only one-third of graduating seniors felt comfortable expressing their opinions about controversial topics during their time at college. Moreover, in a class where less than 10 percent self-identified as conservative, the chilling effect was further exacerbated by political ideology. According to the *Crimson* reporting, "while 41 percent of liberal students reported feeling comfortable discussing controversial topics, only 25 percent of moderates and 17 percent of conservatives felt similarly."[2]

On campus ratings regarding freedom of speech, Harvard fared even worse. In 2024, Harvard was ranked dead last by the Foundation for Individual Rights and Expression (FIRE), falling to the absolute bottom of the barrel of higher education institutions in the nation. FIRE's report implores, "If this prestigious university hopes to turn things around, it should reflect on its traditional scholarly purpose and direct its attention toward reviving the free speech norms that make fulfilling that purpose possible." The culture at Harvard had gotten so bad that seventy intrepid professors defied the university establishment by launching the Council on Academic Freedom, co-led by the widely published psychology professor Steven Pinker—hardly a conservative himself. The co-founders of the council announced that the organization "will encourage the adoption and enforcement of policies that protect academic freedom. . . . When activists are shouting into an administrator's ear, we will speak calmly but vigorously into the other one, which will require them to take the reasoned rather than the easy way out." This group's launch in April 2023 foreshadowed the crisis later that year when Harvard seemingly allowed pro-Hamas activists to take over the college.

After Hamas's terrorist attacks against Israel on October 7th, Harvard's President Claudine Gay became the poster child for how universities mishandled their response. When Harvard's Undergraduate Palestine Solidarity Committee posted the "Joint Statement by Harvard Palestine Solidarity Groups on the Situation in Palestine" declaring that "We, the undersigned student organizations, hold the Israeli regime entirely responsible for all unfolding violence" less than twenty-four hours after the attacks, Claudine Gay and the university remained stunningly silent. This days-long silence allowed the antisemitic statement to essentially speak for Harvard and set the tone for the university's response. The silence was deafening and widely criticized.

The headlines critical of Harvard blared flashing red. For Harvard's PR folks, it was the textbook definition of what it means to be in the jet stream of crisis communications: "Harvard University's president has come under fire for being slow to issue a statement following Hamas's attacks on Israel last weekend and then for not condemning Hamas when university leadership did speak out. President Claudine Gay's handling of the situation has even drawn criticism from former president Larry Summers on X. He wrote that Harvard had appeared 'at best neutral towards acts of terror against the Jewish state of Israel. . . . In nearly 50 years of @Harvard affiliation, I have never been as disillusioned and alienated as I am today,' wrote Summers, who noted Gay's predecessor, Lawrence Bacow, quickly released a statement denouncing Russia following its invasion of Ukraine the previous year."[3]

On October 9, 2023, two days after Hamas's terrorist massacre, Harvard released "A Statement from Harvard University Leadership" that failed to condemn Hamas and equated Hamas's terrorist attacks with Israel's righteous self-defensive military actions. This statement caused the outcry against Harvard to become even more intense and widespread.

Our congressional investigation subsequently found through testimony and subpoenaed documents and emails that Harvard's leaders purposefully chose not to condemn Hamas, proactively cut out language regarding the capture of Israeli hostages, and deleted the description of Hamas as "violent." In the course of drafting the statement with a small group of Harvard's most senior leaders, the sentence reading "We denounce this act of terror" had a comment with a question from Claudine Gay's Chief of Staff Katie O'Dair that asked, "Can we have a letter and not say unequivocally that we denounce this?" Harvard's Vice President and Chief Administrative Officer Marc Goodheart was concerned that the failure to condemn Hamas would be compared with former President Bacow's explicit condemnation of Russia's invasion of Ukraine. He further pushed that "this might be slicing things too fine. But I also wonder whether, if the judgement is not to express an institutional condemnation of Hamas's act of terror, there might be a way to dissociate the university from the 'Israel is entirely responsible' statement reportedly issued by 31 Harvard student groups—and attracting widespread media attention (not to mention denunciation by Rep. Stefanik)."

Ultimately, after much discussion over email, Harvard purposefully chose not to condemn Hamas and not to distance themselves from the student groups' statements solely blaming Israel for the Hamas October 7th terrorist attacks. Moreover, language referencing Israeli hostages was removed by top Harvard leadership because of the "absence of equivalent language regarding the possibility of Palestinians being harmed." Harvard continued down this road of moral equivalency, equating Hamas terrorists with Israel's defensive retaliatory military actions. Lastly, the description of Hamas as "violent" in the draft statement was heavily debated. The dean of Harvard Medical School, George Daley, suggested removing language characterizing Hamas's attack as violent due to the fact that "it singl[ed] out Hamas 'violence' and assigned 'blame.'" One dean doubled down, applauding the removal of "violent" as a "very good catch." The holier-than-thou moral rot truly takes your breath away.

Claudine Gay agreed to remove language describing Hamas's terrorist attacks as violent. Harvard's then-provost, Alan Garber, disagreed but acquiesced after Claudine Gay asked if he could "live with it." Garber responded, "Yes I don't love it but can live with the change. Frankly I'm more disturbed by this logic than the wording change." Calling the logic disturbing is an understatement.

Eventually, Penny Pritzker, the senior fellow of the Harvard Corporation, which is essentially Harvard's most important governance board, testified in our committee's transcribed deposition months later. In this deposition, where I was the only member of Congress in attendance, Pritzker confirmed that Harvard's initial response was "massively inappropriate at the time and insufficient." As we were setting up this deposition, it was revealed to our committee that Harvard had failed to even

dents didn't even get an acknowledgment, let alone receive a substantive response. While Harvard proudly and publicly promoted its embrace of the politically fashionable "diversity, equity, and inclusion" movement, the university specifically chose to exclude Jewish students from qualifying for this initiative.

The significant and growing strains of antisemitism percolating through Harvard today harken back to an era in the early twentieth century when the university explicitly instituted antisemitic admissions policies under then Harvard President Abbott Lawrence Lowell. In the early twentieth century, the number of Jewish students at Harvard increased significantly. According to in-depth reporting in *The Harvard Crimson*, "these were sons of immigrants from Eastern Europe, largely from public high schools in cities on the East Coast. In the 1921-22 school year, Harvard's student body was 21.5 percent Jewish. By comparison, in the mid-1920s, Jewish people made up approximately 3.5 percent of America's population. University officials worried about this 'overrepresentation' of Jewish people on campus." This caused significant consternation among Harvard's leaders, who instituted admissions policies to specifically limit the percentage of Jewish students. In 1922, on the day after commencement, Harvard's top leaders, including President Lowell, began an official meeting with "Is there a problem? Is it a Jewish problem? Does the problem involve a principle?" They unanimously agreed the answer was yes. An echo of this antisemitic history at Harvard would rear its ugly head a century later with Claudine Gay testifying in front of Congress.

As one of the most senior and longest-serving members of the Education Committee, I sit on the top row of the hearing room dais. Typically, members of Congress ask hearing questions in the order of seniority on the committee, starting at the top. Focusing primarily on my alma mater Harvard, I began with direct questions to President Claudine Gay. Typically, committee questions begin with a long opener, a soliloquy of sorts by the member asking them. I do the opposite and have found over the years that I prefer very short and to-the-point questions, which allows me to plow through quite a bit of material. In my first round, I wanted to highlight the antisemitic double standard that was apparently applied only to Jewish students on Harvard's campus. President Gay acknowledged that protesters' chants of "Intifada," a call to violent resistance against the State of Israel, was "hateful speech" and "personally abhorrent." But she tried to wriggle out of acknowledging that it was explicitly in violation of Harvard's Code of Conduct. "We embrace a commitment to free expression," said Gay, "and give a wide berth to free expression even of views that are objectionable, outrageous, and offensive."

Nonsense. Everyone listening to that exchange knew that Harvard cracked down ruthlessly on disfavored speech. And no one thinks that Harvard would tolerate a Ku Klux Klan rally on Harvard Yard. The simple fact is that Harvard suddenly rediscovered its free speech principles only when they were useful to defending anti-Israel and antisemitic speech.

In reality, Harvard had become the mecca of cancel culture in higher education with its legacy of running out and canceling conservative faculty, students, and alumni, and silencing right-leaning viewpoints on campus. It struck me that the only time Harvard had so vociferously and passionately defended freedom of speech was when it was calling for the genocide of Jews.

In congressional hearings, each member of Congress usually gets their five minutes for questions and then they are done. It's a traditional one-and-done mentality to ensure every member on each committee has their chance to conduct oversight and send their clip home to their constituents. Typically, members of Congress come and go, popping in and out throughout hearings so that we can attend other meetings or hearings that are scheduled simultaneously. I believe this practice and schedule are in need of reform on the congressional calendar because they perpetuate surface-level oversight and a perception by witnesses that they just have to survive the five-minute round with the tougher, more effective representatives before moving on to another member's questions that are often on a totally different topic. Over the years, I have learned to clear my schedule for very important hearings to ensure not only that I am asking questions for my allotted five minutes, but also that I am able to listen to the rest of the hearing questions and witness testimony. This close attention often leads to lightbulb moments and timely follow-ups.

In one follow-up exchange, another member yielded me time and I had one minute. So I decided to focus on the flow of foreign dollars to Harvard that I believe had partially caused antisemitism to be infused in academic coursework and curricula.

At the time of the hearing, some $1.5 billion in foreign dollars had poured into Harvard's coffers in the past three years, no small part of it from countries such as Qatar. President Gay seemed purposefully ignorant of that fact.

My time for this round of questions had expired, but there was a lot more to dig into on this issue. My gut told me that when I was asking questions on the particular topic of foreign funding sources, Claudine Gay was extremely uncomfortable answering with any specifics. Her responses were highly rehearsed, and she refused to give direct answers. This was a prescient moment, as our overall congressional investigation would uncover billions of dollars pouring into America's elite higher education institutions from foreign governments that clearly undermine our American values.

I listened to other questions as the witnesses continued to evade giving any direct answers. Another Republican member yielded me an additional one minute. For this round, I recalled that as I reviewed material to prepare for the hearing, I had been shocked to read that as president of Harvard, Claudine Gay had visited the Jewish campus organization Hillel only after October 7th. It struck me as odd. My experience during undergrad was that lots of students were invited to join classmates at Hillel, especially for Shabbat dinner on Fridays. Like the various dining halls where we would join friends who lived in different campus housing or participate in various student organizations' meal meetings, I had been to Hillel a few times starting my freshman year and through college with lots of friends who were active in the community. So I asked about it in my third round of questions.

President Gay shrugged off my concern, which was that during her tenure, and even before, since I had been a student, as the number of

Jewish students steadily declined (starkly in recent years), they had been increasingly ostracized and ignored by the highest echelon of Harvard University's leadership.

At this point in the hearing, nearly every Republican member was saving their remaining time to yield to me for additional questions since I had done so much preparation, and my questions were particularly revealing and effective.

To every question I asked, Gay offered non-answers. At this point, we were hours into the day-long hearing. It was only when I returned after voting on the House floor to ask my final question that I got a direct answer when I specifically asked the last question to Claudine Gay: "Does calling for the genocide of Jews violate your university's code of conduct on bullying and harassment?" Her unforgettable final answer was: "It depends on the context."

The shock and outrage at Harvard and Claudine Gay were swift and deserving.

Pickup trucks with digital billboards featuring video of Claudine Gay's answers on repeat circled and parked in Harvard Square for weeks. Prop airplanes with banners calling for Claudine Gay's resignation started flying in circles over Cambridge. Hordes of prominent alumni withheld funds, with many canceling multimillion-dollar financial pledges to the university totaling hundreds of millions of dollars. I was told by a major donor that one of Harvard's largest donors even called him in disbelief, saying, "Please tell me it's not true! Tell me that I misheard and it didn't really happen!"

It was true, he hadn't misheard, and it really happened.

An overwhelming chorus of calls for Gay's resignation broke out from alumni, students, prominent business leaders, and senior elected officials, particularly from the Republican Party. Harvard's Rabbi David Wolpe, whom, just two weeks earlier, Claudine Gay had appointed to serve on the university's official advisory group to combat antisemitism, publicly resigned. Yet astonishingly, at the same time, hundreds of the woke Harvard faculty circled the wagons to protect Claudine Gay.

I was determined to continue demanding accountability every day after the hearing. And I had some help in that. Bill Ackman, for example, a prominent activist billionaire hedge fund investor and Harvard alum, posted relentless and effective four-thousand-plus-word screeds on X that were viewed by millions.

But despite full-saturation media coverage in every major paper and broadcast and network TV channel, the day after the bombshell hearing President Gay didn't apologize. On the contrary, she instead released a curt statement doubling down on her testimony and blaming her critics for misunderstanding her botched testimony. Titled "Statement on Congressional Hearing," she wrote, "There are some who have confused a right to free expression with the idea that Harvard will condone calls for violence against Jewish students. Let me be clear: Calls for violence or genocide against the Jewish community, or any religious or ethnic group are vile, they have no place at Harvard, and those who threaten our Jewish students will be held to account." No one was confused about Claudine Gay's testimony. And her tone-deaf doubling down and blaming others' "confusion" in the aftermath poured kerosene on the raging public relations bonfire, only hastening widespread calls for her resignation.

The following day, on December 7, 2023, two days after the hearing, Claudine Gay was finally forced to issue an apology, which she did in an interview in *The Harvard Crimson*, stating "I am sorry" and "Words matter. When words amplify distress and pain, I don't know how you could feel anything but regret. . . . Substantively, I failed to convey what is my truth." Harvard's motto of *Veritas* had certainly fallen a long way to "my truth."

Not to be outdone by Harvard's jump into the amoral abyss of antisemitism, on the Saturday night after the hearing, the weekend comedy show *Saturday Night Live* (*SNL*) made history with what is now known as its worst cold open in history. There is a long-running professional pipeline of *Harvard Lampoon* students who go on to write and perform on the Lorne Michaels–produced sketch comedy show that over the years has included the likes of Harvard alumni Conan O'Brien, Jim Downey, and Colin Jost (who was an undergraduate at the same time that I was).

I don't even watch *SNL* and only rarely catch rerun clips online. But my iPhone started going haywire with incoming messages that *SNL* was spoofing the hearing. The skit essentially applauded the university presidents' antisemitic testimony and instead attacked the hearing and specifically me. The next day's headline in the *New York Post* screamed, "*'SNL' swings and misses with cold open attempting to skewer antisemitism hearings hours after UPenn President Liz Magill resigns: 'Abysmal.'*"

The *SNL* cold open was nearly universally panned on social media. One X user tweeted, "The worst cold open on SNL I've ever seen the audience was barely laughing"; another agreed, tweeting, "Gotta be the worst cold open I've ever seen on SNL absolutely abysmal." Radio host Mark Simone tweeted, "Only a hate-filled, anti-Semitic SNL could do a sketch about the anti-Semitic college presidents testifying in front of Congress and make the questioner Congresswoman Stefanik the target of the sketch." It was later revealed that this was the *SNL* debut for novice actress Chloe Troust, who played me in the sketch. She was the last-minute understudy and was heavily criticized. The longtime *SNL* cast member Cecily Strong had originally played me in the skit in the live dress rehearsal right before the show and then dropped out, forcing the part on the understudy. Smart of Cecily Strong to apparently recognize how heinous the content of the antisemitic sketch was.

On Sunday after the hearing on December 10, 2023, the Harvard Corporation and the Harvard Board of Overseers were slated to meet to determine the fate of Claudine Gay's presidency after her atrocious testimony at our congressional hearing. The intensely secretive and opaque Harvard Corporation is chock-full of senior Obama administration officials. It was later reported by the *New York Post* that President Obama called the Harvard Corporation Board before their meeting to directly lobby and pressure them to keep Claudine Gay as president, to "keep the broader [Harvard] administration stable—including its composition." Many of that "administration" were either former high-ranking Obama officials, including members of his cabinet, or prominent supporters and donors of President Obama. I was told directly from a Harvard Corporation board member that Obama shared that he felt it was important "not to give her [me] a win." Again, no concern about Jewish students or the importance of combatting antisemitism, but the typical partisan demagoguery against an effective elected Republican standing up on a moral issue.

After reviewing the notes and emails regarding the December 10th Harvard Board of Overseers meeting as part of the congressional investigation, the House Education Committee found that while Claudine Gay publicly "projected respect for the process by emphasizing that she had been pleased to appear before the Committee for questioning. . . . Behind closed doors in a formal meeting of the University's Board of Overseers . . . Gay launched into a stunning personal attack on the Member of Congress whose questioning yielded those damaging answers, Representative Elise Stefanik, herself a Harvard alumna." The official notes from the meeting revealed that Claudine Gay acknowledged "her truth" that should have been conveyed was "that calls for violence against the Jewish community shouldn't be allowed," before pivoting to lashing out with an apparent reference to me, whom she falsely smeared as a "purveyor of hate" and "supporter of proudboys."[4] These offensive, wildly inaccurate, and arguably defamatory statements had already leaked out to me in real time from sources in the room, prior to the congressional investigation documents that confirmed them. The Harvard Corporation and Board of Overseers were leaking like a sieve straight to my office in the Capitol.

But neither *SNL*'s worst cold open ever nor the Harvard Board of Overseers meeting with Claudine Gay on the hot seat was the biggest news of the weekend related to Harvard's compounding self-inflicted scandals.

The same day that Claudine Gay was in front of the Harvard Board of Overseers, independent journalists Christopher Rufo and Christopher Brunet broke the bombshell news story published on Substack uncovering Gay's alleged plagiarism of large portions of her Ph.D. dissertation, "Taking Charge: Black Electoral Success and the Redefinition of American Policies." This intrepid reporting drew more than one hundred million impressions on X. Full paragraphs had allegedly been lifted from various scholars and writers, as well as an entire appendix copied in full.

This was the tip of the iceberg. There would be nearly fifty instances of alleged plagiarism found in various Claudine Gay publications throughout her academic career. She seemed to be a serial plagiarist. Any one instance of plagiarism would have a student at Harvard facing stiff disciplinary action, often including a requirement to withdraw from the university.

While the president of Harvard's alleged serial plagiarism was shocking news to the general public, it became even more of a bombshell when it was later revealed by *The Washington Free Beacon* that, stunningly, this was already a well-known and well-kept secret by the Harvard Corporation. Even before the public reporting, the *New York Post* had reached out to Harvard in late October 2023 with credible allegations of twenty-five instances of Claudine Gay's plagiarism. According to independent reporting by *The Washington Free Beacon*, when the Harvard Corporation learned about the accusations, "they responded by hiring the 'leading defamation firm in the United States,' which repped clients like the disgraced NBC News anchor Matt Lauer and Putin crony Oleg Deripaska, to threaten and intimidate the *Post*. (It worked.)"[5]

Did Harvard follow established protocols for investigating academic misconduct? Of course not. That would be too honest and fair! Instead the Harvard Corporation fabricated a completely separate process by appointing a so-called independent panel of experts whose identities were never revealed to "review" the allegations. After a span of two weeks, by mid-November, the independent panel released a memo to the Harvard Corporation gushing that Claudine Gay's works were "sophisticated and original" with "virtually no evidence of intentional claiming of findings that are not President Gay's." According to a report eventually released at a later date by Harvard, "the Independent Panel observed that certain allegations were 'trivial,' concerned 'commonly used language' or 'sentence fragments,' or arose from the 1993 publication to which they devoted 'less attention.'"[6] The Independent Panel identified nine of the twenty-five allegations presented by the *Post* as allegations "of principal concern," which "paraphrased or reproduced the language of others without quotation marks and without sufficient and clear crediting of sources," failing "on occasion" to "provide citations according to the highest established scientific practice." It noted further that, with respect to one allegation, "fragments of duplicative language and paraphrasing . . . could be read as Gay claiming findings that are actually those of Schwartz," although "there is no evidence that was her intention." Moreover, the Harvard Corporation would use software to uncover even more instances of Claudine Gay's alleged plagiarism than the original twenty-five. So what did the Harvard Corporation do? Of course, there would be no accountability or basic application of academic standards. They found that many of the allegations were "meritless," and in the instances when they did not adhere to Harvard's College Guide, Claudine Gay would be given a second chance that no other Harvard student or faculty was given; she would be allowed to make "corrections."[6]

This entire episode is the prime example of academic rot at the highest levels of the most elite higher education institution in the world. Mind you, this all happened *before* Claudine Gay's Harvard plagiarism scandal even broke in public.

When the news finally broke and after Gay's appearance before Harvard's Board of Overseers, the Harvard Corporation published a message to the entire Harvard community, unanimously "reaffirming" support for Claudine Gay and calling her "the right leader to help our community heal." The message acknowledged that the university's initial post–October 7th communications had been inadequate but excused them. It also acknowledged the plagiarism accusations against Gay but downplayed them. It was, in other words, a cleanup effort that tried to make the right noises while avoiding saying anything of substance about the real, alarming situation that had been revealed. It was a shameful display of turning a blind eye. The Harvard Corporation tolerated allegedly systemic plagiarism by its president. It tolerated failure to combat antisemitism and failure to protect American Jewish students by its president. It tolerated morally bankrupt congressional testimony that brought shame to the university. And it did so unanimously. The Harvard Corporation's oversight had rotted from within, throwing moral and academic integrity completely by the wayside.

But after allegations of additional plagiarism in late December, it took only one brave board member to crack the Harvard Corporation's sustained, irrational, and undeserving closing of ranks around Claudine Gay. According to *New York Times* reporting, Tim Barakett, "Harvard's treasurer and relatively new member of the corporation . . . didn't think keeping Dr. Gay was tenable. He told his fellow board members that Dr. Gay's poor leadership and academic conduct might disqualify her from the presidency. . . . Barakett didn't think Dr. Gay's apologies got it right and argued that she was failing to take full responsibility for her [alleged] plagiarism."[7] Other board members began to agree with Barakett, and on December 27, Harvard's Senior Fellow Penny Pritzker called President Claudine Gay, who was on vacation over the holidays with her family in Rome, Italy, to ask her, "Did she think there was a path forward with her as the school's president?"[8]

And just like that, it was over for Claudine Gay. On January 2, 2024, Gay resigned, ending the shortest term for any Harvard president in history. President Trump was one of the first phone calls I received when this news broke. Harvard offered her the golden parachute of a lucrative $900,000-per-year salary to serve as the Wilbur A. Cowett Professor of Government and of African and African-American Studies, a position she still holds today.

Harvard's Provost Alan Garber was named Harvard's interim president and then promoted permanently to the role. While not nearly as inept as Claudine Gay, Alan Garber's first months were not smooth sailing and were marked by allowing a pro-Hamas encampment in Harvard Yard during the spring of 2024. Our congressional committee investigation found that Garber conceded that the pro-Hamas encampment "disrupted [Harvard's] education activities and operations . . . created safety concerns that required limiting access to Harvard Yard, and noted that encampment participants . . . were reported to have intimidated and harassed other members of the Harvard community." However, Garber failed to take disciplinary action against those individuals who clearly violated university rules. According to our report, of the "68 students against whom Harvard brought disciplinary cases related to the . . . Harvard encampment, none received non-rescinded suspensions, 53 received disciplinary probations (of which 35 were later significantly shortened), eight received no sanctions, three received warnings, two were found not responsible, one was admonished, and one is on leave." Harvard would continue to fail to mete out discipline for students breaking campus rules, which would only invite more and more egregious rule-breaking.[9]

Understanding that for years, Harvard had totally shredded its relationships with the many Republican elected officials who were alumni, Alan Garber overhauled the university's government relations team to help him proactively reach out to Republican members of Congress. Garber and I met in my Capitol office, and I shared my concerns about the direction of Harvard and the extensive oversight I would continue to conduct and why. I also told Garber that I felt strongly that President Trump was going to win the upcoming election and that we were working directly with his team on how to build off my extensive oversight work regarding college antisemitism. Garber seemed surprised and dismissive when I told him that Trump would win, and he insinuated that was not what he was hearing from Harvard's pollsters and professors about the presidential election. Boy, did my prediction turn out right.

After President Trump was inaugurated for his second term, my office worked closely with his administration and my friend Secretary of Education Linda McMahon on reining in Harvard's failed leadership to help right the sinking ship. In April 2025, the Trump administration sent a letter to Harvard outlining reforms that they must take to maintain access to federal funding. These included reforming governance and leadership, merit-based hiring and admissions, international admissions, viewpoint diversity in hiring and admissions, student discipline, whistleblower protections, elimination of DEI, and reforming programs with egregious antisemitism.[10]

Cheered on by the radicalized Trump-deranged faculty, Harvard's President Alan Garber faced significant internal pressure to reject these commonsense requirements for federal funding and instead upped the ante by publicly stating "the University will not surrender its independence or relinquish its constitutional rights. . . . No government—regardless of which party is in power—should dictate what private universities can teach, whom they can admit and hire, and which areas of study and inquiry they can pursue."[11] President Trump froze $2.2 billion in federal grants and $60 million in federal contracts. Negotiations and lawsuits are currently ongoing to see if Harvard will come to an agreement with the federal government.

One of Harvard's true heroes in this dark chapter for *Veritas* is Shabbos Kestenbaum, an observant Jewish undergraduate student and lifelong Democrat whom I have come to know well as he stands up for what is morally right. Shabbos sued Harvard with a group called Students Against Antisemitism for their failure to protect Jewish students on campus.[12] The group settled with Harvard, forcing the university to adopt the International Holocaust Remembrance Alliance definition of antisemitism. Shabbos further pursued the case, and ultimately Harvard was forced to settle with him individually. After Claudine Gay resigned, he shared his firsthand experience at Harvard in his testimony before our committee.

His testimony was a litany of horrors. Fellow students called Jews "pedophiles" and "baby killers" in online forums. Posters bringing attention to antisemitism on campus were vandalized. On social media, a Harvard employee posted a video featuring himself waving a machete at Kestenbaum and other Jewish students. For several days, Shabbos had to be escorted around campus by private, armed security guards. He testified about students who had ceased to wear recognizably Jewish garments, changed majors to escape anti-Israel or antisemitic hatred, been spat on for being Jewish, and more.

Shabbos's great-great-grandfather was an Orthodox rabbi in Germany. His grandfather had been arrested by the Nazis on Kristallnacht. His family escaped the Third Reich and found refuge in the United States. He acknowledged the horrible irony in his experience. Kristallnacht, he reminded our committee, did not begin with shattered glass and burning books. It began with "the acceptance and normalization of Jew-hatred."[13] Harvard had shamefully allowed this antisemitic hatred to be accepted and normalized.

CHAPTER 4

University of Pennsylvania

Founded 1791
Leges sine moribus vanae
"Laws without morals are in vain"

In 1749, Benjamin Franklin published a pamphlet titled *Proposals Relating to the Education of Youth in Pensilvania*. In it, he sketched his vision for a new type of institution of learning. This school, wrote Franklin, would be unlike the best-known colonial colleges, Harvard and Yale. Instead of focusing on training ministers, it would prepare students for lives in business or public service. Instead of the narrow traditional curriculum (Latin, Greek, divinity, etc.), it would offer a wide-ranging curriculum with lots of subjects for study, including geography, drawing, surveying, mechanics, and the natural sciences. The students would be encouraged to learn in new ways—for example, by observing nature or visiting workshops or courts. And the school would open its doors to a much wider range of young men.

Franklin's *Proposals* were the blueprint for what became, in 1791, the year after Franklin's death, the University of Pennsylvania. Penn, as it is now known, combined two earlier schools, one of which Franklin himself had helped establish in 1740.

The famously broad-minded Franklin, at about the same time he was helping found new schools, was also supporting Philadelphia's growing Jewish community. He signed a petition encouraging citizens of all faiths to help raise Philadelphia's first synagogue, Mikveh Israel ("Hope of Israel"), and he donated to the cause himself. During the Revolutionary War, as occupying British forces made life difficult for them in other colonies, Jews flocked to Philadelphia, a safe haven. Many of them became steadfast patriots.

Franklin's tolerant spirit pervaded the university in its early days. In 1769, when it was still known as the Academy of the College of Philadelphia, the school enrolled its first Jewish student, Moses Levy, who graduated three years later. He became a judge and a much-respected civic leader. He also, in 1802, became Penn's first Jewish trustee, serving until his death in 1826.

Historically, Penn has been known as an especially friendly destination for Jewish students. In the 1960s, Jewish enrollment at Penn is estimated to have grown to approximately 40 percent of the student population.

But, as in the rest of elite academia, it has cratered since then. By 2010, about 20 percent of Penn's students were Jewish. Today, the number is about 15 percent.

The strain of antisemitism at Penn began long before October 7th.

....

An eighty-four-page civil complaint filed against Penn in December 2023 by students Eyal Yakoby and Jordan Davis includes dozens of antisemitic incidents from 2015—when the Boycott, Divestment, and Sanctions (BDS) movement was introduced at Penn—to October 7, 2023. It's a list of alleged horrors in the lawsuit. A few examples:

In April 2017, following Penn's Students for Justice in Palestine's second annual "Israeli Apartheid Week," flyers with swastikas and messages including "join your local Nazis" appeared across campus. Penn's leadership claimed that "the content of student speech or expression is not by itself a basis for disciplinary action."

On July 23, 2020, a Penn graduate student posted to Instagram about a recent classroom experience:

> *During my [master's in social work] program, I was given a "privilege quiz" by my professor who taught a mandatory course on rac-*

ism. The quiz listed several categories based on identity (e.g. religion, race, ethnicity). In each category, the quiz then listed possible identities (e.g. Judaism, Christianity, Islam, etc.). Next to each of these possible identities, the quiz assigned a positive or negative value. The higher the value, the more we would need to "check our privilege," according to our professor. Under the religion category, Judaism was ranked as the most privileged identity, with 25 points assigned. Christianity was ranked as the second most privileged category, with only 5 points assigned. When I voiced my concerns to the classroom, I was met with laughter and eyerolls.[1]

A few months later, a different student posted to the same page: "On the first day of [German] class, my professor noticed my yarmulke and advised me, only me, that I should 'be on my best behavior.' I sat in class for a few more days, only to be met with more uncomfortable remarks: 'something tells me you never liked gefilte fish.'"

The student dropped the class.

In March 2023, Penn Students Against the Occupation hosted an event featuring Noura Erakat, a Palestinian American professor at Rutgers, and Mohammed El-Kurd, a Palestinian writer. Jewish groups asked Penn to distance itself from the event, citing El-Kurd's past comments, including false claims that Israel "harvest[s] Palestinian organs," has an "unquenchable thirst for Palestinian blood," and that "there is no difference between a Zionist and a Nazi." According to the complaint, "During Erakat's speech, she stared at the noticeably Jewish students wearing yarmulkes who sat in the back of the lecture room. Although these students were sitting quietly and doing nothing to disturb Erakat's lecture, she repeatedly encouraged them to challenge her, saying, 'I'm ready for you and will destroy you.'"

As Yakoby and Davis argue in their complaint: "It is inconceivable that Penn would allow any group other than Jews to be targeted for abuse or allow students and professors to call for the annihilation of any country. When it comes to the protection of Penn's Jewish students, the rules do not apply."[2]

These and many other alleged incidents culminated, prior to October 7th, in the September 2023 Palestine Writes Literature Festival at UPenn. Ostensibly a celebration of Palestinian culture, it was in reality a platform tailor-made for open antisemitism. The lineup of speakers included, among others,

- Roger Waters, the Pink Floyd front man, is not an expert on Palestinian culture, but he is a well-known antisemite. He has repeatedly suggested that a "Jewish lobby" controls the American mainstream press and the music industry. He has attacked Israel as an "apartheid state" and Israelis as "settler-colonialists." During shows in 2010, he played video showing a Star of David next to dollar signs. Waters claimed that "there are no hidden meanings in the order or juxtaposition of these symbols." That is true: the meaning was very much out in the open. At a May 2023 concert in Berlin, just months before he was scheduled to appear at Penn, he marched around on stage in a mock-Nazi uniform intending to draw a comparison between Israel and the Third Reich. (Unsurprisingly, Waters has justified the October 7th attacks.)
- Marc Lamont Hill, an ex-CNN commentator who was fired by the network when he called for a "free Palestine from the river to the sea" during a 2018 appearance. He had previously praised Nation of Islam leader Louis Farrakhan, who has called Adolf Hitler "a very great man." Hill has also characterized major news organizations as "Zionist outlets."
- Aya Ghanameh, a Palestinian children's book author who tweeted "'israeli civilians' don't exist. militant settler armed society who r all drafted = everyone is a soldier. even if they're not officially in the army, they are a militia as a society."[3] She praised a terrorist attack on a Jewish synagogue in Jerusalem in January 2023 that left seven civilians dead.

- Wissam Rafeedie, who has had long-standing ties to the Popular Front for the Liberation of Palestine (PFLP), a U.S.-designated foreign terrorist organization since 1997.[4]

And more.

The festival also planned to screen the 2022 film *Farha* by Darin J. Sallam. Critics rightfully pointed out that the film perpetuated the age-old blood libel of Jews as bloodthirsty baby-killers. In the fictional film, a family, including a newborn child, is murdered in cold blood by IDF soldiers during the 1948 "*Nakbah*," the Arabic word for the establishment of the State of Israel. The filmmaker falsely claimed the story was based on "true events."

Following significant outcry from students, alumni, and donors, the university acknowledged "several speakers who have a documented and troubling history of engaging in antisemitism by speaking and acting in ways that denigrate Jewish people," adding that "we unequivocally—and emphatically—condemn antisemitism as antithetical to our institutional values." But the university allowed the event to go forward, under the sponsorship of multiple Penn departments.[5]

Predictably, antisemitism was roundly on display at the event. Dana Dajani, a Palestinian actress and writer, declared: "You orphan-making orphans because you have never known the sanctuary of a home, and it's no wonder you want our land for your own"—invoking the same baby-killer trope as *Farha*'s filmmakers. Salman Abu Sitta, a Palestinian academic, condemned "European Jews" and "the settlers from Europe." He also compared Israeli Jews to Nazis, as did Australian poet Lorna Munro.[6]

A festival panel celebrated the writings of Ghassan Kanafani, who served as a spokesman for the terrorist group PFLP and was likely involved in the organization of the 1972 Lod Airport massacre, a mass shooting carried about by PFLP-trained terrorists who killed twenty-six people and injured eighty others. Panel member Louis Allday has praised Kanafani as a "hero."[7]

If there was any question about Palestine Writes, it was answered two weeks later, when Hamas attacked Israel on October 7th. As prominent UPenn Wharton alumnus and CEO of Apollo Global Management Group Marc Rowan wrote, "It took less than two weeks to go from the Palestine Writes Festival on UPenn's campus to the barbaric slaughter and kidnapping of Israelis." On October 12, 2023, festival Executive Director Susan Abulhawa published an op-ed in *The Electronic Intifada* praising the attacks: "Palestinian fighters finally broke free on 7 October 2023 in a spectacular moment that shocked the world," she wrote. "In a stunning display of low-tech guerilla warfare, a few dozen sparsely armed commandos disabled Israeli watchtowers and paraglided over the electrified fences. . . . These brave Palestinian fighters overtook Israeli colonies built on their ancestral villages, seeing their stolen lands for the first time in their lives."[8]

Abulhawa has tweeted about "Jewish supremacist vampires,"[9] called defenders of Israel "parasites,"[10] and traded in antisemitic conspiracy theories.[11]

....

As at so many campuses, the Hamas attacks against Israel on October 7, 2023, unleashed an unprecedented wave of antisemitism at Penn.

While Hamas forces were still inside Israel's borders, Penn Students Against the Occupation held an "Emergency Solidarity Rally" at Philadelphia's Rittenhouse Square Park, where speakers and participants celebrated enthusiastically. One pro-Hamas speaker said: "I think we should all give an applause right now, to Hamas, for a job well done. When they woke up in the morning, and they found the field hands in the house, with a knife, ready to cut their fucking throats. I was late to the news, but when I heard it, I smiled. I don't want to hear that bullshit, 250, 250, innocent Israelis are dead. Fuck 'em. Again, I swear. I salute Hamas. A job well done."

Following the lead of Harvard, the following week eleven Penn clubs signed onto a "Statement of Solidarity with Palestine" that euphemized

Hamas's attack as a "dignified fight" and blamed Penn for advancing "Zionist media propaganda."

Meanwhile, several Penn faculty took to social media to declare similar sentiments.

Huda Fakhreddine, an associate professor of Arabic literature and a faculty member involved with the Palestine Writes Literature Festival, tweeted: "While we were asleep Palestine invented a new way of life." Ten days later, she wrote that "Israel is antisemitic, anti-human, anti-children, anti-life!"

Two weeks after the attacks, Robert Vitalis, a professor in Penn's political science department, posted a photo of the emblem of Hamas's military wing, alongside the caption: "A quick and easy way to reduce my friends list (and it will look cool on your jacket, too)."

Two days after October 7th, a group of keffiyeh-clad antisemitic demonstrators confronted freshman Jordan Davis, who was wearing a Star of David necklace. "You are a dirty Jew!" one yelled at her. "Keep walking, you dirty little Jew!" said others.[12]

In mid-October, a library assistant for circulation at the University of Pennsylvania's Carey Law School was recorded tearing down posters of kidnapped Israeli hostages that had been hung on a fence.[13]

Less than one month later, a Penn student stole an Israeli flag from the residence of a Jewish student and burned it at a rally. During the flag-burning, she lauded the "joyful and powerful images which came from the glorious October 7." She declared that Hamas's attack caused her to feel "so empowered and happy." And she encouraged the crowd to "hold that feeling in your hearts" and "bring it to the streets." The student was a member of anti-Israel student group Penn Students Against the Occupation. She was arrested and charged with theft, but she was let off of any meaningful discipline by Penn. The student was a foreign student from Jordan. Did Penn shield her from disciplinary consequences for that reason? If so, that would raise serious legal questions.[14]

In early November, according to the university, several Penn staff members received "vile disturbing antisemitic emails threatening violence against members of our Jewish community." The messages included bomb threats targeting Penn Hillel and Penn's Lauder College House, a dormitory named for the Lauder family, members of which were among Penn's well-known Jewish alumni and donors.[15]

A few days later, pro-Hamas groups projected messages onto several Penn buildings. According to *The Daily Pennsylvanian*, Penn's student newspaper, the messages included "Let Gaza live," "From the river to the sea, Palestine will be free," "Zionism is racism," "Penn funds Palestinian genocide," "From West Philly to Palestine, occupation is a crime," "Free Palestine," and "10,000 murdered by Israeli occupation since October 7." The university condemned the messages as "antisemitic" and "vile."[16]

The next day, dozens of students, faculty, staff, and alumni staged a multiday occupation of Penn's student union, Houston Hall.

Penn's administrators did not issue an official statement until three days after the October 7th attack. Much like Harvard, what Penn came up with was a muddle of moral confusion—the statement did not condemn Hamas explicitly—and absurd self-congratulation: President Liz Magill praised the "leaders and administrators who quickly and thoughtfully mobilized, identifying and reaching out to students, faculty, and staff with connections to the region to offer assistance and resources."

That was not the experience of many Jewish students.

Long before she appeared before our committee, Liz Magill was under fire for her handling of on-campus antisemitism. Marc Rowan, the CEO of private equity firm Apollo Global Management and at the time a member of the advisory board of Penn's prestigious Wharton School of Business, had already petitioned the university aggressively to shut down the Palestine Writes Literature Festival because of its rank antisemitism. When Magill's statement appeared, he blasted it as inadequate and increased the stakes, calling on Magill to resign.

Rowan began a very effective pressure campaign in concert with other alumni appalled by Penn's slouching approach to the problem of antisemitism on campus. "Microaggressions are condemned with extreme moral outrage," Rowan said during an October 2023 appearance on CNBC's

Squawk Box, "and yet violence, particularly violence against Jews, antisemitism, seems to have found a place of tolerance on the campus."

On October 11, 2023, Rowan published an open letter to the Penn community on eJewishPhilanthropy.com. (The letter was submitted to *The Daily Pennsylvanian* on October 10 but not run, according to Rowan.) In the letter he took Penn's leadership—Magill and Board of Trustees Chairman Scott Bok—to task for their failure to secure Penn against the corruption of antisemitism. He lamented that Penn, "once a place of critical reasoning, objective proof, considered debate and moral leadership," had given way to "hate, racism and, ultimately, violence." Rowan called on "all UPenn alumni and supporters who believe we are heading in the wrong direction to 'close their checkbooks' until President Magill and Chairman Bok resign."[17]

That was the background against which Liz Magill appeared before our committee on December 5, 2023.

Of the three university presidents who testified, UPenn's Liz Magill was, by far, the worst. "It's a context-dependent decision" was her answer to my repeated questioning of whether calling for the genocide of Jews violated UPenn's code of conduct. Her smirk when answering questions regarding the genocide of Jews was near universally criticized.

According to *Politico*, which ran a sympathetic profile of Magill in June 2025, it was not until hours after the hearing that Magill realized that her answers were insufficient. "After the hearing, Magill immediately drove back to Philly. At first, she got messages from board members congratulating her on having done a good job. But, around five o'clock, [Magill's chief of staff, Mike] Citro called and told her that her answers were 'blowing up' on Instagram and that she might need to issue an apology. . . . 'I hadn't seen any of the Instagram stuff,' Magill said, 'but it was quick.' Soon, she said, she understood that the situation was exploding."[18]

Hundreds of millions of dollars of donor commitments to Penn vanished overnight, coupled with outraged alumni and student condemnation.

The explosion not only rocked Penn, it boiled over into the top news stories in national politics.

I called for Liz Magill's immediate resignation at the hearing. Republicans nationwide were unified in an immediate cacophony of outrage, with demands of accountability. Even Biden White House spokesperson Karine Jean-Pierre, while declining to comment on whether the university presidents should be fired, did say: "We do not stand for calls for genocide. That is unacceptable. That is vile. We will call that out."[19]

In a statement, Pennsylvania Democrat Senator John Fetterman wrote: "There is no 'both sides-ism' and it isn't 'free speech,' it's simply hate speech. . . . It was embarrassing for a venerable Pennsylvania university, and it should be reflexive for leaders to condemn antisemitism and stand up for the Jewish community or any community facing this kind of invective."[20]

During a visit to Philadelphia restaurant Goldie, which had been the site of an antisemitic protest the day before (pro-Palestinian demonstrators stood outside the Jewish-owned restaurant chanting: "Goldie, Goldie you can't hide, we charge you with genocide!"), Governor Josh Shapiro condemned Magill's remarks: "Frankly, I thought her comments were absolutely shameful," he said. "It should not be hard to condemn genocide." Magill should've given a "one-word answer," he went on, but "failed to meet that test." Penn's leaders "have seemingly failed every step of the way to take concrete action," Shapiro added. "The testimony yesterday took it to the next level. It was a failure of leadership, clearly."[21]

Under pressure from all sides, Magill tried to clean up her mess. The day after the hearing, she hastily released a poorly filmed video speaking straight to the camera while seated in a corner that attempted to calm the storm. She promised to "get it right."[22]

But Magill had not gotten it right. In fact, Penn had failed for years to get it right.

Liz Magill was forced to resign as president of the University of Pennsylvania on December 9, 2023, four days after her disastrous testimony. Penn quietly and cowardly kept Magill as a tenured faculty member, and less than one year later, Harvard hired Magill as a senior fellow at Harvard

Law School. Talk about the revolving door of a broken higher education system.

....

Penn's antisemitism problem, and the university's incompetent response, did not begin with Liz Magill. It also did not end with her.

Months later, ten pro-Hamas students stormed into a Penn Board of Trustees meeting, bringing the meeting to a halt. The students, who chanted "endowment transparency now, divest from genocide," refused to stop when asked by Penn officials. Two students were placed on short-term probation, while others were assigned "reflective essays."

In May 2024, a group of pro-Hamas rioters broke open the gate to the house of Penn's interim president, trespassed onto the grounds, and disobeyed police commands. Police described the scene as a "riot." Two students broke into the house and vandalized it, causing $18,000 in damage.

A week later, nineteen people—including seven Penn students—were arrested for attempting to occupy Fisher-Bennett Hall, one of Penn's main academic buildings. Four students were arrested for the attempted occupation, while the other three were arrested for ignoring police instructions. According to our House Education Committee report: "During the attempted occupation of Fisher-Bennett Hall on May 17, 2024, protesters obstructed the building's windows with cardboard and barricaded multiple building entrances using barbed wire, wooden pallets, bike racks, furniture, and zip ties. Protesters resisted removal by police, shouted expletives at police officers, and chanted 'there is only one solution, intifada revolution.'"

I mentioned Eyal Yakoby earlier in this chapter. Eyal is one of the fearless Jewish students I have met and worked with. He has bravely confronted and chronicled antisemitism on Penn's campus since October 7th. Today, Eyal has one of the most informative X accounts that track this important issue.

On May 15, 2024, he testified before the House Judiciary Subcommittee on the Constitution and Limited Government about antisemitism at our elite universities. After recounting several horrible episodes on campus—"Bigotry, violence, and harassment have become part of Penn's daily syllabus," he said—he declared that he would not be cowed: "I refuse to let hatred drown out my love for freedom."[23]

Eyal testified before the House just two days before those vandals stormed Penn's Fisher-Bennett Hall. Eyal and students like him are the opposite of criminal vandals: They help to preserve and sustain what is best about our institutions of higher learning. They are beacons of courage, independence, and the spirit of toleration and mutual respect who live up to Benjamin Franklin's founding principles for UPenn.

Liz Magill's resignation within days of her testimony in response to my questions and others at the hearing was the first of many dominoes to fall in higher education and lead to the beginning of accountability for these institutions.

One down, so many to go. And so much work to do.

From the reckoning of the most prestigious business school in the world touting graduates who become titans of industry, like Elon Musk, let's take a stroll from Philadelphia, Pennsylvania, to New York City.

CHAPTER 5

Columbia

Founded in 1754
In lumine tuo videbimus lumen
"In thy light we shall see light"

"To the stewards of Columbia*—a once great institution founded by Alexander Hamilton in 1754; a place where so many members of my family, even my grandfather, received such excellent education and made such lasting friendships—what is happening today is on you. You, the trustees, the officers, the deans, the faculty and the admissions directors, have caused this university to fail. As you watch today as the campus goes up in proverbial smoke, understand that you invited hatred into your school and hatred has now consumed it. Columbia is now bankrupt, if not yet financially, then certainly morally and intellectually. You gave scholarships to foreigners who hate America while hardworking American parents took multiple jobs just to realize the dream (a dream my parents had as well) for their kids to advance. Shame on all of you."*

—David Friedman, Former U.S. Ambassador to Israel (April 18, 2024)[1]

A stunning statue of Alexander Hamilton proudly stands in front of his namesake Hamilton Hall, harkening back to Hamilton's studies at what was then called King's College, founded in 1754. Hamilton's studies were interrupted. In 1775, before he could complete his degree, King's College was closed down by British troops occupying New York City. Hamilton joined the colonial American militia. He would go on to be Continental Army leader George Washington's aide-de-camp and, of course, one of the most famous of our nation's Founding Fathers.

Hamilton was just one of several Founders who could claim King's College as an alma mater. Robert R. Livingston, who was part of the five-member committee that drafted the Declaration of Independence, and later became the U.S. ambassador to France, as well as the young nation's first secretary of state (called then the "secretary of foreign affairs"). Gouverneur Morris, who enrolled at Columbia at just twelve years old, was a key member of the Continental Congress. And John Jay, who with Hamilton and James Madison co-authored *The Federalist Papers*, helped negotiate the Treaty of Paris that ended the Revolutionary War.

Columbia is different today. The university that helped educate America's first patriots has embraced an entirely different, even opposite, mission. Today, much of what passes for education at Columbia University is designed to instill hostility toward the United States, our Founders, and our founding ideals. An institution that helped educate the men who put their lives at stake for liberty and equality is now a breeding ground of race hatred and violence. You won't find Alexander Hamiltons at Columbia anymore. Instead, you'll find a lot of people who want to tear down his statue.

In the months after October 7th, Columbia became a sorry spectacle. The whole nation saw as one ugly episode after another played out on its Manhattan campus, and as its leaders fumbled and floundered to assert themselves against antisemitic protests and violent mobs.

None of this was inevitable. Columbia was once home to legendary Jewish faculty, such as the literary critic Lionel Trilling and the art historian Meyer Schapiro. For more than a century the Upper West Side, where Columbia is located, has been a center of Jewish life in New York City. Many European Jews who fled Adolf Hitler found safe harbor there. As Matt Schweber, a member of the Columbia University Jewish Alumni Association, told the *New York Post*: "Who could have ever imagined that Columbia University would be the site for rallies calling for Intifada, for swastikas scrawled on campus property and for Jewish students to be intimidated and followed as they walk home from class?"[2]

The chaos and dangerous antisemitism that took over Columbia's campus were the result of failed leadership. The moral rot on display was an indictment of the university's total embrace of radical progressivism, which came at the expense of ordinary students.

....

When Columbia's pro-Hamas encampments sprang up in the spring of 2024, Columbia University President Minouche Shafik was in Washington, D.C.

Shafik was supposed to be under oath at the December 2023 congressional hearing, seated alongside her fellow university presidents from Harvard, Penn, and MIT. Instead, citing a "scheduling conflict," President Shafik stayed far away. In fact, we later uncovered that, rather than answer questions from Congress in Washington, D.C., President Shafik chose to travel halfway around the world to Dubai to participate in the United Nations Climate Change Conference, where speakers discussed climate change's impact on women.[3]

Columbia was crystal clear on its priorities. Jewish students, faculty, and staff being harassed, assaulted, and engulfed in antisemitic threats on a daily basis on campus? Not a priority. Climate change? That deserved a seven-thousand-mile trip by Columbia's president, with a university entourage in tow.

Days after the disastrous university presidents hearing, *The New York Times* published a fawning piece applauding President Shafik's strategic foresight: she had cleverly avoided attending the hearing and submitting to congressional oversight featuring questions that led to the immediate ouster (at that point) of Penn's president and the firestorm currently facing the Harvard and MIT presidents who were barely hanging on to their positions. The *Times* wondered whether individuals in high-profile positions ought to testify at all, given the risk from "lawmakers with political agendas" who might be "setting prosecutorial traps for their witnesses." We might also call it: doing our job! Calling university presidents to testify, because their schools aren't honoring their legal obligations, is

Congress's duty. That's what oversight authority means. Congress is responsible for overseeing all federal laws related to higher education, and for ensuring that American higher education institutions are complying with the Higher Education Act, the Clery Act, and the Civil Rights Act of 1964. Moreover, billions of hard-earned U.S. taxpayer dollars go directly to fund higher education institutions, especially our most elite institutions. Columbia enjoys more than $1 billion in U.S. taxpayer dollars, much of it in the form of federal grants and contracts.[4] Congress has the responsibility to keep an eye on that money on behalf of hardworking U.S. taxpayers. Our supposed national "paper of record" is disconnected from the concerns, and moral common sense, of everyday Americans.

In the days and months after October 7th, while President Shafik was waxing poetic about the history of climate change nomenclature in Dubai, Columbia's Manhattan campus was consumed by horrifying antisemitic crimes.

Immediately following Hamas's terrorist attacks on Israel on October 7th, American Jewish and Israeli students at Columbia faced vile slurs and constant threats to their physical safety. Less than one week after October 7th, a former Columbia undergraduate assaulted an Israeli student with a stick while tearing down posters of the Israeli hostages taken by Hamas. According to a report, "the violent assailant shouted 'F*** you. F*** all you prick crackers.'" The perpetrator was eventually prosecuted for charges including second-degree and third-degree assault.[5]

This was hardly the only incident. A few days later, during an anti-Israel protest, a Jewish student wearing an Israeli flag was yelled at and called a "murderer." Another Jewish student wearing an Israeli flag had it torn off and thrown down a subway staircase. One week later, a Columbia student inside Columbia Law School screamed "F**ck the Jews" at a law student wearing a yarmulke.[6] Antisemitic posters appeared on campus featuring an image of a blue-and-white skunk with a Star of David on its back. Underneath, the captions read "Beware! Skunk on Campus" and "brought to you in collaboration by Columbia University and the IOF [Israeli Occupation Forces]."

When students at Columbia Law School tried to organize Law Students Against Antisemitism, the law school's student senate denied the group recognition. The litany of antisemitic acts at Columbia continued to skyrocket. According to the *Columbia Spectator*, nine organizations had requested recognition, and Law Students Against Antisemitism was the only one not to receive approval.

Columbia University Apartheid Divest (CUAD) partnered with Students for Justice for Palestine and hosted an "All Out for Palestine" rally immediately outside Columbia's gates. A Jewish Columbia undergraduate wearing a shirt with an Israeli flag at a pro-Israel counterprotest was harassed by an antisemitic protester wearing a keffiyeh. After the Jewish student broke free and escaped, his assaulter shouted "Keep running, keep f**cking running." Pro-Hamas protesters chanted "Long live the intifada," "Settlers, settlers go back home—Palestine is ours alone," "NYPD, KKK, IDF they're all the same," and "NYPD burn in hell!" Trucks drove by blaring antisemitic messages, including "Israel is the new Nazi Germany" and "Israel steals Palestinian organs." The New York Police Department arrested three pro-Hamas protesters and charged a dozen with disorderly conduct, including a Columbia undergraduate.[7]

It was not just encampments, physical assaults, and threats of violence that targeted Jewish students at Columbia, but also vile online antisemitic harassment that was pervasive and tolerated by the university. Within the weeks following October 7th, Columbia social media was flooded with heinous antisemitism. And the university turned a blind eye. "On the anonymous messaging platform Sidechat, which requires a Columbia e-mail address to access, posts included 'say it with me: F**CK ISRAEL,' 'f**ck the Jews,' and 'wish we had some way to indicate Zionists and the Zionist supporting shops in Morningside so we can actively avoid them and not give them our business . . . perhaps with a Star of David from the Israeli flag, idk why I even engage with Zionists, their stupidity literally gives me migraines." When the author of the post was asked about their "problem with Zionists," the author wrote back, "my problem is their existence." Another post wished that "any IDF veterans" at Columbia "die a slow death" and identified by name a student currently serving in Gaza.[8]

How could Columbia's faculty, staff, and administrators tolerate this kind of blatant, raging antisemitism? The simple fact is, key parts of Columbia were already infected by this poison. Antisemitism wasn't a new arrival. It had been a presence in Columbia's classrooms for years.

....

The problem of anti-Jewish bias, and even abuse of Jewish and pro-Israel students, is long-standing at Columbia. Antisemitism has found homes in whole departments and fields of study, to the extent that students dare not enter, for example, the notorious Department of Middle Eastern, South Asian, and African Studies (MESAAS) if they hold pro-Israel opinions. The episodes I've chronicled below are not isolated incidents: they're part of a widespread pattern of hostility and harassment.

Take, for example, Joseph Massad, professor of modern Arab politics and intellectual history in the Middle Eastern Studies Department. He began teaching at Columbia in 1999, after earning his doctorate there a year earlier. He was granted tenure in 2009. Massad's history of antisemitism is well documented and apparent in his work. In the early 2000s, Massad allegedly asked a student who had served in the Israeli Defense Forces, "How many Palestinians did you kill?"[9] He has called IDF soldiers "baby-killing Zionist Jewish volunteers for Israeli Jewish supremacy" and labeled Zionism a "genocidal cult."[10] When Columbia was asked by the media about these heinous statements by a professor, instead of condemning the statements, they cowardly refused to comment.

In 2005, a series of student complaints forced Columbia's then president Lee Bollinger to establish a five-person committee to investigate Massad. The investigation was designed to exonerate him, not to assess his behavior. The members of the committee were two professors who had signed an anti-Israel BDS petition, a professor who had publicly blamed Israel for worldwide antisemitism, Massad's dissertation advisor, and a university administrator who had previously been accused of ignoring student complaints of antisemitism on campus. "The man who handpicked the committee, Nick Dirks," the *New York Post* added, "is married to a professor who co-teaches a class with Massad."

Unsurprisingly, Massad was not disciplined.[11]

So it could hardly come as a shock that, on October 8, 2023, just twenty-four hours after Hamas launched its terrorist attack on Israel, Massad published an online op-ed at the website *The Electronic Intifada* celebrating Hamas's "resistance." Massad praised the attacks in paragraph after paragraph.[12] At no point does Massad mention any of the particular acts of violence and terror committed by Hamas—for example, slaughtering whole families in their homes or butchering elderly peace activists. All of that is hidden under the word "resistance."

Massad was hardly alone. A few weeks later, he joined 170 other Columbia faculty in signing an open letter "in Defense of Robust Debate About the History and Meaning of the War in Israel/Gaza." The bulk of the letter is spent defending a student-written statement that had appeared earlier in the month. At no point in this letter are Hamas's crimes mentioned or acknowledged. According to the letter, Hamas's "armed resistance" is "anticipated" by "international humanitarian law"—a way of saying that Hamas's acts are implicitly righteous. Whether the "prohibition against the intentional targeting of civilians" applies to Hamas or only to Israel is, notably, left ambiguous.[13]

This is just one egregious example of Columbia professors who fully embrace and foment antisemitism on campus. Unfortunately, there are many more cases.

One incident was described in *The Atlantic* (the faculty member in question was left unnamed): "One student left class in the middle of a professor's broadside against Israel in a required course in the Middle East studies department. Afterward, he sent an email to the professor explaining his departure, to which the professor wrote back, saying they could discuss it in class later. When the student returned, the professor read his email aloud to the whole class and invited everyone to discuss the exchange. It felt like an act of deliberate humiliation."[14]

Hamid Dabashi, Columbia's Hagop Kevorkian Professor of Iranian Studies and Comparative Literature, has a decades-long record of antisemitism in his classroom. In 2004, Dabashi wrote that Israelis have "a vulgarity of character that is bone-deep and structural to the skeletal vertebrae of its culture." A decade later, he wrote, "from now on, every time any Israeli, every time any Jew, anywhere in the world, utters the word 'Auschwitz,' or the word 'Holocaust,' the world will hear 'Gaza.'" In 2018, he wrote, "Every dirty treacherous ugly and pernicious act happening in the world just wait for a few days and the ugly name of 'Israel' will pup [*sic*] up as a key actor in the atrocities."[15]

At Columbia's Graduate School of Architecture, Planning and Preservation, after a student shared her family's heritage from Israel, one professor asked: "So you know a lot about settler colonialism. How do you feel about that?" Another professor declared, "It's such a shame that your people survived just in order to perpetuate genocide."[16]

None of these teachers faced any disciplinary action.

There's one other professor whose name might sound familiar. Mahmood Mamdani is the Herbert Lehman Professor of Government in the Department of Anthropology at Columbia. He is also the father of New York City's pro-Hamas, defund-the-police, Socialist, I believe jihadist, new mayor Zohran Mamdani.

The elder Mamdani's bona fides are, naturally, impeccable: anti-American, anti-capitalist, and anti-Israel fanaticism have animated his entire career and shaped his son's.

For example, in *Good Muslim, Bad Muslim*, published in 2004, Mamdani asserted that "we need to recognize the suicide bomber, first and foremost, as a category of soldier."[17] Mamdani rejected the idea that suicide bombing is barbaric. It's probably not a coincidence that the book appeared at precisely the time that Hamas, Palestinian Islamic Jihad, PFLP, and other terrorist groups were embracing suicide bombing as the central tactic of the Second Intifada, during which time they killed more than one thousand Israelis.

In *Neither Settler nor Native*, published in 2020, Mamdani claimed that in Israel "the expunging of non-Jews has taken the form of ethnic cleansing, dispossession, segregation, fragmentation, apartheid, and denial of identity."[18]

At an event in 2022, taking a moment away from attacking Israel to go the next step and attack America, he explained: "America is the genesis of what we call 'settler colonialism.' The American model was exported all around the world." He claimed that Hitler modeled the Holocaust on American precedents, specifically Abraham Lincoln's Native American policies.[19]

And that's far from the worst of it.

Mahmood Mamdani is a member of the Advisory Policy Council of the Gaza Tribunal, the goal of which "is to awaken civil society to its responsibility and opportunity to stop Israel's genocide in Gaza." Other members of the council include the virulently antisemitic ex–UK Labour Party leader Jeremy Corbyn and Ramy Abdu, a human rights lawyer with close ties to Hamas. The Gaza Tribunal hosted a conference in Istanbul in late October 2025. Among its featured speakers were several with present or past ties to designated terrorist organizations.[20]

When it comes to Mayor Zohran Mamdani's radicalism—for example, when he refuses to condemn Hamas or when he peddles antisemitic conspiracy theories such as: "When the boot of the NYPD is on your neck, it's been laced by the IDF"—the apple does not fall far from the tree.[21] In fact, Zohran Mamdani's dangerous ideology was developed in a petri dish of antisemitic, anti-American indoctrination from his parents, whom he himself has described as having shaped his political worldview.

For years, Columbia has welcomed professors like those above, treating them as superlative members of Columbia's academic community. Pro-Israel professors have not received the same welcome. Consider what happened to former Columbia Business School Professor Shai Davidai.

On the evening of October 18, 2023, Professor Davidai, who grew up in Israel, gave an impassioned speech at an anti-terror vigil on Columbia's campus. He posted the speech to YouTube titled "An Open Letter to Every Parent in America."

"I want this message to get to every parent who sent their kids to Columbia University," he said. "I want this message to get to every parent in America who sent their kids to NYU, to Harvard, to Stanford, to Berkeley. And I want you to know one thing: we cannot protect your child.

"I'm speaking to you as a dad," Davidai continued: "I want you to know we cannot protect your children from pro-terror student organizations, because the president of Columbia University will not speak out against pro-terror student organizations, because the president of Harvard University, because the president of Stanford, because the president of Berkeley will not speak out against pro-terror student organizations."

In the course of his ten-minute oration, he accused then Columbia President Minouche Shafik of being a "coward" and said that he feared for his safety on campus, given the indisputable evidence of anti-Israel and anti-Jewish hatred.[22] Davidai's stirring speech, and his fierce advocacy on behalf of Columbia's Jewish community, made him a well-known presence on campus. Unlike the tenured professors spewing vile antisemitism for decades, Shai Davidai became a target of Columbia's administration. In December 2023, Columbia University launched an investigation of Davidai, alleging harassment based on "national origin and/or shared ancestry." The charges reflected accusations from pro-Palestinian students and faculty that Davidai had "doxxed" and "harassed" them—charges that Davidai denies.

Davidai and his wife identify as liberals. Writing in *Tablet* in February 2024, while the investigation was still ongoing, they articulated their position this way: "As leftist, liberal Zionists, we have always made a clear distinction between the people of Palestine and the inhumane terror organizations that falsely purport to speak in their name. Our support for a two-state solution has never wavered, and to this day we remain staunchly opposed to Israel's occupation of the West Bank, refrain from buying products manufactured beyond the 1967 armistice line, and protest any governmental policy that we see as oppressive or unjust." They simply think that Israel has the right to exist—a belief they share with the majority of Americans.

That was all it took to set off an avalanche of vicious hatred from supposed allies.

Davidai and his wife reported receiving everything from antisemitic caricatures to threats of violence: "Shai is regularly called a Nazi, a Zionist pig, a genocidal baby murderer, a kike. Thousands have called for his death." They pointed to the hypocrisy in their supposedly "progressive" circle. For their friends, they said, it wasn't a problem of Davidai's politics, but of their very identity, not of what they believed but of who they were.[23]

In October 2024, on the first anniversary of October 7th, antisemitic protesters surrounded and intimidated a group of students holding a university-sanctioned memorial. Pro-Hamas protesters sat on the steps of Columbia's library holding mock newspapers that read, in a full-page advertisement, "Glory to the Martyrs. Victory to the Resistance." Davidai broadcast much of the protest on his X account. When Columbia chief operating officer Cas Holloway happened to cross Columbia's plaza, Davidai challenged him to explain why pro-Hamas protesters were permitted by the university to harass Jewish mourners and accused Holloway of being "indifferent" to "hatred." A few days later, Davidai's campus access was suspended. A university spokesman alleged that Davidai had "repeatedly harassed and intimidated University employees in violation of University policy."[24]

Eventually, exhausted by Columbia's mistreatment, Davidai left the university. Writing in *Tablet* in July 2025, he explained his decision: "Columbia's failed leadership, morally bankrupt faculty, and indifferent majority have shattered my respect for an institution I once called home. I no longer trust its leaders to do what's right, or my colleagues to show them the way. With that respect lost, I have no choice but to leave. Staying would betray everything I stand for."[25]

The pattern is clear. Those who attack Jewish students are treated with kid gloves and allowed to remain in positions of privilege and influence.

But those who stand up for the civil rights of Jewish students are bullied—then accused of being the bullies, suspended, canceled, and driven out.

Columbia's topsy-turvy moral code declares that those who bully and harass—often in violation of students' civil rights—are really the victims of bullying and harassment. But the actual victims are accused of being the bullies and harassers. Likewise, when American Jewish or pro-Israel students request permission to engage in university-sanctioned activities like anniversary memorials, the university enforces its regulations to a T. But when pro-Palestinian, and even pro-Hamas, students and faculty break university rules and violate standard time, place, and manner restrictions, the university simply turns a blind eye. The moral judgment of these university leaders is utterly upside down.

This is not 1930s Germany. This is the 2020s in New York City at one of the most prestigious universities in the United States of America. And just to remind you: Columbia University's undergraduate tuition is an eye-watering $70,000 per year—for this antisemitic, anti-American, and vile anti-West hate.

....

The culture that Columbia's faculty and leadership created on campus did not stop brave students from taking a stand. While the lack of any action by Columbia's president, Board of Trustees, and the vast majority of faculty and staff allowed antisemitism to fester, and subsequently to explode after October 7th, some undergraduate students boldly and bravely stepped forward to speak out, telling the world what they were being forced to endure as American Jewish students at Columbia.

Over the course of our congressional investigation, I had the opportunity to meet many of these inspiring young leaders who refused to be silenced and who shared their stories with poise and moral clarity.

Eden Yadegar is one of those extraordinary young leaders. Eden, a junior at Columbia in early 2024, was a Middle East studies major and one of the university's many Jewish and pro-Israel students. Speaking before

Congress, Eden gave testimony that encapsulated the antisemitic rot on Columbia's campus. She recounted appalling stories of student and faculty bigotry, and of open harassment of Jews and supporters of Israel. On various occasions, the university facilitated chaotic antisemitic protests while actively discouraging peaceful gatherings of Jewish students.

Like Harvard student Shabbos Kestenbaum, Eden Yadegar is the child of a family who fled antisemitism abroad—this time from Iran, a half century ago. "I thought coming to Columbia would enable me to pursue the American dream in the same way my parents did when moving to this country," Eden testified. "Instead, it has turned into a nightmare."[26]

Every American should be proud of Eden Yadegar for bravely speaking the truth to the representatives of the American people in the U.S. Congress. Her own university failed to listen, but her bold decision made sure the story of what she and other students experienced on campus was heard. I am grateful for her strength and courage of conviction.

But not even Eden's powerful testimony could shock Columbia's leadership into disciplinary action or toward real accountability. Instead, Columbia continued to ignore antisemitism on campus and the brave students calling attention to it.

On March 24, 2024, a month after Yadegar testified to our committee about widespread antisemitism at Columbia, Columbia University Apartheid Divest held an event called "Resistance 101" at the Barnard Center for Research on Women. The ninety-minute event featured two speakers with proven connections to terrorist groups. Khaled Barakat, who called into the event via Zoom from his home in Vancouver, is a known partner of the Popular Front for the Liberation of Palestine (PFLP), a U.S.-designated foreign terrorist organization. At the event, he recounted conversations with "friends and brothers in Hamas, Islamic Jihad, the PFLP" and praised airplane hijackings as "one of the most important tactics that the Palestinian resistance [has] engaged in" and "heroic."[27]

Charlotte Kates, his wife, is the international coordinator for Samidoun, the Palestinian Prisoner Solidarity Network, considered a terrorist organization by Israel. "There is nothing wrong with being a fighter in Hamas," she told attendees.[28]

Under public pressure, Columbia claimed that they suspended at least six students involved in organizing the event. Yet almost all of them had their suspensions lifted.[29]

The failure to hold those students accountable was part of the larger failure to recognize what was really happening with on-campus antisemitism at Columbia and elsewhere. "Resistance 101" made the situation crystal clear: the student activists on campus saw themselves as the allies and friends of actual terrorist organizations. To the members of Columbia University Apartheid Divest, people like Khaled Barakat and Charlotte Kates are not terrorists. They're role models. They're partners. They're comrades-in-arms in a shared struggle. Over and over, student activists showed their true colors. But campus leaders, like Columbia's president Minouche Shafik, refused to see what was right in front of them.

....

Eventually, the degrading situation at Columbia became impossible to ignore. Encampments were disrupting normal campus life. Jewish students were forced to dodge the shouts and slurs of classmates and former friends. Finally, on April 17, 2024, more than six months after Hamas's terrorist attack and nearly two months after undergraduate Eden Yadegar's shocking testimony, Columbia President Minouche Shafik entered the congressional hearing room to testify to the House Education Committee. At her side were Board of Trustees Co-Chairs Claire Shipman and David Greenwald, and Professor David Schizer, who served as co-chair of the Columbia University Task Force on Antisemitism.

Minutes before the hearing commenced, Claire Shipman went out of her way to introduce herself to me. I doubt she was just being friendly. She wanted to make it known to me that they had come highly prepared and lawyered up, and were ready for any and all tough questions.

President Shafik had an obvious advantage over Presidents Gay,

Magill, and Kornbluth (Harvard, Penn, and MIT). She had watched them implode. Presumably, she would not make the same mistakes. Like them, Columbia had hired a team of lawyers who spent months preparing Shafik for her appearance. In fact, one of her lawyers I knew professionally quite well.

It is worth mentioning that a few weeks prior to this hearing, I received a friendly call from a former White House colleague, Bill Burck, a defense lawyer for top executives facing white-collar cases and an avowed expert at congressional investigations and preparing high-profile witnesses for testimony. "Burck," as he is well known in Washington circles, is an uber-successful attorney with pristine credentials and an exceptional professional reputation. He's also a personal friend whom I have known for nearly two decades. As happens a fair amount prior to hearings, Burck informally called me to discuss his client Columbia President Shafik's upcoming hearing and that, unlike the presidents of Harvard, Penn, and MIT, she would come prepared with answers. I told Burck that I would have tough questions for her like the other college presidents because I was concerned by the rise of antisemitism at Columbia and her failure to address this scourge of hate.

This type of pre-call to members or members' offices prior to hearings is fairly commonplace on Capitol Hill. My policy is that I don't share my questions or topics ahead of time, and I often review the hearing preparation materials, absorb them, think about things independently for some time leading up to the hearing, and then draft my questions late the evening before or draft them in real time as the hearing is ongoing, for what strikes me at the moment. After a decade in Congress, I have found that my most effective questions are usually done on the fly and not pre-written. My dedicated legislative team conducts a tremendous amount of research and makes recommendations of potential questions or topics prior to the hearing, but for nearly every major hearing, I end up writing and asking my own questions.

Over the years, I have honed a questioning style that is the opposite of the typical legislative-speak "legislativese" in congressional hearings, with paragraph-long statements followed by a two-minute question. Instead I prefer to keep my questions short and to the point. I want the questions to be fact-based, direct, and pertinent to the American people, often requiring a yes-or-no answer. I also typically outline what I call my "question tree" of what my many follow-up questions will likely be so that I can use my five-minute allotted time most judiciously. After the first hearing with university presidents, many fellow committee members and particularly freshmen members of Congress reached out to me directly to adjust and better hone their questioning style to more effectively cut to the chase. One particular freshman member of Congress who told me that he studied my questioning style at length to help hone his hearing presentations is rising star Brandon Gill from Texas, who has already earned deserved recognition for his excellent hearing questions. I make it a habit to try to always work with members when they reach out asking for guidance regarding committee hearing strategies.

My colleague Representative Tim Walberg, a former pastor from Michigan, opened the Columbia hearing with a line of questioning similar to what I had planned. He pointed to Professor Joseph Massad's praise for Hamas's October 7th attacks, his long track record of antisemitic statements, and his allegedly abusive behavior toward Jewish students. Were there any consequences at Columbia for that kind of conduct? President Shafik said Massad "has been spoken to," but nothing more.[30]

In these university hearings on antisemitism, I was usually the only member of Congress other than the chair of the committee who sat through every hearing in its entirety. The daily schedule of most members of Congress includes multiple hearings and meetings scheduled simultaneously. Members time their appearance for their five minutes of allotted questioning. It is far from an ideal schedule, but it's the unfortunate reality of how Congress functions today with various hearings happening all the time. Still, I felt it was a priority for me to hear the complete back-and-forth with other members' questions and the witnesses' answers. Most of the time, the witness thinks they are off the hook for any follow-ups after they get through five minutes of an individual member's time. As the attorneys who prepped these various university presidents who appeared before the education committee would have told their clients, that is not the case with the way I prepare for and adjust my questions on the fly to do timely follow-ups throughout the hearing.

Congressman Walberg's line of questioning laid a trail I could follow. So I did. I grilled the witnesses further about Joseph Massad and about multiple other Columbia faculty members, one who had declared support for terrorist organizations, another who had called for discrimination against Israeli students. Had they suffered any consequences?

No was the answer. In fact, I learned a few minutes later via text message that one of those professors was, at that very moment, participating in an unsanctioned pro-Hamas protest on campus.[31]

Like most hours-long congressional hearings, the hearing had a short break in the middle. Columbia's witnesses huddled in the Education Committee anteroom. Columbia President Shafik and Board Co-Chair Claire Shipman were privately celebrating with one another how well the hearing was going from their perspective. "It's going very well, better than we could have imagined," I overheard.

Were they experiencing the same hearing? It was a trainwreck! The American people and Columbia students watching the hearing were absolutely appalled. It was sickening to me that rather than reflect and consider what actions should be taken to address the pervasive antisemitism on campus that had been highlighted during the hearing, they were arrogantly treating it as just something to get through behind closed doors, to check the box and congratulate themselves on avoiding the fate of the Penn and Harvard presidents (now former presidents).

Little did they know how out of touch they really were, as they could not have imagined what the aftermath of the hearing would be for Columbia.

In reality, the hearing was a disaster. President Shafik equivocated on antisemitism, was inconsistent in her testimony about disciplinary action taken against antisemitic students and faculty, and even declared that there had been no "anti-Jewish" activity on campus—before turning around and acknowledging that campus protesters had chanted slogans such as "F*** the Jews!" and "Death to the Jews!"

The hearing caused an eruption on campus. That night pro-Hamas agitators set up Columbia's first major encampment. A few days later, the NYPD was finally called in to clear the site, leading to violent attacks on law enforcement and the subsequent arrest of more than one hundred encampment participants. Before long, the campus descended into outright chaos. "As you watch today as the campus goes up in proverbial smoke, understand that you invited hatred into your school and hatred has now consumed it," wrote former U.S. ambassador to Israel and Columbia alumnus David Friedman on X.[32] It was clearer than ever that Columbia leaders' abject failure to address antisemitism early and forcefully was enabling bigger, bolder, and more dangerous agitation.

....

One of those agitators was a foreign graduate student: Mahmoud Khalil, a master of public administration student at Columbia's School of International and Public Affairs. Khalil became a left-wing celebrity in early 2025 when the Trump administration detained and began the process of deporting him—one of a number of students detained for violating the terms of their student visas.

What did Khalil do? The left-wing media has cried endless crocodile tears for him, treating Khalil like the innocent victim of a corrupt government. The position of the U.S. government is that Khalil broke the law. As a leader of Columbia's pro-Hamas encampments, he participated directly in the violation of American Jewish students' civil rights. On several occasions, Khalil acted as a spokesperson and negotiator for the encamped students as they petitioned Columbia's administration. He was identified as such by several media outlets.

In reality, as a leader of Columbia University Apartheid Divest (CUAD), Khalil was at the forefront of antisemitic and anti-American activism from the first moment he arrived on campus. Photos show Khalil leading chants in demonstrations in the days immediately following October 7th. His student organization, CUAD, has called for the "total eradication of Western Civilization." As we saw above, it was the organization responsible for inviting Khaled Barakat and Charlotte Kates to campus in March 2024.

On March 7, 2024, Khalil was a speaker at the "Palestine 101" event held on Columbia's campus. "Israel and their propaganda always find something to attack. . . . They—we—have tried armed resistance, which is, again, legitimate under international law, but Israel calls it terrorism." (Note that "we.")

On October 7, 2024, Khalil played a leading role in the "Al-Aqsa Flood Walkout," an event intended to "commemorate the historic Al-Aqsa Flood operation." (Al-Aqsa Flood was Hamas's name for the terrorist attack against Israel.) Protesters chanted, "Resistance is glorious! We will be victorious!" The protest was openly and explicitly pro-Hamas.[33]

In other words, Khalil was an open supporter of terrorism—in spite of the best efforts of the mainstream media to cast him as a peacemaker and bridge-builder.

Despite being several times in violation of university policy, there is no record that Mahmoud Khalil was ever disciplined by Columbia for any of this obviously illegal conduct. Columbia simply turned a blind eye to the many ways in which pro-Hamas protesters such as Khalil broke the law, violated American students' rights, violated Columbia policy, and stoked an atmosphere of antisemitic harassment and physical intimidation.

It was only when President Trump took office for the second time that real accountability began. In Khalil's case, federal prosecutors uncovered that Khalil intentionally omitted his time spent working for the antisemitic United Nations Relief and Works Agency for Palestine Refugees (UNRWA) from his green card application. From June to November 2023, he was a political affairs officer for the organization.[34] The Trump administration rightly ceased funding to UNRWA given the organization's direct ties to terrorism.[35] It is well documented that UNRWA employees participated in the October 7th Hamas attacks against Israel.[36] Lying on a visa application is grounds for rejection.

Khalil spent over one hundred days in the custody of Immigration and Customs Enforcement before being released. The radical Left showered him with attention. Socialist Congresswoman Alexandria Ocasio-Cortez greeted him immediately after his release from detention.[37] Khalil was a prominent guest at Zohran Mamdani's mayoral victory party.[38]

Its full embrace of a terrorist sympathizer is an indication of just how radical the Left has become.

....

One of the most dramatic episodes on campus in the months after October 7th happened in late April. On the night of April 29, 2024, Columbia janitors Mario Torres and Lester Wilson were working the night shift on the third floor of Hamilton Hall. A little after midnight, they heard noises: yelling, breaking glass, stampeding. Dozens of anti-Israel activists, most of them wearing masks and hoods, invaded the building. They used furniture and vending machines to barricade the doors. They locked the exits with zip ties and bike chains. When they discovered Torres and Wilson, who initially refused to leave, they shouted at the men, threatened them, and shoved them. Torres was accused of being a "Jew-lover" and a "Zionist." Both men were held against their will overnight and into the morning hours. In an interview with *The Free Press* in the days following the episode, Wilson said he thought he "could have been killed in there."[39] They later filed a lawsuit against more than three dozen Columbia students, including leaders of Columbia University Apartheid Divest and Students for Justice in Palestine. According to the suit, the two men suffered physical injuries at the hands of the occupiers and subsequently developed post-traumatic stress disorder.[40]

The occupation of Hamilton Hall was one of the most dramatic episodes during the several weeks when encampments against university policy took over Columbia's Manhattan campus, as well as elite campuses across the country. It was also the predictable result of the environment of disorder, chaos, and lawlessness permitted and fostered by Columbia's inept administration. For nearly two weeks, hundreds of antisemitic demonstrators were camped out on Columbia's Butler Lawn. Most were students, mostly from Columbia but also from nearby campuses, such as Barnard and City College of New York. Some were faculty. Some were outside agitators, eager to make a bad situation worse. The encampments were an intimidation tactic. Their purpose was to make campus life difficult for others—for administrators, for fellow students who just wanted to get on with their studies, and, in particular, for anyone with pro-Israel sympathies. All along, campus leaders failed to rein in these encampments, which from the very beginning demonstrated a total disregard for campus rules, civic norms, and civil rights law. Violent demonstrators were permitted to run amok, and innocent bystanders suffered the consequences of their lawlessness.

The occupiers remained in Hamilton Hall until the evening of April 30, 2024, when the New York Police Department received permission from Columbia to clear the building. More than forty students and outside agitators were arrested on charges of trespassing. But Manhattan District Attorney Alvin Bragg ultimately dropped most of the charges.[41]

....

It's tempting to think that the problems at our elite universities can be solved with a resignation or two. But when you look beneath the surface, it's clear how deep the rot goes. Columbia would churn through a few presidents in short order.

When Columbia's beleaguered President Minouche Shafik resigned in August 2024, she was replaced by Katrina Armstrong, a physician and then head of Columbia University Irving Medical Center. Armstrong's tenure lasted less than a year. After agreeing to a set of accountability measures with the Trump administration, including placing the Middle Eastern, South Asian, and African Studies (MESAAS) Department in receivership, it emerged that Armstrong had informed Columbia faculty during a Zoom meeting that she did not intend to follow through with her commitments as the administration understood them.[42]

When Armstrong resigned as interim president in March 2025, she was succeeded by Clare Shipman—the Board of Trustees co-chair who had testified before our committee alongside Shafik in April 2024. Shipman, a graduate of Columbia and left-leaning journalist, was previously married to President Obama's Press Secretary Jay Carney.

Shipman had been active behind the scenes at Columbia since October 7, 2023. But the nature of her activism was deeply troubling.

"People are really frustrated and scared about antisemitism on our campus and they feel somehow betrayed by it," she wrote to Minouche Shafik on October 30, 2023. "Which is not necessarily a rational feeling but it's deep and it is quite threatening."

Shipman did nothing to address those concerns, as subsequent communications made clear.

In January, she advised Shafik: "We need to get somebody from the middle east [*sic*] or who is Arab on our board. Quickly I think. Somehow." This was advice that, if followed, would raise questions about Columbia's compliance with Title VI of the Civil Rights Act of 1964, which prohibits discrimination "on the ground of race, color, or national origin."

A month earlier, Shipman suggested that "we should think about . . . how to do some things with Rashid [Khalidi]. Events. That won't be popular in some groups but he is a respected academic." Khalidi, who joined Columbia as a professor in 2003 and ultimately retired in 2024, is well known for two reasons. First, his book *The Hundred Years' War on Palestine: A History of Settler Colonialism and Resistance, 1917–2017* is a work of anti-Israel propaganda that became a standard resource post–October 7th when President Joe Biden was spotted carrying it during a visit to Nantucket. Second, Khalidi allegedly served as a spokesman for the Palestinian Liberation Organization in the 1980s—an organization that has been designated by the United States as a terrorist group. (Khalidi denies the allegation.)

And, perhaps worst of all, Shipman repeatedly attacked in private Shoshana Shendelman, a Jewish member of Columbia's Board of Trustees. Asked in April by the board's vice chair, Wanda Greene, whether she thought Shendelman was “a mole? . . . A fox in the henhouse?” Shipman agreed: “I do.”[43]

What is one to make of references to the board’s sole Jewish member as a “mole”—for whom or what? There is no answer to that question that isn’t repulsive.

Shipman apologized for her messages about Shendelman, but only *after* my staff reviewed and uncovered all the Columbia documents and correspondence the committee subpoenaed and I publicly exposed them. Columbia’s board stood behind her. She remains acting president of Columbia as of this writing.

Can Jewish students, faculty, or alumni have any confidence that Shipman’s successor will be any better?

....

In August 2024, the Columbia Task Force on Antisemitism released a report detailing its findings based on more than five hundred interviews and firsthand accounts. The report made clear that, in its responsibility to treat every member of the campus community with respect and civility, Columbia University had failed. After October 7th, Jewish and Israeli students had reported harassment, abuse, and even violence to campus leaders, but many of those leaders responded “sluggishly and ineffectively” even to obvious violations. The report called Columbia’s problems “serious and pervasive.”[44]

When he returned to office in January 2025, as promised during his campaign, President Donald Trump rightfully took direct aim at Columbia University. In early 2025, the Trump administration froze Columbia’s federal research funding and federal contracts, worth more than $400 million. The administration cited Columbia’s record of antisemitism in doing so.[45] By July 2025, Columbia and the federal government struck a deal. Columbia was required to pay more than $200 million and institute a suite of reforms, in exchange for restoration of its research funding and permission to apply for new federal contracts in the future. Among the promised reforms are, in the university's words, "enhancements to campus safety, changes to disciplinary processes, and renewed efforts to foster an inclusive and respectful learning environment."[46]

The deal is a start. The Trump administration is, as with Harvard, correctly using the federal government's considerable power to ensure that universities are adhering to civil rights laws. Columbia had made clear it was incapable and unwilling to fix itself. For too long these institutions have engaged in systematic antisemitic discrimination, but no one could impose any cost. President Trump finally has, with the support of Congress.

There's an opportunity for still more. Columbia should be forced to make concrete investments in viewpoint diversity—for example, by establishing a center that would elevate dissenting voices at Columbia—not just pay lip service to the idea. The complete elimination of DEI is crucial, as is the fundamental reform of hiring and admissions. On the matter of admissions, our office worked with President Trump to require a 15 percent cap on foreign students. Columbia's current cap is 40 percent. Reducing the number of foreign students on Columbia's campuses would make a significant difference in reducing antisemitism.

The faculty-run University Judicial Board acts as a shield for antisemitic students who violate Columbia policies. Dozens of students who have occupied buildings including Hamilton Hall in strict violation of university policy have been let off by the University Judicial Board. It should be terminated and a real disciplinary process established.

Furthermore, what accountability measures can be put in place to ensure the enforcement of penalties against faculty and students responsible for antisemitic conduct? As we've seen, enforcement has been shamefully inconsistent.

Finally, the Middle Eastern, South Asian, and African Studies (MESAAS) Department, where known antisemite Professor Joseph Massad and others serve, should be put into full receivership. The department long ago swapped rigorous intellectual standards for ideological indoctrination, and it needs to be overhauled from the ground up. No department should be a locus of antisemitism and open support for anti-American terrorism.

....

In September 2025, Columbia appointed religion scholar Jonathon S. Kahn senior associate dean for community and culture. In that role he will "build and lead initiatives that cultivate curiosity, civic purpose and meaningful dialogue—facilitating student engagement with faculty outside the classroom."[47]

Dialogue with some faculty might be difficult.

In May 2021, when Kahn was teaching at Vassar College, he signed onto a letter "affirm[ing] that the Palestinian struggle is an indigenous resistance movement confronting settler colonialism, apartheid, and ethnic cleansing." Kahn and his fellow signatories rejected "the fiction of a 'two-sided conflict.'" The announcement and the letter were posted to X by a Jewish student group. They asked: "Did anyone even bother vetting [Kahn] before hiring? Or was this done on purpose?"[48]

Good question.

We mentioned Katrina Armstrong above. After her clumsy presidency ended, and despite misleading the federal government about Columbia's promised reforms, she was simply reinstated as dean of Columbia Medical School. Yet another example of the revolving door of failing up in American academia.[49]

These episodes are just two signs, among many, that it's back to business as usual at Columbia. In spite of the pressure imposed by the Republican Congress and the Trump White House, and in spite of the admission of Columbia's own antisemitism task force that the university failed to uphold its obligations to Jewish students and faculty, nothing has dramatically changed. The university is either oblivious to its mistreatment of its Jewish community—or, worse, it simply doesn't care.

There is a hard but necessary lesson here for anyone who wants to see real, lasting reforms at our elite universities. These institutions' problems are systemic. It's not just administrators, it's not just faculty, it's not just students—it's the whole university body and ecosystem. Anti-Americanism and antisemitism, whether latent or explicit, are like a cancer that has spread to the bone. Without strong measures and long-term vigilance, they will be extremely difficult to root out.

Our elite universities are not likely to change on their own. Many of them will have to have their hands forced. Investigations, as our work on the Education Committee has shown, can help shed a light to publicly shame them into taking action. So can lawsuits. So can accountability by student and alumni groups. But real change will not happen until these universities can no longer wriggle out from underneath their commitments. Promises and handshakes are not enough.

It will take vigilance, rigor, and dogged accountability for years to come to dig out of decades of this academic and moral decay.

CHAPTER 6

The Other Ivies and Beyond

"I'm worried about the future insofar as our academically most promising students are being funneled through the cookie-cutter Ivy League and other elite schools and emerging with this callow anti-American, anti-military cast to their thinking."

—Camille Paglia

In the previous chapters, we plunged deep into the dysfunction of three of America's most elite universities in the Ivy League. We saw that the moral and academic rot is wide and deep. However, what is so important to understand is that what happened at those schools wasn't the exception. It was the rule. It set the tone and the standard, and most other higher education institutions across the country followed suit.

In this chapter, we take a glimpse behind the curtain at other prestigious schools, some in the Ivy League, some not, but all members of the elite class of colleges and universities. Each school is a variation on a common theme. At each one, antisemitism and anti-Americanism exploded after October 7th. American Jewish students and faculty found themselves face-to-face with hostility, harassment, and in many cases violence, and without any meaningful support from their respective institutions.

This chapter does not document every incident at every school. In fact, it doesn't even come close. But it gives a bird's-eye view of the dire explosion of antisemitism and radical Far Left ideology that is pervasive and widespread on college campuses. Critics seeking to downplay the moral crisis within American higher education claimed that there were just a few incidents that garnered outsized media attention at a handful of high-profile, name-brand schools; that these cases were the exception and not the rule. This is not accurate; the stark reality is that the rise of antisemitism and academic rot became the norm across America's top universities. Working from student testimonies, congressional oversight work, news reports, social media posts, interviews, and more, I've highlighted episodes that reveal the true, poisoned character of these once-great institutions. Each school has its own dysfunctions and challenges with a unique twist, but when brought together, they tell a common, concerning, and very important story about what has become of the American higher education constellation that was once the envy of the world.

Yale

Founded 1701
Lux et veritas
"Light and truth"

Yale has long been a battleground in America's culture wars. In 1951, William F. Buckley Jr. published *God and Man at Yale*, a scathing indictment of his alma mater's descent into left-wing ideology. The book was explosive: a frontal assault on the Ivy League and therefore on America's elites. Buckley stood up for traditional religion against Yale's trendy "secularism" and for individualism against Yale's Soviet-friendly "collectivism." Buckley's book helped lay the foundations of the modern conservative movement, which has been fighting Far Left radicalism on campus ever since.

If you were trying to identify the moment when the Ivy League tipped over into madness, you could do worse than October 2015 at Yale. That month Yale undergraduates received a message from Yale's Intercultural Affairs Council urging students to rethink Halloween costumes that could be considered culturally insensitive. In response, Erika Christakis, an expert in early childhood development, wrote to the undergraduates of Yale's Silliman College, where she and her husband were faculty leaders, to push back. Christakis argued that the Intercultural

Affairs Council's nudge was patronizing to students and contributed to an atmosphere that stifled free expression. She wondered whether universities any longer trusted students to be able to exercise mature judgment without intervention from on high.

All hell broke loose.

Students petitioned the president to remove the Christakises from Yale. More than four hundred faculty signed a letter effectively denouncing the couple.

A month later, a group of undergraduates surrounded Erika Christakis's husband, Nicholas, a professor of sociology at Yale. They yelled at him, berated him, cursed at him. It was a public temper tantrum by highly privileged Ivy League students. Christakis, by contrast, stood calmly, listened, and patiently attempted to explain his position on free speech. The students would have none of it. Unable to strong-arm an apology from him, they stormed off.

Video of the encounter went viral on YouTube and social media, and the episode became a source of nationwide conversation. Why? Because to many it was a perfect microcosm of the elite university campus: increasingly authoritarian students attempting to cow university leaders into groveling apologies and concessions to radical progressive views. The failure of university leaders to stand up to student bullies and to forthrightly defend the principles of free speech on campus opened the door to exactly the sort of ugly behavior that has consumed the Yale campus since October 7th.

....

During the spring immediately following Hamas's terrorist attack against Israel, Sahar Tartak, then a sophomore undergraduate at Yale, was stabbed in the eye with a Palestinian flag by an anti-Israel protester in the middle of campus.

As the editor of Yale's independent newspaper, *The Yale Free Press*, Sahar was engaged in nothing more than standard on-campus journalism when she attempted to film one of Yale's antisemitic demonstrations. Several pro-Hamas encampers formed a barricade to block her path. They shoved Sahar and a friend repeatedly. Then "one of them takes their Palestinian flag and waves it in my face, and then jabs it in the face," she told *The Jerusalem Post.* Sahar was taken to a local hospital by ambulance.[1]

Thankfully Sahar did not suffer any long-term damage to her eyesight. But violence like this was a natural endpoint of Yale administrators' disgraceful negligence. University leaders, at Yale and many other schools, refused to confront the mobs who overran their campuses for fear of being seen as "on the wrong side" of a hot-button political issue. That refusal to act decisively had consequences—consequences suffered by the universities' students.

When Sahar Tartak testified before our committee on November 14, 2023, she observed that mourning the events of October 7th had become impossible under the continual assault of antisemitic episodes at Yale. She testified to receiving death threats for her pro-Israel activism and to "the hundreds upon hundreds of individual stories of Jewish students who are living in constant fear and intimidation, who have begun calculating their every move since October 7 through a lens of fear."

The attack on Sahar took place as voices on Yale's campus outwardly defended Hamas's October 7th terrorist attack.

On October 25, 2023, then junior Netanel Crispe went to Yale's quad to pray in public. It was intended to be a peaceful witness to the power of faith in a time of extreme difficulty.

Shortly, a rally led by Yalies4Palestine arrived on the quad. Protesters surrounded Netanel. One protester shoved him repeatedly. Netanel threatened to call campus police.

Here is what the antisemitic agitator who pushed Netanel posted online after the encounter:

> *Through his nasally voice he stutters out that he would call the police . . . to embroil his whiteness to weaponize the fear of polic-*

ing in communities of color and assert his position as the white male archetype . . . racist, patriarchal hegemony is what keeps police brutality, ethnic cleansing, and other forms of oppression alive.[2]

This, in addition to repulsive antisemitism, is the language of someone completely brainwashed by left-wing DEI ideology, which at its core is racist and antisemitic. Is this what students are learning from their Yale Ivy League education?

More episodes piled up. In a shocking incident, Yale students dropped a heap of fake "bloodstained" hundred-dollar bills on the heads of American Jewish undergraduates as they passed underneath the balcony of one of Yale's dining halls. According to Sahar Tartak, a dean told her that Yale considered the blatantly antisemitic act "political speech." The dean's only stated objection was to the littering.[3]

The graduate student chair of DEI declared in an online post that "all zionists must be institutionalized. they are a severe threat to all humans," and "zionists are the lowest form of human existence [*sic*]."[4]

A few weeks later, during a "press conference" held by demonstrators, one student shouted: "To the people who financed, encouraged, and facilitated this mass killing against us: May death follow you wherever you go. And when it does, I hope you will not be prepared." The university, in a statement issued two days later, described the incident as "a public statement that was taken as a threat" and promised a police investigation. Ultimately, the student received a slap on the wrist with minimal academic probation.[5]

Antisemitism in the encampments that sprouted later in the month in New Haven was impossible to ignore. The encampment at Beinecke Plaza, dubbed "Gaza Solidarity Plaza," featured memorials to Leila Khaled and Walid Daqqa. A terrorist, Khaled participated in two plane hijackings in 1969 and 1970. Daqqa, who died of cancer in prison in early April 2024, was convicted of participating in the August 1984 kidnapping, torture, and execution of nineteen-year-old Moshe Tamam, an off-duty Israeli soldier.

The antisemitic encampers blasted British rapper Seb's song "Free Palestine!" Here's a sample of the anti-Israel and antisemitic lyrics:

Free Palestine, bitch, Israel gon' die bitch
Bullshit prophets, y'all just want the profit

A Jewish freshman was called a "dumbass Jew."[6] Fake revolutionary "newspapers" circulating through the encampment claimed that Jews were responsible for the Holocaust.[7]

At the same demonstration in Beinecke Plaza where Sahar Tartak was stabbed in the eye, Netanel Crispe was also abused. "I was wearing my black hat; I was very identifiably Jewish," Crispe told *New York Times* columnist Bret Stephens. "I was yelled at, harassed, pushed and shoved numerous times. Every time I tried to take a step someone confronted me inches from my face, telling me not to move."[8]

At a second encampment, set up on Yale's Cross Campus after the Beinecke Plaza encampment was cleared by police, students were required to declare their support for Palestine in order to enter. Straight out of scenes of checkpoints in Nazi Germany, student "marshals" patrolling encampment checkpoints demanded assurances that students were "committed to Palestinian liberation and fighting for freedom for all oppressed peoples" before allowing them to pass. One marshal told the *Yale Daily News*, "We want to make sure . . . they believe in divestment, and they believe in Palestinian liberation."[9]

In a notice delivered to demonstrators, Yale administrators "wrote that the demonstration 'impedes' the ability of other students to study for finals," according to the *Yale Daily News*, and mentioned explicitly "the exclusion of students from using parts of Cross Campus, a public space, unless they declare political agreement with the protesters." Despite that lip service, exactly zero students were ever disciplined for these breaches of university policy.

Amazingly, Yale allowed something similar to happen one year later. A short-lived encampment was established to protest a visit to New Haven by Israeli National Security Minister Itamar Ben-Gvir.[10] In the following days Yale revoked the official status of Yalies4Palestine, writing in a statement that Y4P had "flagrantly violated the rules to which the Yale College Dean's Office holds all registered student organizations." The university also cited "concerns" about "disturbing antisemitic conduct" at the Ben-Gvir protests, although the details are unclear.[11]

Princeton

Founded 1746
Dei sub numine viget
"Under God's hand she flourishes"

Soon-to-be graduates attending Princeton's May 2023 commencement might have expected a commencement address appropriate to the dignified and celebratory occasion. Princeton President Christopher Eisgruber had something else in mind. After a school year of Ivy League institutions allowing a skyrocketing of antisemitism on their campuses and subsequently bending to the will of the pro-Hamas movement threatening American Jewish students' right to exist, let alone study in peace, Princeton's president exhibited absolutely no self-reflection and instead blamed the critics of American higher education for the widespread problems: "There is a movement afoot in this country right now to drive a wedge between the constitutional ideals of equality and free speech," he declared to the assembled crowd. "There are people who claim, for example, that when colleges and universities endorse the value of diversity and inclusivity or teach about racism and sexism, they are 'indoctrinating students' or in some other way endangering free speech. That is wrong."

As Eisgruber called for tolerance and mutual understanding, he castigated his political opponents and treated them in bad faith. Rising to a peak of sanctimony, he called on the graduating seniors: "So, as you go forth from this University, let your voices rise. Let them rise for equality. Let them rise for the value of diversity. Let them rise for freedom, for justice, and for love among the people of this earth."[12]

In *The Daily Princetonian*, Matthew Wilson, Class of 2024, called the address "an invective tirade delivered with the fervor of a preacher's sermon, excoriating the sins of those who would dare to disagree with his views on a wide array of highly contestable topics."[13]

The reality is that Princeton's President Christopher Eisgruber is the head of a badly rotted fish. The month before his commencement address, *The Daily Princetonian* released the results of its annual Senior Survey, which polled 571 graduating seniors (close to half of the year's graduating class) about an array of issues, including Princeton's campus climate surrounding speech. The findings were alarming.

The vast majority of the small number of students who self-identified as "libertarian," "somewhat conservative," or "very conservative" said they felt somewhat or very uncomfortable sharing their political views on campus. Compare the results of this same question with just 3 percent of self-identifying "leftist/socialist," 5 percent of "very liberal," and 18 percent of "slightly liberal," students who said they felt uncomfortable sharing their political views. Similar statistics at top universities are widespread and should be a wake-up call. These same university leaders who bellow and lecture on their high horse about the merits of free speech have in fact, inculcated campus environments that hamper free speech, creating a chilling effect for conservative students.

Furthermore, 45 percent of graduating seniors reported growing "more left-wing" during their time at Princeton; just 17 percent said they had grown more right-wing. For context, among graduating seniors who had voted in 2020, just 6 percent voted for Donald Trump, compared to 73 percent who voted for Joe Biden.[14]

So it's not surprising that the campus-wide response to the Hamas terrorist attacks against Israel was troubling at Princeton.

One week after October 7th, Princeton Students for Justice in Palestine (SJP) published one of the more outrageous statements in the wake of the Hamas attacks: a four-page screed that labeled the attack "an unprecedented uprising," accused Israel of "imminent genocide," and called for "the full dismantling of the Zionist apartheid state." The letter included links to the Instagram page of noted antisemites and to Al-Jazeera, the Qatari-funded outlet that was subsequently banned in Israel in May 2024 for national security reasons.[15]

Because Princeton SJP made illicit use of a school-wide listserv, the statement arrived in the inbox of every Princeton student. Despite the obvious violation of university policy, there is no evidence that the students responsible for breaking the rules were disciplined.[16] A few days later, Princeton SJP sponsored a "teach-in" that celebrated the "strong, vocal Palestinian resistance"—at the same time as a pre-planned vigil for Israeli victims of October 7th.[17] According to students Danielle Shapiro and Yonah Berenson, writing in *The Wall Street Journal*, "Friends of ours who tried to film the vigil were harassed into putting down their cameras."[18]

During an anti-Israel rally later that month, American Jewish students reported being heckled by protesters: "*you* are committing genocide."

At a rally on November 9, student reporter Alexandra Orbuch was stalked, harassed, and stepped on by an antisemitic demonstrator who was trying to prevent her from reporting on the rally. Her incident report, filed with Princeton's administration, was dismissed by Princeton's elaborate DEI apparatus. Princeton then went a step further. Rather than disciplining the perpetrator who harassed and stepped on Orbuch, Princeton instead punished the victim of harassment and physical aggression and issued a "no contact order" against Orbuch herself.

No contact orders, until recently, were one of Princeton's go-to measures in the domain of campus censorship and administrative repression. An "NCO" can be requested by any student for any reason, or for no reason—although officially they are mechanisms for preventing contact "if conflict persists after an individual communicates in writing to the other individual that they wish to have no communication with that individual."

In practice, no contact orders have been used by Princeton as a tool to silence inconvenient members of the campus community: for example, American student reporters reporting and blowing the whistle on antisemitic, anti-American activities on campus.

That was Danielle Shapiro's experience, which she chronicled in *The Wall Street Journal* in an article titled "I Committed Journalism, and Princeton Told Me Not to Communicate." In February 2022, Shapiro, a reporter for *The Princeton Tory*, Princeton's conservative newspaper, attended a protest held by an activist student group with a history of antisemitism. The group's target was the Israel Summer Programs Fair hosted by the Center for Jewish Life. Shapiro interviewed one of the student organizers for her article, and the two exchanged emails briefly after the event, for the purpose of correcting quotations before publication. According to Shapiro, "While she disagreed on some points concerning context, she remained cordial throughout our exchange and never indicated that she felt threatened or wished to terminate our conversation."

But after the article appeared, Shapiro was hit with a no contact order. The notice said that neither Shapiro nor the protest leader "may have any communication with each other in person or through another party, by telephone, letter, e-mail, or other electronic media, or by any other means, including via social media." The no contact order, as Princeton administrators later made clear, included Shapiro's on-campus journalistic activity.

And, as Shapiro writes, no contact orders are extremely wide-ranging. As of 2022, the policy defined "contact" to include "studying in the same section/floor of the library as the other party" and "standing next to the other party in line at a food servery."[19]

In January 2024, the Anti-Defamation League and the Foundation for Individual Rights in Education (FIRE) co-wrote a letter to Princeton, challenging the school's manifest abuse of no contact orders and threatening legal action. Since both Shapiro's and Orbuch's no contact orders were occasioned by reporting about antisemitic activity on campus, the letter pointedly observed that Princeton seemed to be issuing no contact orders with the purpose of "stifling" certain viewpoints.[20]

Following this intervention, Orbuch's no contact order was eventually lifted, but it was neither a brief nor a simple process, and it revealed a blatant double standard at work in administration policy. As Orbuch wrote: "I had to fight for months to remove an unjustly imposed university order, yet I have witnessed errant anti-Israel protesters who seem to violate university policy and the law being privileged with an expedited disciplinary process, often resulting in no discipline at all." As of November 2024, Princeton still had a robust no contact order policy on its books.[21]

That was before the encampments, which sprung up in late April 2024, eventually swelling to a few hundred students, who held out until commencement weekend. The "Popular University for Gaza," as it was dubbed, was uneventful compared to the chaos that erupted at other campuses. But there was more than enough to raise concerns. One student strummed a guitar while sitting in front of a Hezbollah flag.[22] (Hezbollah, a U.S.-designated foreign terrorist organization, was responsible for, among other things, the 1983 Beirut barracks bombing in Beirut, Lebanon, that killed 241 U.S. military personnel.) Another protester sang the praises of the totalitarian North Korean regime.[23] The encampment featured a "liberation library" with titles such as *The Wretched of the Earth* by Frantz Fanon, *How to Be an Antiracist* by Ibram X Kendi, and *How We Get Free* by Keeanga-Yamahtta Taylor, a Princeton professor of African American studies. Several Princeton faculty held classes within the encampment.[24]

On the exact same day and just a few hours before demonstrators in Manhattan rampaged through Columbia's Hamilton Hall, approximately a dozen Princeton students, a postdoctoral researcher, and a seminarian were arrested for occupying the campus's historic Clio Hall. They were accompanied by Princeton Professor Ruha Benjamin, Princeton's Alexander Stewart 1886 Professor of African American Studies (who was not arrested).

According to *Princeton Alumni Weekly*, a little after 4:30 p.m., the student and faculty rioters, accompanied by two student journalists, entered the Office of the Dean of the Graduate School. The demonstrators demanded that staff in the building's administrative suite exit immediately, counting down sixty seconds while employees scrambled to leave. The protesters used a large conference table and filing cabinets to barricade the door leading to the administrative suite. Other doors were hijacked with bike locks.

Elsewhere in Clio Hall, between twenty and forty staff emailed each other in a panic: "Something's happening, get safe, and stay where you are," one recalled. Several were trapped inside, but Princeton Public Safety hesitated to act. A crowd of demonstrators was closing in on the building from outside, threatening to rush officers if they acted recklessly. Staff members waited helplessly. "They were not in a good place," one later said of his colleagues. Eventually, Public Safety was able to smuggle them out through a back door.[25] Hours after the events at Clio Hall, Princeton's President Eisgruber published a campus-wide statement: "This incident was and remains deeply upsetting to many people, including especially the staff of the Graduate School. It is also completely unacceptable. Everyone on this campus needs to feel safe and be safe."[26]

The next day, Princeton's Vice President for Campus Life Rochelle Calhoun condemned the occupation as "an escalation . . . into unlawful behavior that created a dangerous situation for protesters, university staff, and law enforcement. As protesters entered Clio Hall, our staff found themselves surrounded, yelled at, threatened, and ultimately ordered out of the building."

"The way [staff members] were treated yesterday was abusive," wrote Calhoun.

Princeton leaders promised action. Wrote Eisgruber: "All those arrested received summonses for trespassing and have been barred from campus. The students will also face University discipline, which may extend to suspension or expulsion," he wrote.

What happened to the rioters who clearly broke university rules?

Just a few short weeks after the occupation, President Eisgruber announced the establishment of a "restorative justice" process for "students arrested in protest-related offenses." The process would "minimize the impact of the arrest on the participating students" by working to "rapidly conclude the University disciplinary process, making it possible for the students to join Commencement and receive their degrees."

Meanwhile, in July 2025, all charges against the thirteen arrested protesters were dropped, in exchange for six hours of community service (which they had already completed) and a written letter of apology to the university. When an initial draft of the protesters' letter was read aloud in court in June, Judge John McCarthy III, Princeton Class of 1969, objected, observing that the letter needed "to be a written apology that is indeed an apology, and not a political manifesto with references to our constitutional rights to take over Whig-Clio." A second draft finally managed to satisfy.[27]

In late April 2025, *City Journal* published an interview between investigative journalist Christopher Rufo and an anonymous Princeton professor, who explained:

> *Anti-Semitism is really a symptom of a deeper malaise at Princeton, which is that the university decided to go woke and—as President Eisgruber wrote in the last few months of the first Trump administration—declare that we were "systemically racist." But if we have been systemically racist, it's been against whites, Jews, Asians, and Indians, in favor of other demographics. I have a colleague in the sciences, and he was told by the department, "You can't shortlist this person. We can't hire a white guy." This colleague went to the chair, who was Jewish, and said to him, "In the 1930s, that's what they used to say about Jews here at Princeton: 'We couldn't hire them because they're Jewish.'"*

That's the situation all across the Ivy League. Radical DEI ideology that is inherently antisemitic and anti-white has led to the reestablishment of the vicious prejudices of a century ago.

One last story.

On April 7, 2025, Naftali Bennett, former prime minister of Israel, visited Princeton as part of an ongoing campus tour, at the invitation of the Center for Jewish Life. The event was co-sponsored by the Scharf Family Chabad House, the School of Public and International Affairs, and the Bobst Center for Peace and Justice.

Outside, about 150 anti-Israel protesters chanted. Some taunted Jewish students, calling them "inbred swine" and shouting, "Go back to Europe!"[28]

Meanwhile, inside McCosh Hall, it took just fifteen minutes for a group of anti-Israel protesters to begin shouting down Bennett during his remarks, interrupting the event until they could be escorted outside by Princeton Public Safety officers. A few minutes later, an outside agitator, a well-known anti-Israel demonstrator, interrupted the proceedings again. Ten minutes later, someone pulled the fire alarm, sending the hall into a panic.

While the alarm rang out and Princeton officials tried to evacuate the hall, something happened. Rabbi Eitan Webb of the Scharf Family Chabad House raised his voice and began to sing: *"Kol ha'olam kulo, gesher tzar me'od. Veha'ikar lo lefached klal."* ("The whole world is a very narrow bridge, and the main thing is not to be afraid at all.")

Students leapt onto the stage and joined in the song, throwing their arms around each other's shoulders. They danced and sang "*Dayenu*," a Passover seder song. As the alarm died out, they launched into "*Hatikvah*," Israel's national anthem.[29]

Center for Jewish Life Executive Director Rabbi Gil Steinlauf said of the spontaneous outburst that he had "never witnessed such a powerful and moving display of the Jewish spirit. Those who tried to silence us could not succeed."[30]

How did Princeton respond to the protesters who attempted to silence the event? President Eisgruber vowed to "pursue disciplinary measures, as appropriate, to the extent any members of the Princeton University community are implicated." Not a single student was disciplined for the night's disruption.[31]

Brown

Founded 1764
In Deo speramus
"In God we hope"

Don't negotiate with terrorists, the saying goes.

What about terrorist-sympathizers?

Brown University has made a habit of putting that piece of common-sense wisdom to the test. Negotiating with terrorist supporters has been their modus operandi.

In April 2024, when encampments broke out at Brown, President Christina Paxson and other university administrators, rather than enforce the rules that Brown's antisemitic protesters had willfully broken, decided instead to negotiate with them. The sides struck a deal: in exchange for rolling up their encampments peaceably, the university would consider Brown Divestment Coalition students' proposal that Brown divest from Israel-linked companies.[32] This is part of the broader antisemitic Boycott, Divestment, and Sanctions (BDS) movement raging on college campuses. With this agreement, Brown went further than any other elite university in bending to protesters' demands.[33]

In other words, Brown's antisemitic encampers used the threat of violence and chaos to extort Brown's leaders—and those leaders buckled immediately.

Calling for boycotts of, divestment from, and sanctions against Israel—the three prongs of the BDS movement—is a longtime weapon of antisemitic forces, aimed at companies and governments that do business with the State of Israel or Israeli enterprises.

BDS often presents itself as one among many movements spearheading human rights reforms. But that's far from the reality. "While many rank and file members of the movement sincerely want peace and are lured in by this human rights façade," explains the American Jewish Committee, "BDS leadership in fact seeks nothing less than the elimination of Israel as a Jewish state."[34] BDS is not one more advocacy project. It is a front for extremism and blatant antisemitism.

While serving as secretary of education during the first Trump administration, Betsy DeVos called the rising BDS presence on university campuses a "pernicious threat." "These bullies claim they stand for human rights," she said during a Justice Department summit on antisemitism. "But we all know that BDS stands for antisemitism."[35]

Over the last decade, more than thirty states have passed into law some form of anti-BDS prohibition, usually requiring the state not to contract with a company engaged in boycotting Israel.

Yet since October 7th, BDS efforts have intensified and accelerated. Calls for divestment have been a regular feature of antisemitic protests on campus as common as "from the river to the sea" genocidal chants.

Writing in *The Wall Street Journal* on September 8, 2024, Joseph Edelman explained his decision to resign from Brown's Board of Trustees in light of the pending BDS vote. "I find it morally reprehensible that holding a divestment vote was even considered, much less that it will be held," he wrote. The decision "was made not based on facts or values but based on weakness toward student activists," he continued. "The university leadership has for some reason chosen to reward, rather than punish, the activists for disrupting campus life, breaking school rules, and promoting violence and antisemitism at Brown." Edelman castigated Brown's administrators for "a stunning failure of moral leadership."[36]

In a letter, twenty-four state attorneys general warned Brown that "adopting that proposal may require our states—and others—to terminate any existing relationships with Brown and those associated with it, divest from any university debt held by state pension plans and other investment vehicles, and otherwise refrain from engaging with Brown."[37]

In October 2024, the Corporation of Brown University, the university's governing body, voted against divestment. In defense of the university's decision, President Paxson and Chancellor Brian Moynihan wrote in a campus-wide letter that a decision to divest would "signal to our students and scholars that there are 'approved' points of view to which members of the community are expected to conform."[38] It was the right decision—after a series of wrong ones. Brown's university leadership and board should have never allowed the antisemitic students to demand or dictate a vote on the matter.

The unfortunate reality was that Brown's friendliness to outrageous antisemitic voices was not new.

In 2012, Professor Beshara Doumani founded Brown's Center for Middle Eastern Studies (CMES), which quickly revealed itself as a center of antisemitic sentiment on campus. In 2021, Professor Doumani, who is Palestinian, was given permission to become the president of Birzeit University, while retaining his post at Brown.

Birzeit University is not your average institution of higher education. In the West Bank, Birzeit University is considered by Israel to be a breeding ground for extremism, and no wonder. In 2019, when students rallied to celebrate the anniversaries of Hamas and the PFLP, replete with military uniforms and cardboard rockets (in honor of rocket attacks on Israel), the university tried to shut the event down. In response, students rioted, damaging campus property.[40]

In early September 2025, two Palestinian men gunned down six people and injured two dozen more at a bus stop in Jerusalem. One of the shooters was a Birzeit student.[41]

This is the university over which Brown's Professor Beshara Doumani presided, with Brown's public blessing. Brown University had no problem with one of its professors heading up an institution firmly tied to terrorist organizations.

Brown has also played host to Dr. Rasha Alawieh, a known associate of the terrorist leader of Hezbollah. In March 2025, Alawieh landed at Boston Logan Airport only to be immediately detained by federal authorities. The Department of Homeland Security revealed that Alawieh, a Lebanese national, had attended the recent funeral of Hassan Nasrallah, the Hezbollah leader killed by Israel in a targeted strike, and had pictures of the event on her cell phone.

A Department of Homeland Security spokeswoman said sensibly: "A visa is a privilege not a right. Glorifying and supporting terrorists who kill Americans is grounds for visa issuance to be denied."

In February 2025, the Department of Health and Human Services opened an investigation into Brown's Warren Alpert Medical School, following a chaotic May 2024 commencement ceremony that saw protesters associated with Brown Alumni for Palestine stage a so-called disruption of scheduled events. In April, the investigation was expanded to the whole university, following what the Rhode Island Coalition for Israel described as "months of disruptive, anti-Semitic and harassing behavior targeting Jewish and pro-Israel students on campus."[42]

In the summer of 2025, Brown reached a settlement with the federal government, promising to pay $50 million over ten years to support "state workforce development organizations," as well as to "take steps to improve the campus climate for Jewish students and combat antisemitism," although the particular steps are still to be determined. In exchange, the government agreed to unfreeze $510 million in frozen research funds.[43]

The particular tragedy of Brown is how far it has fallen from its founding ideals.

Founded in 1639 by religious dissidents, the Rhode Island colony was forward-thinking. Having known the experience of persecution on account of their religious beliefs, its colonists committed themselves to religious toleration. A commitment to liberty of conscience was written into the colony's royal charter in 1662. Here, more than anywhere else in colonial America, religious pluralism flourished, and believers of all sorts came to Newport. As early as the seventeenth century, one could find, living shoulder to shoulder, Anglicans, Baptists, Quakers, and many more, including Sephardic Jews.

So it was natural, though still extraordinary, that the Charter of Brown University, which established Rhode Island's oldest institution of higher education in 1764, should contain the following declaration:

> *And furthermore, it is hereby enacted and declared that into this liberal and catholic institution shall never be admitted any religious tests: But, on the contrary, all the members hereof shall forever enjoy full, free, absolute, and uninterrupted liberty of conscience: . . . And that youth of all religious denominations shall and may be freely admitted to the equal advantages, emoluments, and honors of the College or University; and shall receive a like, fair, generous, and equal treatment during their residence therein, they conducting themselves peaceably, and conforming to the laws and statutes thereof.*

What has become of Brown University's commitment to "a like, fair, generous, and equal treatment" of all students?

Northwestern

Founded 1851
Quaecumque sunt vera
"Whatsoever things are true" (Philippians 4:8)

The pro-Hamas encampment tents went up across Northwestern's idyllic, two-acre Deering Meadow on the morning of April 25, 2024.

Within a few hours, President Michael Schill announced in an email to the campus community that tents on Deering Meadow had been removed by police. Outside, a pro-Hamas demonstrator asked the crowd: "He said we've left. He said we've put our tents down. Is that true?" "No!" they replied.

It was the first example of the weakness and bungling that characterized Northwestern's failed response to its antisemitic protest movement and set a disastrous precedent for universities nationwide of negotiation with the pro-terrorist encampments rather than disciplinary action.

That weakness culminated five days later, on April 29, in the "Deering Meadow Agreement." Northwestern's President Schill had empowered "radical anti-Israel faculty members Jessica Winegar and Nour Kteily to serve as negotiators with the encampment."[44] Professor Winegar is the Hamad Bin Khalifa Al-Thani chair, named for the former emir of Qatar, in Middle Eastern Studies at Northwestern and was well known for her public support of the anti-Israel BDS movement. Additionally, Nour Kteily used his negotiator position to try to encourage Northwestern to boycott the Israeli-co-owned Sabra hummus brand on campus. The final agreement was negotiated by Schill, Provost Kathleen Hagerty and Vice President of Student Affairs Susan Davis, and encampment leaders (including radical faculty members who appointed themselves spokesmen for demonstrating students). The agreement was treated by Northwestern as a victory for sanity and good-faith negotiations.

In fact, it was a stunning capitulation by university leaders to the demands of the pro-Hamas encampers responsible for what President Schill later called "the major antisemitic event on our campus."[45] As the first negotiated compromise between university leaders and antisemitic protesters at any campus, it set a catastrophic example. It gave permission to other university leaders nationwide to bend on their own policies surrounding permissible demonstrations and to negotiate with pro-Hamas students violating university rules, disrupting learning environments, and endangering Jewish students. It empowered the pro-Hamas encampments to go further in their violations.

In exchange for continued "peaceful demonstrations" that "compl[y] with University policies," Northwestern agreed, first, to reestablish the Advisory Committee on Investment Responsibility (ACIR) and to disclose "specific holdings, held currently or within the last quarter, to the best of its knowledge and to the extent legally possible." The Northwestern University Divestment Coalition cheered the "concrete measures" as "the first step toward divestment."

Northwestern additionally agreed to fully fund two Palestinian faculty per year for two years and five Palestinian undergraduates; to establish a long-term space for MENA/Muslim students; and to "include students in a process dedicated to implementing broad input on University dining services, including residential and retail vendors on campus." The last provision did not name but was intended to target Sabra hummus, which is produced by an Israeli company.[46]

The agreement was lauded by pro-Hamas encampment leaders: "Schill just released a statement proving tangible steps toward divestment today," one organizer told protesters on April 29. "We have been working tirelessly to bring you this statement we are very proud of and hope you guys can be very proud of this milestone we made." The agreement was approved by a 17-to-1 vote of the Northwestern Divestment Coalition. In a statement, demonstrators called the agreement's terms "the floor for our progress going forward, not the ceiling."[47]

"We have fought for years and years for a seat at the table, and being able to even get to where we got today is historical," said a leader of Northwestern's SJP chapter. "There is always more to come."[48]

What was a resounding victory for antisemitic forces on campus was felt as a betrayal of American Jewish students. At no point was the university's antisemitism task force, set up precisely to help guide Northwestern's administrative policy, consulted about the negotiations with the pro-Hamas encampment. When the agreement was announced, all the committee's Jewish members resigned in protest.

As our congressional Education Committee wrote in our October 2024 investigative report, Northwestern's agreement with the demonstrators put the school in danger of violating its Title VI obligations. The agreement arguably gave preferential treatment to people of certain backgrounds, while creating conditions for future actions that could violate federal nondiscrimination law. And, beyond all that, it gave a shot in the arm to campus actors who were actively engaged in creating a hostile environment for American Jewish students and faculty.[49]

The failure of the Deering Meadow Agreement to shield Northwestern's Jewish community from further mistreatment has been manifest.

In 2025, following the promises of the agreement, Northwestern hired political scientist Mkhaimar Abusada, a Gaza native and scholar of the Israeli-Palestinian conflict, as a visiting lecturer.[50]

In addition to this position, *The Washington Free Beacon* reported in May 2025:

> *Abusada also serves on the boards of two organizations that present themselves as human rights groups—the Independent Commission for Human Rights (ICHR) and the Palestinian Center for Human Rights (PCHR)—that, in reality, maintain close ties to terrorists. ICHR has praised Hamas and met with the terror group's leaders, including Ismail Haniyeh, while PCHR has Popular Front for the Liberation of Palestine (PFLP) members on its payroll—with one serving as its leader.*

A little background: ICHR was founded by former Palestinian Liberation Organization Chief Yasser Arafat. A well-known political figure on the world stage during his lifetime, Arafat participated in terrorism against Israel through the al-Aqsa Martyrs' Brigades, which are a U.S.-designated foreign terrorist organization. The Brigades have fought alongside Hamas during the Gaza War. In December 2018, ICHR members met with Ismail Haniyeh, the political head of Hamas, to discuss "Hamas's commitment to human rights values."

Abusada is also the deputy chairman of PCHR's board of directors. His predecessor in the role was Jaber Wishah, who led the PFLP's military wing in the Gaza Strip. According to Jerusalem-based nonprofit NGO Monitor, Wishah was convicted by Israel in 1985 of "holding a leading position in a terrorist organization of which he was a member, intentionally attempting to kill an Israeli Staff Sergeant in Gaza, configuring a bomb and planting a bomb, possession of firearms and conspiring to commit murder."[51]

Commenting on Abusada's appointment by Northwestern, Gerald Steinberg, president of NGO Monitor, told the *Free Beacon*: "His employment as a faculty member is a heinous violation of basic academic norms and moral principles."[52]

Northwestern claims to have made significant strides in addressing antisemitism on campus since 2023. "Coming out of the encampment, we recognized . . . that our rules were just—fell way short. I mean, they really fell way short. Our demonstration policy was laughable. . . . Our Code of Conduct was insufficient to capture antisemitic harassment." So said President Schill during his transcribed testimony before our committee in August 2025. As a result, Northwestern imposed new constraints on campus demonstrations, instituted campus-wide antisemitism training, and created new processes for enforcement and accountability.

But the reality is that the campus climate is still a problem. In May 2025, Northwestern's student newspaper published the results of its survey of campus attitudes: 58 percent of Jewish students reported that they or someone they knew had experienced antisemitic conduct on campus, and 63 percent described antisemitism as a "somewhat" or "very serious" issue, compared to just 30 percent of the overall student body.

As for the campus climate around matters of free speech, 30 percent of students said they have felt pressure to conform to majority political views on campus. Among self-described moderates and conservatives, it was 58 percent.[53]

In early September 2025, Michael Schill was forced to resign as president of Northwestern. As of this writing, he has yet to be replaced.

Cooper Union

Founded 1859

"Free as air and water"

One of the most harrowing episodes of post–October 7th antisemitism took place in Manhattan, but not at Columbia. Rather, the incident happened a few blocks south, at the Cooper Union for the Advancement of Science and Art.

Jacob Khalili was a senior at Cooper Union on October 7th and was one of the victims of the hateful events that took place later that month.

He testified before our committee in February 2024. I've drawn directly from his deeply disturbing testimony for this account.

In the wake of Hamas's attack on Israel on October 7th, Cooper Union's administration, led by President Laura Sparks, was noticeably quiet. The administration had spoken out forcefully about public events on past occasions, including Russia's invasion of Ukraine in 2022 and the death of George Floyd in 2020.

It was October 9, 2023, when, after an outcry from Jewish students and alumni, the administration issued a statement. Cooper Union's leadership did not say anything about Hamas, about terrorism, or about the Israeli or American victims. In as milquetoast a fashion as possible following Harvard's abysmal lead, the statement lamented "the upsetting news of war between Israel and Hamas in the Middle East as well as reports of devastation and aggressions in many other parts of the world."

Over the next few weeks, American Jewish students on Cooper Union's campus watched as posters featuring the images of hostages held by Hamas were defaced. They saw protesters vandalize the Foundation Building's windows, hanging posters that featured antisemitic messages. And they reported heinous graffiti in a bathroom stall, written in the style of Hitler's *Mein Kampf.*

Cooper Union's nonresponse set the stage for what happened later that month. On October 25, 2023, student protesters gathered around lunchtime for a student walkout for "Palestinian Liberation." Some were masked. They chanted "Globalize the intifada from New York to Gaza," "Resistance is justified when people are occupied," and "From the river to the sea, Palestine will be free."

Nearby, a small group of Jewish students stood by, some holding a silent vigil for the Israeli and American hostage victims.

Late in the afternoon, the antisemitic protesters who had been marching outside the Foundation Building then turned into rioters and stormed inside. They ran to the seventh floor and the office of the president.

It was about that time that Jacob and his Jewish peers, some of whom were wearing observant Jewish attire, went into the Cooper Union library, located in the basement of the Foundation Building. In a lawsuit subsequently filed by ten Jewish students against the school, the events are described this way:

> *The demonstrators "attempted to enter the library, banging on and rattling the locked library doors and shouting 'let us in!'" They then spread out along the floor-to-ceiling windows separating the library from the hallway and banged loudly on the glass while waving a Palestinian flag, holding up signs critical of Israel, and continuing their chants, this time plausibly directed at the visibly Jewish students inside the library. This ordeal, which lasted approximately twenty minutes, was sufficiently threatening that a Cooper Union administrator locked the library doors as the mob approached, and the Jewish students left inside, some of whom were crying, contacted their loved ones and attempted to call the NYPD for help. Indeed, two school employees suggested that those Jewish students, and those students alone, should "hid[e] in the windowless upstairs portion of the library out of the demonstrators' sight" or attempt to "escap[e] the library through the back exit."*[54]

Eventually, the one hundred or so rioters dispersed without intervention, and the students were escorted out by campus security. But this act of blatant antisemitic harassment and intimidation inspired no response from the administration. President Sparks and the school's administrators did nothing.

In fact, it was later discovered that when the pro-Hamas mob rushed upstairs to confront her, President Sparks allegedly snuck out the back door while Jewish students were barricaded. For the rest of the semester, President Sparks had a security guard posted outside her office while Jewish students were on their own.

The day after the incident, the Jewish students did not show up for class. Over the following weeks and months they suffered "'intense anxiety and panic attacks,' 'had difficulty concentrating during their exams,' 'engaged therapists,' 'missed and/or dropped classes,' and 'failed to complete and perform on assignments,' among other harms," according to the lawsuit.

In April 2025, a court ruled that the students' lawsuit alleging that Cooper Union "created a pervasive environment of intimidation and hostility" toward the school's Jewish community and was in breach of contract with those students could proceed.

When Jacob Khalili testified before our committee in February 2024, he said: "I, along with other Jewish students, are still dealing with the repercussions of this traumatic incident. It is very troubling to feel unsafe on your own college campus, threatened by students with whom you share the campus on a daily basis."

But he added, defiantly: "Jewish students, as all students at Cooper Union and elsewhere, have the fundamental right to pursue their education free from threats of violence and harassment. They should never be in fear that they will be targeted simply because they are Jewish or because they identify with their ancestral homeland—Israel."[55]

MIT

Founded 1861
Mens et manus
"Mind and hand"

President Sally Kornbluth was the only university president who escaped from my questions at the university presidents committee hearing still with her job. She should have been fired.

President Kornbluth's answers to my questions were cold comfort to the Jewish community at MIT who had heard calls for violence against them echoing across campus for months.

Kornbluth pretended not to hear those calls. She fell back on hypotheticals and that all-purpose excuse, "context."

Despite Kornbluth's protests to the contrary, there was no need for hypotheticals. The situation at MIT was obvious for anyone with eyes and ears.

Less than twenty-four hours after the murderous Hamas terrorist attack on October 7th, Palestine@MIT and MIT Coalition Against Apartheid (CAA), along with other Students for Justice in Palestine chapters at Brandeis, Wellesley, and Boston University, released a statement that they "hold the Israeli regime responsible for all unfolding violence" and "unequivocally denounce the Israeli occupation, its racist apartheid system, and its military rule." They declared solidarity with the attackers: "We are committed to supporting decolonization efforts in Palestine, and we recognize our role to oppose Zionism from within the imperial core."[56]

The next day, one of the groups posted an advertisement on its Instagram page for a rally and march in celebration of the "victory" of the "Palestinian resistance." Accompanying the text was a colorized image of a man standing on a tank, waving a Palestinian flag. The image was a rendering of a photograph taken three days earlier of a Hamas terrorist celebrating the October 7th massacre. The Hamas terrorist was celebrating the murder of innocent Jews, and MIT's Coalition Against Apartheid was glorifying him.

Within a month of October 7th, antisemitic students launched a campaign of harassment against the MIT International Science and Technology Initiatives (MISTI) Israel program, which sends MIT students to Israel to study. According to a staff member who was present at the time, protesters swarmed the MISTI Israel offices. They "insistently rattled the door handles of offices that were closed with staff inside; and they congregated outside of and entered the office that facilitates MISTI's programming in the Middle East, and at least one other office. Their chants included: 'From the river to the sea . . . ,' 'MISTI, MISTI, you can't hide,' and cries associating MISTI with genocide."

Later, antisemitic protesters demonstrated outside the office of the faculty director of MISTI Israel. He felt so threatened that he fled campus and did not return for weeks.[57]

The events of November 9, 2023, were especially instructive. At 8 a.m. that day, MIT CAA launched a sit-in—"in solidarity with our siblings in Palestine facing genocide and a total blockade orchestrated by the US and Israel"—inside MIT's Lobby 7, the campus's main entrance. The event was part of a larger "Global Day of Jihad" sponsored by major anti-Israel organizations, including National Students for Justice in Palestine. It was well known to the protesters that Lobby 7—a central thoroughfare of MIT's campus—was not a permitted site for demonstrations. They didn't care.

MIT's response to lawlessness and antisemitism on its campus was toothless. Rather than break up the illicit assembly and enforce university rules, MIT put the burden of events on the victims. MIT's Hillel sent a note to the university's Jewish community: "MIT Hillel recommends that you do not directly engage the protesters for your physical safety and well-being. You may want to choose paths around campus that avoid Lobby 7 and the Infinite."[58] Around 5 p.m., MIT Advisory, an official campus-wide emergency alert system, warned all students to steer clear of Lobby 7, for their own safety.

MIT administration warned that any MIT-affiliated protesters who did not leave Lobby 7 by 12:15 p.m. would face disciplinary action. Some left, but others refused to go—and, as a further act of defiance, invited in outside agitators.

Late in the day, MIT President Sally Kornbluth issued a statement on the protest. It was "disruptive, loud and sustained through the morning hours," Kornbluth wrote, and "was organized and conducted in defiance of those MIT guidelines and policies." As "face-to-face confrontation between the protesters and counter-protesters intensified," MIT's leadership "had serious concerns that it could lead to violence." According to President Kornbluth, "the administration felt it was essential to take action."

In a message directly to demonstrators, Kornbluth wrote: "By choosing to violate our policies and guidelines, you have chosen to accept the consequences, and made yourself subject to MIT disciplinary action."

What sort of action? Originally, the administration planned suspensions, wrote Kornbluth, but "because we later heard serious concerns about collateral consequences for the students, such as visa issues, we have decided, as an interim action, that the students who remained after the deadline will be suspended from non-academic campus activities. The students will remain enrolled at MIT and will be able to attend academic classes and labs."

In other words, the students who had "chosen to accept the consequences" of defying university policies didn't have to suffer the consequences after all. MIT let them off with a slap on the wrist, deferring "final adjudication" to the Committee on Discipline. Unsurprisingly, there is no indication that any demonstrators suffered any further discipline.[59]

Meanwhile, real consequences were suffered by MIT's American Jewish students. The X account @StopZionistHate advertised an $800 "bounty" to identify a Jewish student who was involved in an altercation during the Lobby 7 protest. A selectively edited video shows the Jewish student pushing a female protester but does not show the Jewish student being shoved by an antisemitic mob moments before.[60] According to MIT Israel Alliance, the student was forced to hide in his dorm for weeks. Check-ins were performed by friends and public safety officers.

This episode of "Jew-hunting" at MIT brings into sharp relief one other salient fact of the protest. The date of the demonstration—November 9—was not a coincidence. Students of history will know that November 9, 1938, was *Kristallnacht*, or the "Night of Broken Glass," when Nazi leadership coordinated a nationwide wave of violence against Jewish communities across Germany, smashing storefronts, vandalizing homes, setting fire to synagogues, and ultimately deporting twenty-six thousand German Jews to concentration camps.[61]

As we've seen elsewhere, antisemitic protesters frequently falsely compare Israel to the Third Reich and Jews to Nazis. But when they associate themselves with one of the most horrifying events in Jewish history, everyone averts their eyes. It's a disgraceful and sickening inversion.

In testimony delivered before our committee in December, MIT graduate student Talia Khan described a campus-wide climate of fear, where "Jewish students are afraid to leave their rooms, walk the hallways with Jewish clothing and jewelry, and speak in Hebrew on campus." She placed the blame squarely on the shoulders of MIT's leadership, calling it "feckless," "cowardly," and "hypocritical."

She was right. MIT's decision to bend to the whims of its antisemitic rioters, and to refuse to come to the aid of its Jewish community, was a deliberate choice. And it was one that was made over and over and over again.

For example, in February 2024, MIT's anti-Israel Coalition Against Apartheid was temporarily suspended for repeatedly violating MIT's restrictions on demonstrations, a welcome if overdue step. But the group simply defied the suspension, continuing to disrupt on-campus activities and engage in protests. MIT merely shrugged.[62]

In March, the Black Student Union Office hung a poster proclaiming its solidarity with the Popular Front for the Liberation of Palestine—a U.S.-designated foreign terrorist organization since 1997.[63]

When encampments against university policy sprung up at MIT in April 2024, one demonstrating student said it all: "We've shown our administrators the power that we hold, and we can't give it up. We are the ones who run this campus, who make the campus what it is. We hold the power, so we have to show them that we won't back down until they meet our demands."[64]

The new school year had barely begun when at the door to their campus orientation, first-year students were handed flyers that condemned Israel and listed additional online "resources," including a link to the antisemitic and shocking Mapping Project, which identifies Jewish organizations in and around Boston, provides their addresses, and in some cases gives names of organization leaders. It is, in other words, a site that specializes in targeting and intimidating Jews akin to labeling with gold stars.

President Kornbluth felt compelled to acknowledge the incident in a letter to the MIT community. "I believe the Mapping Project promotes antisemitism," she said, and noted that "antisemitism is totally unacceptable in our community. It cannot be justified, and it is antithetical to MIT's values."[65]

But antisemitism has become entrenched in MIT's campus culture.

On November 7, 2024, *The Tech*, MIT's student newspaper, published an op-ed authored by the MIT Coalition for Palestine. The article reported that "MIT's Computer Science and Artificial Intelligence Laboratory (CSAIL) conducts research funded by the Israeli Ministry of Defense (IMoD), with direct applications to the ongoing genocide in Gaza." The Coalition demanded that CSAIL Director Daniela Rus "end her IMoD-sponsored research."

But the op-ed went on to accuse Rus, by name, of being party to Israeli crimes: "To Daniela Rus and the world: no more labor for apartheid and genocide! At the end of the day, MIT's racism and racist discipline cannot counteract one fact: Daniela Rus is complicit in doing research for genocide."

The article was titled "Daniela Rus, The People Demand: No More Research for Genocide."

Over the next several weeks, a targeted harassment campaign was executed against Professor Rus. "WANTED" posters with her name and image appeared on campus, and campus facilities were vandalized with messages aimed at her.

On December 6, Sally Kornbluth wrote again to the MIT community, decrying "an unacceptable pattern of escalations" against Rus and CSAIL. "Let me be clear," Kornbluth wrote: "Harassment, intimidation and targeting are unacceptable at MIT, and the accusations against Professor Rus are unfair, willfully mischaracterizing the content and purpose of her work."[66]

On December 9, *The Tech* retracted the Coalition for Palestine's op-ed, "in light of increasing hostile rhetoric and action against Professor Daniela Rus and her laboratory," and published a list of corrections to "factual errors"—including the central accusation in the piece: that Professor Rus's research was in any meaningful way connected to Israel's military.[67]

But it gets worse.

In early July 2025, "Death to the IDF!" was spray-painted across the doors into the Stata Center, which houses CSAIL. Direct Action Movement for Palestinian Liberation (DAMPL), a non-MIT group, claimed credit. To accompany the vandalism, DAMPL posted a video to its Instagram that showed the Coalition for Palestine's November op-ed, next to images of the vandalized doors. "Death to the IDF!" plays on a loop in the background. An accompanying caption claims credit for the vandalism, recites false facts about Rus and CSAIL from the Coalition for Palestine's article, and closes with a threat of violence against the university: "This was not symbolic. *This was a costly warning shot.* . . . We will meet you with forceful resistance, not polite requests. The resistance is alive. And it knows exactly where you work."[68]

In a campus-wide message, Kornbluth called the episode "extremely troubling," adding that the university would work with authorities to hold perpetrators accountable.[69] (In early August 2025, one of the vandals was arrested.)[70]

On September 12, Kornbluth wrote again to the MIT community:

> *Over the last week, we have seen several instances of disturbing imagery and text on campus—in two cases, a hand-drawn swastika; a sign wishing violence on a conservative non-profit; and multiple cases, in graffiti and on an email list, of messages celebrating violence. . . . Because a swastika is an unambiguous symbol of hate, particularly antisemitic hate, it is therefore a tool of intimidation, as is advocating violence against those with whom one disagrees.*[71]

The pattern of continued antisemitic activity at MIT, two years after October 7th, is outrageous. Sally Kornbluth is a failed university president. MIT deserves better.

Cornell

Founded 1865

"I would found an institution where any person can find instruction in any study." —**Ezra Cornell**

Maybe it's my Upstate New York bias, but Cornell is located in one of the most beautiful regions of America. Perched on a hill in Ithaca, New York, it looks out over the state's famous Finger Lakes. Surrounding the campus are hundreds of gorges with trickling waterfalls. It's a truly breathtaking place. Cornell has also educated many multigenerational Upstate New York agricultural families who proudly till the earth and feed their communities and the world today. Many Cornell alumni have worked for and with my congressional office over the past decade.

Cornell is also an institution that has its roots deep in America's best democratic traditions. The school was chartered in April 1865, just weeks after the assassination of Abraham Lincoln and just weeks before Union forces secured victory in the Civil War. Its founders were two New York State senators, Ezra Cornell, a wealthy businessman and philanthropist, and Andrew Dickson White, a distinguished scholar and educator. They had a shared vision: to build a new kind of university that would be accessible to a wide range of students and offer instruction in a broad array of subjects.

Cornell famously said, "I would found an institution where any person can find instruction in any study." This was a bold idea at the time. It challenged the standard model of higher education, which focused on classical studies such as Greek and Latin, and which was typically reserved for the sons of privilege. Cornell and White envisioned something different.

For them, "any study" meant areas of study beyond the normal classical disciplines. They envisioned a school where, in addition to traditional subjects, students could gain experience in hands-on fields such as agriculture and engineering. That was made possible by Cornell's recognition as an early land-grant institution. Their vision is responsible for Cornell's unique situation today, as both an Ivy League research institution and a major technical school.

For them, "any person" meant students of either sex and of any race or religion. In 1870, two years after opening its doors, Cornell became the first Ivy League university to admit female students. That same year Cornell enrolled one of its first Jewish students, John Frankenheimer of New York City. Frankenheimer was the son of Bavarian immigrants. During his time at Cornell he distinguished himself academically, winning several prizes and election to prestigious academic organizations. After graduating in 1873, he earned his law degree from Columbia and practiced law in New York City until his death in 1917.

Cornell can claim a host of distinguished Jewish alumni. Philanthropist Harold Tanner, Class of 1952, became national president of the American Jewish Committee. Attorney Nadine Strossen, Class of 1972, led the American Civil Liberties Union for nearly twenty years, from 1991 to 2008. And, of course, there's Supreme Court Justice Ruth Bader Ginsburg, Class of 1954.

Today, according to Hillel International, there are about 2,500 undergraduate and 500 graduate Jewish students at Cornell, who make up about 16 percent of the student body. There are also more than thirty different Jewish student organizations.

Cornell's commitment to the education of "any person" has aided generations of strivers—young men and women of every background who desired to climb the ladder of American life.

But is Cornell still making good on that commitment today?

As with many other schools, the problems post–October 7th ignited on social media.

Derron Borders, a staff member of Cornell's Johnson Graduate School of Management, took to Instagram to celebrate the attacks. Hamas had struck back "against settler colonization, imperialism, capitalism, white supremacy, [for] which the United States is the model," he wrote.

He added: "F–k your fake outrage at Palestine when you've literally been silent about the violence perpetuated by Israel against Palestine every day."

Did I mention that Borders was Cornell's director of diversity and inclusion?[72]

Antisemitism at Cornell became national news a week later. On October 15, 2023, a Cornell history professor, Russell Rickford, took the microphone at an anti-Israel rally held off campus.

"Hamas has shifted the balance of power!" Rickford declared. "Hamas has punctured the illusion of invincibility. . . . Nothing will be the same again! . . . We are able to breathe—for the first time in years.

"It was exhilarating," he continued, gushing. "It was exhilarating, it was energizing. And if they weren't exhilarated by this challenge to the monopoly of violence, by this shifting of the balance of power, then they would not be human. I was exhilarated."

Following an outcry, Rickford apologized—sort of. He admitted to a "horrible choice of words," but he did not rescind his comments. Rickford went on voluntary leave, but Cornell allowed him to return to the classroom teaching students in the fall of 2024. Again, no consequences or accountability.[73]

Rickford's remarks, as we've already seen, are emblematic of a type of professor who can be found across elite academia: a fanatical ideologue with a moral compass that has gone wildly out of whack.

Toward the end of October, the situation for Cornell's Jewish community turned dangerous. Online messages posted to Greekrank, a forum dedicated to fraternity and sorority life, threatened to "bring an assault rifle to campus and shoot all you pig jews." The messages specifically threatened to "shoot up 104 west," referring to the university's kosher dining hall. The messages also threatened to "bomb Jewish house"—that is, the Cornell Center for Jewish Living, located next door to 104 West, which houses Jewish students. The same author threatened to "stab" and "slit the throat" of male Jewish students on campus, to rape female Jewish students, and to behead Jewish babies, according to the Department of Justice.

For days the threats loomed over the university's Jewish community. Campus police stood guard outside the Center for Jewish Living, backed up by state law enforcement. Later in the week, a student was arrested: Patrick Dai, a junior. He is, as of this writing, serving a twenty-one-month prison sentence "for posting threats to kill or injure another person using interstate communications." The U.S. attorney responsible for the case said that Dai had "terrorized the Cornell campus community for days and shattered the community's sense of safety."[74]

It was one of the worst incidents to take place across America's campuses. But, astonishingly, it seems to have done nothing to stem the swelling tide of antisemitism, at Cornell or elsewhere.

In early December, student protesters occupied Cornell's Day Hall, in an effort to force changes to university policy, including the adoption of a narrower definition of antisemitism. Outside the hall, members of the Coalition for Mutual Liberation staged a mock trial of Cornell President Martha Pollack. She was, they insisted, guilty of complicity in "genocide against Palestinian civilians." The plaza resounded with chants of "From the river to the sea, Palestine will be free!"

The occupation ended two days later, when the university agreed to organize a meeting between university administrators and the student occupation organizers. No students were disciplined for the episode.[75]

If Cornell's administrators had enforced university rules, they might not have suffered a repeat of the situation the following March. Again, pro-Hamas students turned rioters occupied Day Hall, demanding that Cornell's Board of Trustees vote to divest from Israel-associated companies.

Cornell took what seemed like a stronger posture. At 6 p.m., the occupiers were removed by campus police. Twenty-two students and two employees were charged with trespassing. But all subsequently reached an adjournment in contemplation of dismissal with the District Attorney's Office, an arrangement whereby the protesters' charges would expire, provided they did not get arrested again before the end of the spring semester.[76]

In other words, they were let off the hook.

That likely encouraged the students who established an encampment on Cornell's Arts Quad. During its eighteen-day lifespan, six students were suspended, but no arrests were made. Some faculty and staff, who proudly proactively held classes in the antisemitic encampment, were referred for violations of university policy, but actual punishments were never meted out.[77]

In April 2025, Cornell's campus faced another uproar. As part of its end-of-semester Slope Day festivities, the university booked R&B star Kehlani to perform. Jewish students objected, citing past comments—for example, "It's f*ck Israel, it's f*ck Zionism, and it's also f*ck a lot of y'all too."—and the music video for her new song "Next 2 U," which featured the phrase "Long Live the Intifada" and Kehlani and backup dancers performing in keffiyehs.

President Michael Kotlikoff, who assumed his role in March 2025, after serving as interim president following Martha Pollack's resignation the previous summer, tried to dodge the situation, pleading that it was "too late to secure another performer." But pressure from student groups mounted. Eventually, Kotlikoff canceled Kehlani's appearance, citing her history of "antisemitic, anti-Israel sentiments in performances, videos, and on social media."[78]

President Kotlikoff might have been responding, too, to new external pressures.

Cornell had watched from the sidelines while the presidents of Harvard, Penn, and MIT were grilled by our committee in December 2023. But in January 2024, Cornell, along with Harvard, Penn, and MIT, received an official notice from the House Ways and Means Committee warning that the schools' failure to address antisemitic conduct on campus could endanger their tax-exempt status. The committee requested information from the universities about what efforts they were making to protect Jewish students, to eliminate DEI programming, and to protect free speech.[79]

Our committee was planning to join the fray, too. More hearings were in the works, and Cornell was on the agenda. When word came that the Education Committee was about to subpoena Cornell's President Martha Pollack to appear for a hearing, she pre-emptively announced her resignation. Perhaps to avoid the deserved public embarrassment that would have ensued.[80]

Cornell was one of some sixty colleges and universities to receive a letter from the Department of Education the following spring warning of "potential enforcement actions if they do not fulfill their obligations" under federal law to "protect Jewish students on campus, including uninterrupted access to campus facilities and educational opportunities."[81]

In April 2025, the Trump administration froze approximately $1 billion in research funding to Cornell, citing its ongoing investigation into whether the university failed to protect the civil rights of Jewish students. In November, the administration announced an agreement. In addition to a renewed commitment to abide by federal civil rights law, over the next few years Cornell will pay $30 million in fines and invest $30 million in agriculture-related research in exchange for the restoration of frozen research funding.[82]

....

Unfortunately, many more schools could be included in the exceedingly long list of institutions that failed to address the pervasive rise of antisemitism on college campuses post–October 7th. In each and every instance, there is weak university leadership at the helm—with university presidents often beholden to the radically woke faculty who encouraged and even participated in the pro-Hamas sentiment fomenting on campus. The crisis in higher education is not limited to the most recognizable schools. It is pervasive and widespread. This is the rotten character of the higher education apparatus in the United States supported by taxpayer dollars. One of the reasons why the first and subsequent congressional hearings on college campus antisemitism were so riveting was because they revealed a disgraceful pattern of weak and out-of-touch university presidents who doubled down, one after another, on their failed approach. In hearing after hearing, with school after school, we heard excuses and moral equivocation without even the semblance of self-reflection.

And the American people, much smarter than these university presidents, said enough is enough.

CHAPTER 7

What Went Wrong?

"The next time some academics tell you how important diversity is, ask how many Republicans there are in their sociology department."

—Thomas Sowell

Over the last several chapters we've related the stories of American Jewish students and faculty on our college campuses since October 7, 2023. What they have been through has in many cases been harrowing and horrifying. In every case, it has been disgusting and un-American. But the rise of antisemitism on college campuses was the culmination of a much broader moral and academic rot in American higher education. It was a symptom of a deep-seated decay that has been happening at elite universities for decades.

These schools were once important institutions for invention, inquiry, research, development, scientific exploration, artistic achievements, and societal advancement. An elite American college education was the envy of the world and a near guarantor of the American Dream. Yet today, American higher education has fundamentally lost its way. The most important questions are Why? and How? Why did our country's campuses become cesspools of antisemitism? How did this happen? What went wrong?

First, radical left-wing political ideology is now synonymous with higher education. Universities are monocultures, where faculty, staff, and administrators operate like a herd. Where there's division in the ranks, it's almost always very Far Left faculty fighting with slightly less Far Left faculty. This problem only grows worse over time, because ideology is fiercely policed through the tenure system, which enables radical senior faculty to hire even-more-radical junior faculty. It also manifests in the batty curricula that can be found in classrooms across American universities. What is actually being taught in our schools has shifted away from academically rigorous coursework toward political and social indoctrination, filled with endless buzzwords and moral relativism. Training in "the best that has been thought and said" has given way to endless electives, where English majors can graduate without having read Shakespeare or Chaucer (as is now the case at Harvard), or history majors can avoid ever having to study the Middle Ages or the Reformation (also Harvard).

Second, the insidious Woke Revolution that culminated in the "Diversity, Equity, and Inclusion" (DEI) agenda insinuated itself into every nook and cranny of the university in the late 2010s and early 2020s. Wokeness was not just another notch in the left-wing ratchet. It was a pseudo-religious movement, and everyone had to bend the knee. DEI reshaped admissions, hiring, the classroom, student life—nothing was allowed to go untouched. "Cancel culture" came not just for the rebels who actively resisted the DEI regime but for innocent professors and students who simply ran afoul of the new dogma of the Woke Left. The purpose of DEI was not to advance racial equality; it was to put a new, radical class in power and establish a culture of fear and racism that would keep dissenters in line.

Third, there has been a historic demographic shift. Elite institutions have deprioritized American students and dramatically increased their attention to foreign students. Part of that is ideological: students need to be "global citizens," the schools insist. But the main driver is—let's be frank—financial: elite universities are competing with each other for access to deep foreign pockets. Countries like China and Qatar are dangling enormous sums of money in front of American universities, and no one can resist. Of course, the result is that foreign donors, including adversarial governments, now have a meaningful say in what happens at American universities, from admissions to curricula to hiring to student discipline.

Finally, the failed governance structure of universities has allowed university presidents to plumb the moral abyss with little accountability.

University boards, which are supposed to be guarding the long-term interests of the university, have largely absented themselves from determining the direction of these institutions. Most university trustees are happy enough to be invited to dinners, have their names in big letters on donor lists, and enjoy premium seats at football games. They don't want to make the hard decisions of governing. But without hands-on trustees, universities will continue to spin out of control.

Each of these challenges in its own way has eaten away at our universities, and together they've combined to do massive structural and existential damage over decades.

....

When I was an undergraduate, I could count the conservative professors I had at Harvard on one hand. Now it's even fewer. The overwhelming left-wing bias of higher education is long standing and well documented. But I don't think that even conservatives who pay close attention fully understand just how bad the situation has gotten at our colleges and universities.

A 2020 study by the National Association of Scholars surveyed more than twelve thousand faculty at American campuses. The study looked at the top two highest-ranked public and private universities in each state. By voter registration, they found 8.5 registered Democrats for every 1 Republican.

That's bad enough. But when you look at professors by discipline, not just faculty in general, the numbers get even more scandalous. In English, there are about 27 registered Democrats for every 1 Republican. In anthropology, it's an astonishing 42-to-1. Humanities and the social sciences tend to be worse than mathematics and the natural sciences. But even Democrat biologists outnumber their Republican counterparts by nearly 10 to 1.

The numbers are even worse at elite universities. At Columbia, there are about 25 Democrats for every 1 Republican. At Yale, there are 31. At

Harvard, it's a staggering 88-to-1 ratio. The only university with a higher ratio of Democrats to Republicans than Harvard is the famously progressive University of Massachusetts (Amherst), where there are 92 registered Democrats for every 1 Republican.

A 2017 study by political scientist Samuel Abrams of Sarah Lawrence College looked at how faculty self-identification has changed over time. According to his research, Democrats outnumbered Republicans by less than 2-to-1 in 1970. By 2014, it was nearly 5-to-1. Certainly, it is much higher today. So, not only are universities left-leaning, they've become much *more* left-leaning over time.

The general population, meanwhile, hasn't really changed. At close to 1 Democrat for every 1 Republican, it's about the same as it was in 1970. So while the relative ideological tilt of the country hasn't moved, American higher education has sprinted to the Left. It's no wonder our elite institutions—not just universities, but all the institutions that pull their leaders and staff from elite campuses—have become disconnected from the values of the American people.

There's evidence to back that up. In a 2021 study of faculty bias that extended across the U.S., Great Britain, and Canada, demographer Eric Kaufman found that "over 4 in 10 US and Canadian academics would not hire a Trump supporter, and 1 in 3 British academics would not hire a Brexit supporter." That's plain political discrimination. The numbers showing academic self-censorship are simply appalling. Ninety percent of pro-Trump academics and 80 percent of pro-Brexit academics say they would hesitate to share their views with a colleague. Among North American and British self-identified conservatives, more than half admit to self-censoring either in their research or their teaching.[1]

A 2024 Foundation for Individual Rights in Education survey of more than six thousand faculty at fifty-five colleges and universities found something similar. According to FIRE, "35 percent of faculty say they recently toned down their writing for fear of controversy, compared to 9 percent of faculty who said the same during the McCarthy era."[2]

Again, that's one-third of conservative faculty not saying what they think, for fear of politically motivated retribution. That's not a climate in which the free exchange of ideas is flourishing.

As Abrams explains in a 2017 essay, political bias and fear of reprisals can shift entire fields of research over time. When faculty all agree on a political agenda, or when certain assumptions go unchallenged, it hurts scholarship by promoting orthodoxy and discouraging dissent. Scholars come to confuse their political biases with established scientific facts, a dangerous situation. This isn't true only in the social sciences. As we've seen in recent years, this sort of thinking has infected the natural sciences as well. No field is safe.

It also obviously has downstream effects on what gets taught to students and how faculty handle disagreement in the classroom. Consider the bias that informs and infects course offerings having to do with the Middle East at elite universities.

In a 311-page report released by its Antisemitism Task Force, Harvard admitted to supporting "departments that taught classes that denied historical facts in service to a political agenda," in the words of *The Wall Street Journal*. "One professor denied Jews have any kind of historical connection to the land of Israel."[3]

At UC Berkeley, a course titled "Leninism and Anarchism: A Theoretical Approach to Literature and Film," offered in spring 2025, promised to examine the genocide of the "indigenous Palestinians by the Israeli Occupying Forces." Hamas is described as "a revolutionary resistance force combating settler-colonialism."[4]

A fall 2023 course at Princeton, "The Healing Humanities: Decolonizing Trauma Studies from the Global South," included on its syllabus the 2017 book *The Right to Maim: Debility, Capacity, Disability* by Rutgers Professor Jasbir K. Puar. That book claims without evidence that IDF soldiers deliberately maim Palestinian civilians "in order to control them." Puar has repeatedly asserted, again without evidence, that the IDF has engaged in harvesting the organs of Palestinians.[5]

In spring 2025, in the notorious Middle Eastern, South Asian, and African Studies (MESAAS) Department at Columbia, "Palestinian and Israeli

Politics and Societies" was taught by none other than the October 7th–celebrating Joseph Massad.

When Massad's course was announced, School of International Public Affairs Professor Laurence Rosenblatt, who is Jewish, resigned in protest. In a Facebook post, Rosenblatt charged Columbia with betraying its responsibilities as an institution of learning. Massad teaching about Israeli politics would be like "having a white nationalist teach about the U.S. Civil Rights movement," wrote Rosenblatt.

But that is not how Columbia's leaders see it. Likewise, it simply does not register to many faculty and administrators that their view of the world is wildly to the left of the American mainstream, or that this could be a problem.

Yet the left-wing monoculture of the university today has an immiserating effect on intellectual life. A pro-Israel student who wants to study the Middle East at an elite American university can expect to have to run a gauntlet of anti-Israel politics, antisemitism, propaganda, misinformation, and even harassment. They certainly cannot expect that their views will be respected, taken seriously, or perhaps even entertained. This is a recipe for increasing narrow-mindedness and bigotry and for a suffocating educational atmosphere.

What's true of these departments is true, to greater and lesser degrees, for others. As conservative students and faculty at universities across the country will tell you, this is just what you should expect if you step onto an American campus, especially an elite campus. This is the climate that the progressive intelligentsia has established at America's elite universities.

Of course, there's also just an enormous amount of unseriousness.

When I was an undergraduate, there was still an expectation, eroding though it was, that a Harvard education meant well-rounded learning in the classical liberal arts tradition. So, students were expected to take a certain number of courses outside their major field. English majors should understand calculus. Physicists should know about the Renaissance. The basic idea was good, but even then the practice of the "Core" belied the theory behind it. Instead of learning about Socrates,

Plato, and Aristotle, or Adam Smith and John Locke and Jean-Jacques Rousseau—that is, the great thinkers and achievements of the Western Canon—students were just as likely to be subjected to extremely specialized courses that were only distantly related to what we might call "liberal education." For many, the Core ended up being just a random assortment of left-wing professors' pet intellectual projects.

That's much of what goes by the name of elite education today. In their 2025 book *Slacking: A Guide to Ivy League Miseducation*, authors Adam Kissel, Rachel Alexander Cambre, and Madison Marino Doan examine the "general education" programs of the eight Ivy League schools. "Core curricula historically guaranteed consistency for undergraduates, reflecting a wise faculty's determination of the knowledge and academic skills most worth having," they write. "Today, however, most general education requirements in the Ivies are so general—some arts here, some sciences there—that they are simply another opportunity for undirected self-actualization. Hundreds of course options can fulfill each 'requirement.'" "Slacking" is their name for what most students prefer to do: steer away from courses on traditional, substantive materials and toward courses on everything from anticolonialism and antiracism to television, movies, and video games. (Cornell, for example, offers "Natural History of the Magic Kingdom: Understanding Animal Behavior Through Animated Films," which includes studying *The Lion King*, and "Queer Girlhood," which includes discussions of Barbie and the 1990s cartoon *The Powerpuff Girls*.)[6] At Princeton, students can learn about being "Black + Queer in Leather: Black Leather/BDSM Material Culture."[7]

There are exceptions to this rule: Columbia still has a robust Core Curriculum, for those who wish to pursue it, and Yale has Directed Studies, an interdisciplinary study of canonical Western texts for a select group of outstanding undergraduates. But these are very much exceptions.

States are beginning to take action to expose outlandish course offerings. Syllabus transparency is one basic measure. Georgia, Texas, Florida, Indiana, and Ohio all have laws on the books mandating that professors make publicly available certain basic course information. In Utah, syllabi for mandatory courses are available through a publicly searchable database.[8] Six public university systems in Texas have undertaken a full curriculum review to ensure that all courses are in compliance with state law.

It's obviously important that universities preserve plenty of space for students to explore controversial ideas and difficult topics. But there's a difference between discussion and indoctrination. For students making decisions about course offerings, and for parents trying to ensure their children are receiving a rigorous education, course catalogues are often a black box. Transparency in syllabi encourages more informed decisions and helps prevent professors from abusing their teaching authority.

....

Unfortunately, structural factors make it difficult to enforce faculty discipline. The long-standing institution of tenure, for example, which was intended to provide job security and to help shield faculty from suffering consequences for disfavored academic work, has now in many cases become a protective blanket for indulgence, indoctrination, and harassment. Many professors think they can attack students in the classroom, and that their conduct is covered by tenure's "academic freedom" provisions.

That's not true. In many cases, these attacks are straightforward violations of universities' codes of conduct—although the universities are loath to enforce them. That's something that needs to change. Moreover, despite what certain elite faculty think, tenure does not trump U.S. civil rights law. The many lawsuits being filed against the universities by victims of harassment and targeted violence are overdue reminders that universities have serious legal obligations, and if the universities refuse to comply with them voluntarily, they will be made to comply with them by judges. That's the way a system of laws works.

But the problem nonetheless grows, because tenure also promotes the increasingly insular self-selection of faculty who share the same ideological and pedagogical viewpoints. Although departments often have to gain approval from administrators for new faculty hires, that process often lacks real oversight. Provosts are fine rubber-stamping faculty selections. That's a problem when faculty use the hiring process to police ideological boundaries. Instead of hiring for diversity, they hire for conformity. Rigor is exchanged for loyalty to the department's ideological priorities. So, over time, departments become more narrow and more brittle.

For all these reasons, tenure is an institution in desperate need of reform. Variations on traditional tenure, such as tenure "terms" after which tenure is renewed or not, have been tried successfully at smaller schools and deserve a more serious look at elite institutions. Unfortunately, this will require the assertive intervention of reform-minded administrators and boards of trustees. Tenure will never be reformed where it remains within the control of a cabal of like-minded faculty and board members, who have a personal interest in keeping the institution exactly as is.

Faculty unions are another example of self-interested faculty trampling dissenters. As of 2024, according to the National Education Association, "about 27 percent of faculty belong to unions, for a total of 402,217 unionized faculty. By comparison, just 11.3 percent of U.S. workers, in general, belong to unions."[9]

The problem with these unions is exemplified by the City University of New York. In 2021, CUNY's faculty union, the Professional Staff Congress, issued the following anti-Israel statement: "PSC-CUNY condemns the massacre of Palestinians by the Israeli state and cannot be silent about the continued subjection of Palestinians to the state-supported displacement, occupation and use of lethal force by Israel."[10]

One might wonder why CUNY's faculty union, whose sole responsibility is to negotiate on behalf of faculty on issues having to do with working conditions, "cannot remain silent" about this entirely unrelated issue.

A year later, in June 2022, the PSC-CUNY issued a resolution condemning "the continued subjection of Palestinians to the state-supported displacement, occupation, and use of lethal force by Israel." The union called for chapters to consider union support for Boycott, Divestment, and Sanctions efforts.

Multiple faculty members objected, calling the resolution and language antisemitic. They sought to leave. In *The Wall Street Journal*, Avraham Goldstein, a tenured professor of mathematics, explained that union officials refused to honor his resignation and continued to automatically collect union dues from his paycheck. He had no way to escape, and no way to obtain other union representation. "I am forced," he wrote, "to rely on a union that says anti-Semitic, hateful things about Israel to negotiate on my behalf."[11]

An Orthodox, Zionist Jew and an ordained rabbi, Goldstein and his family were victims of Soviet antisemitism when he was a boy. This kind of situation imposes an obviously intolerable burden on him. In effect, forced faculty union membership means that Professor Goldstein and his fellow plaintiffs are forced to sign onto political speech with which they disagree, and they are unable to go outside the union to find alternative representation. The unions could of course avoid this situation by simply refraining from political speech that is outside their remit. But for many faculty, forcing like-mindedness in the form of "solidarity" is the point. No one can be allowed to dissent from the antisemitic company line.

....

The grab bag of rules, programs, slogans, and dogmas that went under the banner of Diversity, Equity, and Inclusion (DEI) overran American campuses so easily because the ground had already been softened by years of progressive assaults on free speech and academic freedom. For years, universities had entertained trigger warnings and safe spaces and other devices intended to ease the burden on students of having to encounter perspectives that they might find uncomfortable. Much of the administrative apparatus of colleges and universities became an enormous machine for making students feel as "safe" as possible—not just physically but emotionally. Professors who dared to teach challenging, inflammatory, or sensitive material were sometimes fired. DEI was a natural successor to this state of affairs: a cancer that struck an already weakened body.

The key to understanding DEI is to see that it does the exact opposite of what it claims to do. In order to promote "diversity," DEI segregates people by race, quashes voices it dislikes, and expels viewpoints it disagrees with. In order to secure "equity," it places certain groups of people (so-called marginalized groups) above others (so-called oppressors) in strict "intersectional" hierarchies of race, sexual orientation, and gender identity. In order to secure "inclusion," it excludes disfavored people (for example, "cis-gender" white males) and opinions. So, in the topsy-turvy world of DEI, "inclusion" means letting biological males compete in women's sports while silencing any female athletes who might object. Likewise, "equity" means giving special privileges to Palestinian students and faculty ("victims") while systematically ignoring the petitions of beleaguered and abused Jewish students and faculty ("oppressors"). DEI is racism under the guise of opposing racism, sexism under the guise of opposing sexism, and antisemitism under the guise of opposing hatred. The not-so-hidden secret of DEI is that it is not about securing greater justice or equality. It is mostly about wielding a club against people and views that the most progressive activists do not like. DEI is a magic wand that can be used to turn ordinary people into "racists," "bigots," "transphobes," "Islamophobes," and more.

DEI has its roots in a variety of academic critical theories that have come to be roped together as "Critical Race Theory." Writing in *City Journal* in 2021, Wilfred Reilly, assistant professor of political science at Kentucky State, pointed to "three baseline assumptions" that propped up CRT. First, the Critical Race Theorist sees racism everywhere. Nothing is untouched by the pollution of racism. If a tool, a system, or an institution claims to be neutral, it has only failed to recognize its own internal bias. Second, to prove oppression one need only show disparities between groups. So, if one group performs better on, say, a standardized test (e.g., the SAT) than another group, it must be the result of bias somewhere in the educational system, from the schools to the test itself. Finally, to solve the problem of racial disparity, we need to impose "equity." Equity isn't equality, which is about opportunities. Equity is about outcomes. Until groups are represented proportionally across all endeavors—from Harvard admissions to NFL coaches to Fortune 500 company boardrooms—oppression still rules the day.[12]

These assumptions are really, as Reilly shows, articles of faith. They are assumed to be true, rather than proven. Thinkers such as economist Thomas Sowell (who is Black) have debunked these assumptions time and time again for decades. Unfortunately, not enough people listened.

During the late 2010s and into the 2020s, the work of figures such as "antiracist" activist Ibram X. Kendi and author Robin DiAngelo became talismans for the progressive left. Kendi's *How to Be an Antiracist* and DiAngelo's book *White Fragility: Why It's So Hard for White People to Talk About Racism* were both *New York Times* bestsellers and received rapturous reviews in mainstream outlets.

Meanwhile, on the university campuses that had incubated these toxic ideas, DEI took over. It was installed in every facet of the university's operations, from hiring and admissions to the President's Office to the classroom experience to athletics, and on and on. Nothing at the university went untouched by DEI.

The goal was not to advance the traditional work of the university: teaching, learning, discovering new knowledge. The purpose was to destroy the university, replacing it with an even more efficient machine for ideological indoctrination. As Princeton "Latinx" Studies Professor Lorgia Garcia Pena told a conference in July 2025, "We want to abolish the university as it is."

Predictably, the results have been disastrous for campus communities and students.

A study by the Network Contagion Research Institute found that exposure to DEI materials can "engender a hostile attribution bias and heighten racial suspicion, prejudicial attitudes, authoritarian policing, and support for punitive behaviors in the absence of evidence for a transgression deserving punishment." The researchers found that, compared to a control group, study participants who were exposed to DEI materials were significantly more likely to engage in antisocial behaviors. "Educational materials from some of the most well-published and well-known

DEI scholars not only failed to positively enhance interracial attitudes, they provoked baseless suspicion and encouraged punitive attitudes."[13]

The University of Michigan also offers an example of how DEI disserved campus communities. A 2021 survey of students and faculty found that the campus climate was perceived as less positive than before DEI efforts were launched. Students said that they interacted less, not more, with people of other races and religions.

Put more simply: DEI encouraged a campus climate of suspicion, discrimination, and, ultimately, civil rights violations.

DEI's hierarchy of victimhood also led administrators and support staff to systematically ignore and suppress the concerns of American Jewish students and faculty. "Michigan community members reported dozens of instances of antisemitic discrimination to the university's DEI bureaucracy. The university investigated and reported on only *one* of these incidents."[14] Some victims don't count.

Happily, we've begun to see a steady stream of anti-DEI victories.

The Supreme Court struck a major blow against the DEI regime. In 2023, in its 6–3 decision in *Students for Fair Admissions v. Harvard*, the court struck down racial preferences in admissions, closing the book on nearly a half century of affirmative action—i.e., legal discrimination. As Chief Justice John Roberts put it bluntly: "Eliminating racial discrimination means eliminating all of it." The court rightly held that race-conscious admissions violate the 14th Amendment's Equal Protection Clause. It was a critical victory for the core principle of equality under law. DEI was a direct attack on that founding principle.

Unfortunately, there is every reason to think that highly selective colleges and universities will continue to take race into consideration, despite the chief justice's warning that "universities may not simply establish through application essays or other means the regime we hold unlawful today." Early post-*SFFA* admissions decisions indicate that admissions departments have not yet gotten the court's message. Comparing admissions data for the Class of 2028 at highly selective schools (including Yale, Princeton, Brown, and Columbia) with data from the pre-*SFFA* Class of

2027, Manhattan Institute fellow Renu Mukherjee found that the racial composition of the admitted cohorts remained largely the same. How was that possible? "For more than two decades, universities claimed that socioeconomic preferences, geographic sorting, and other race-neutral alternatives could not achieve the same level of racial diversity on campus as could affirmative action. Yet the demographics of many schools' Class of 2028 suggest otherwise. It raises an awkward question: Did America's top universities mislead the Supreme Court then, or are they breaking the law now?"[15]

It's a question that the Department of Justice is likely to pursue.

A return to—hopefully—merit-based and race-blind admissions is being accompanied by the surprise return of standardized testing as a key admissions criterion. Gulled by DEI claims that standardized tests were purveyors of racism, and responding to the exceptional educational circumstances brought on by Covid-19, many elite schools moved to a "test-optional" admissions policy in the early 2020s. Admissions offices would no longer demand SAT or ACT scores from applicants.

But starting with MIT in 2022, selective institutions began reinstating standardized tests as part of their admissions criteria. Harvard brought back its testing requirement in 2024. What happened? Evidence from classes admitted under "test-optional" policies revealed that, without standardized tests, cohorts became *less*, not more, diverse. Studies suggest that a standardized testing requirement boosts the chances of low-income students, even when their score is below the median score of the school to which they are applying. Standardized tests are also much better predictors of college performance than other metrics, such as high school GPA.[16] MIT's admissions director announced in 2022 that MIT's research showed exactly that, and that it also helped the university identify students from disadvantaged backgrounds who could thrive at the school: "We believe a requirement is more equitable and transparent than a test-optional policy."[17]

This is all to say, the protests of elite universities that they can't establish diverse student bodies without race-conscious admissions is absurd, and often misleading. What they tend to mean, in reality, is that they can't socially engineer classes according to ideological dictates. However tentative it may be, the shift toward merit-based admissions processes is a welcome change of direction.

As soon as President Trump took office in 2025, his administration began to take a much-needed jackhammer to the DEI infrastructure, too. One early executive order struck a massive blow against preferential treatment based on race and sex in the federal government and among federal contractors. According to the order, contractors are no longer permitted "to engage in workforce balancing based on race, color, sex, sexual preference, religion, or national origin." That includes universities. The order attacked DEI as "dangerous, demeaning, and immoral," and antagonistic to "traditional American values of hard work, excellence, and individual achievement."

This marks a sea change in federal policy and deserves praise.

It's also having an impact. In August 2025, the Department of Education's Office for Civil Rights found George Mason University had violated Title VI of the Civil Rights Act of 1964 "by illegally using race and other immutable characteristics in university practices and policies, including hiring and promotion." The Department of Education cited specifically George Mason's aggressive implementation of DEI programs.

The finding was a shot across the bow of universities across America. Many policies encouraged by DEI advocates are patently illegal under existing nondiscrimination law, and the colleges and universities that implemented these policies knew that. Now the government is holding them to account.

Again, though, there are reasons to be wary when it comes to these victories.

There is clear evidence that colleges and universities have simply taken DEI underground. Schools renamed their DEI offices and eliminated familiar buzzwords, but they continue to operate like before—even in red states that have passed aggressive anti-DEI laws. According to an April 2025 report from Defending Education, 245 colleges and universities—

including every Ivy League school, as well as elite universities such as Stanford, Duke, the University of Chicago, and MIT—still have active DEI offices.[18]

A recent survey found that one out of five academic jobs still requires some form of DEI statement. Many colleges and universities have retained mandatory course requirements put in place for DEI purposes. Likewise, the administrative apparatus is still thoroughly dyed in DEI propaganda. At Princeton at the beginning of the 2025 semester, residential college advisors were required to undergo a training in the "Four I's of Oppression": "ideological, institutional, interpersonal, and internalized oppression." The mandatory training was one of two designated "DEI training" sessions.[19]

At Northwestern, a required anti-discrimination training for all employees promised to address "antisemitic, anti-Muslim, anti-Arab and anti-Palestinian biases," but noticeably omitted "anti-Zionist" prejudice—the name under which antisemitism is usually smuggled (as we've seen above). Michael Teplitsky, head of the Coalition Against Antisemitism at Northwestern, criticized the policy, saying that it "trivializes documented discrimination and neglects the lived experiences of Jewish, Israeli, and Zionist students." He added: "By prioritizing certain biases over others, Northwestern sends a clear message: some forms of hate clearly matter more than others."[20]

Unfortunately, no matter what these schools may say to cover their own skin, it's clear that we will be suffering the lingering effects of the Woke Revolution for a long time.

....

At a certain point in their history, America's most prestigious institutions of higher learning stopped being institutions first and foremost by and for Americans. Buzzwords like "global citizenship" became ubiquitous, as universities stopped thinking of themselves as primarily national institutions and started to think of themselves as global villages. Students are encouraged to "change the world," not their neighborhoods, their cities, or their country. They are encouraged to work on behalf of an abstract "humanity," rather than on behalf of concrete neighbors and fellow citizens.

This change in self-understanding is reflected by changes in the composition of our elite universities. Today, foreign students make up a large part of the student body of our most prestigious schools, and foreign money constitutes a key part of campus budgets.

According to the Migration Policy Institute, the "number of international students pursuing degrees in the U.S. has increased from just 26,000 in the 1949-50 school year, to an all-time high of more than 1.1 million in 2023-24, with an additional 18,000 international students working toward a U.S. degree online from abroad." Those students account for 6 percent of all students enrolled at American colleges and universities.[21]

At elite universities, however, the numbers are dramatically different. According to *The New York Times*, at Yale and Princeton, 24 percent of the student body were international students as of 2023. At Harvard, it was 28 percent. At MIT, 30 percent. Columbia was a staggering 40 percent foreign.[22]

(The proportion of Chinese students among international students is noteworthy, too. At Harvard, 23 percent of international students are from China. At Columbia, it's 47 percent.)

All these foreign students may bring in tuition dollars, but they also make universities beholden to foreign interests. If the federal government were to eliminate the student visa program, several elite universities would watch a quarter or more of their student body evaporate. I believe that those slots could and should be filled by American students. Since international students pay higher tuition than domestic students, that's a body blow to these schools' bottom lines. The National Association for Foreign Student Affairs estimates that the economic contributions of international students to Harvard in 2023 added up to $384 million. At Columbia, it was $903 million.[23]

Despite a drop in international enrollment at most colleges and universities since the Trump administration placed more constraints on student visas, the number of international freshmen at Columbia remained steady, as of the 2025 fall semester, and at Princeton had risen slightly.

But are the dollars these students add to university coffers the only relevant metric? Absolutely not. Does it matter that American universities are educating the sons and daughters of Chinese Communist Party leaders and Qatari royalty? Yes. Should it matter to us that foreign students bring with them their own—sometimes very strong—ideological programs and anti-American cultural biases? Yes. Does the presence of foreign students have an effect on the educational culture of American campuses? Absolutely.

Let's not be naive. The fact is that American universities are no longer prioritizing American students. They are also no longer educating international students, as they once did, into core American principles and values, because the universities themselves no longer believe in American principles and values. So, very often, the foreign students end up "educating" the institutions—that is, changing the universities to fit their own ideological priors.

That's a big problem.

The direction of influence is obvious when it comes to foreign money. Billions of dollars from foreign countries have poured into American colleges and universities in recent years. That money has consequences.

A 2024 Heritage Foundation report explores the way that foreign money shapes American campuses. The report identifies five ways foreign outfits attempt to exert influence through donations: gifts directly to the institutions; indirect gifts to nonprofits that funnel the money to the universities; tuition payments; funding for U.S. campuses in foreign countries; and research grants to faculty. These various forms of donation are obviously intended to serve the donor's interests. And those do not always align with American interests.

According to a study by the Network Contagion Research Institute (NCRI), foreign donors gave almost $29 billion to American colleges and universities between 2021 and 2024—as much as they gave in the previous four decades combined. Since the federal government began tracking foreign donation data in 1986, almost $60 billion has flowed into American universities from foreign sources.

Where is that money coming from?

Since 2014, China, Qatar, and Saudi Arabia have been among the top four foreign donors to American universities. From 2021 to 2024, the four largest foreign donors to American universities were, in order: Germany ($3.3B), China ($2.3B), Qatar ($2B), and Saudi Arabia ($1.9B). Both Chinese and Qatari funding have risen dramatically since 2021.

This is a big deal and cause for grave concern.

"This isn't just a financial issue—it's a national security crisis," NCRI co-founder Joel Finkelstein told *The Free Press* in 2025. "Hostile powers are buying influence on American campuses at an industrial scale."[24]

What does this look like? Take the two most troubling examples: China and Qatar.

. . . .

Let's start with China.

The Chinese Communist Party's influence operation in American universities has been going on for decades, mainly through its network of Confucius Institutes. In 2004, the Chinese Communist Party began planting on-campus centers for the purposes of, so the story went, promoting Chinese language and culture. In fact, as the Department of State wrote in 2020, the institutes "push out skewed Chinese language and cultural training for U.S. students as part of Beijing's multifaceted propaganda efforts." Then Secretary of State Mike Pompeo called them "part of the Chinese Communist Party's global influence and propaganda apparatus."

At more than one hundred campuses across the United States, Confucius Institutes have acted as veiled instruments of Communist China's soft power, teaching doctored lessons about Chinese history and culture, while exerting pressures on the campus culture that favor Chinese Communist interests.

Columbia's Global Center in Beijing has reportedly canceled lectures for fear of displeasing Communist Chinese leaders.[25] In 2017, a report from the National Association of Scholars found that faculty associated with Confucius Institutes felt pressure to self-censor. Confucius Institutes threaten "the independence and integrity of academic institutions," the American Association of University Professors said in 2014.[26]

In 2018, I worked in Congress from my perch on the House Armed Services Committee to prohibit Confucius Institutes from receiving funding from the Department of Defense.[27] Since then, almost all Confucius Institutes in the U.S. have closed—or, at least, seemed to. As of 2023, 111 Confucius Institutes had closed nationwide, but according to the National Association of Scholars, "of these, at least 28 have replaced their Confucius Institute with a similar program, and at least 58 have maintained close relationships with their former Confucius Institute partner."

....

Then there's Qatar.

Billions of dollars have flowed from Qatar to American universities in recent years. Between the late 1990s and early 2000s, six American universities established campuses in Qatar, with the additional benefit of tens of millions of dollars in subsidies and research support.

Hamas might be part of Iran's terror network, but for a long time it's Qatar that has been its most important source of financial and political support. Since 2012, key Hamas leaders have resided in Qatar. For several years Ismail Haniyeh, Hamas's top political leader, lived in Doha. He was killed by Israel in 2024 when a bomb exploded in his hotel room during a trip to Tehran to visit with Iranian leadership. Qatar has served as the chief mediator for negotiations between Israel and Hamas since October 7, 2023.

Several universities have been happy to climb into bed with Qatar, including elite universities such as Cornell, Northwestern, and Georgetown, all of which have campuses there.

Since 2008, Doha has been the site of Northwestern University Qatar, or NU-Q. A 2022 Canary Mission report on NU-Q faculty found—surprise!—that the school's faculty are overwhelmingly anti-Israel. Some have justified or glorified terrorism. Students who attend NU-Q are immersed in a viciously antisemitic environment, then ushered into internships through Northwestern's extensive professional network.[28]

NU-Q is an influence operation: a mechanism for channeling Qatar's money and Qatar's worldview into elite American institutions.

It has serious consequences. Inquiries by the National Association of Scholars have found that Qatar's "influence led to compromises on freedom of expression [on American campuses] to appease Qatar's authoritarian government."

According to the Institute for the Study of Global Antisemitism & Policy (ISGAP), "foreign donations from Qatar, especially, have had a substantial impact on fomenting growing levels of antisemitic discourse and campus politics at US universities, as well as growing support for antidemocratic values within these institutions of higher education."

A NCRI study found that, from 2014 to 2019, receiving foreign donations "was strongly associated with higher levels of antisemitic acts than on campuses that did not receive such funding." Receiving donations from member countries of the Organization for Islamic Cooperation (OIC) and from authoritarian countries was "strongly associated with scholars and campus speakers being targeted for disinvitation" and also "strongly associated with higher levels of antisemitic activity on campus than on campuses that did not receive funding from such countries."[29]

These correlations suggest deeply troubled campus cultures, and the money likely contributes to environments characterized by divisive, antisemitic sentiment or creates further perverse incentives for crackdowns on disfavored speech.

All this has had a direct impact on campus life post–October 7th. The Heritage Foundation reports that universities have regularly declined to impose consequences on foreign students who, in the course of participating in antisemitic campus encampments, violated campus policies, state laws, and even federal civil rights laws. The universities cared more about shielding foreign students from the consequences of their rule- or lawbreaking than about upholding the legal rights of American Jewish students.[30]

For evidence of the above, look no further than Columbia's treatment of Mahmoud Khalil.

....

Foreign influence is also closely connected to the pervasive antisemitism online. Even before October 7th, antisemitic comments, memes, videos, slogans, and more could be found lurking in social media's darkest and ugliest corners. But since October 7, 2023, social media platforms have witnessed an explosion of antisemitism. Users no longer have to go searching for it. It is so pervasive that it shows up almost inevitably in users' threads and feeds. Antisemitism on social media platforms is no longer the exception; it's the norm.

Because social media plays an outsized role in the lives of young adults, it is shaping and reshaping their politics in profound ways.

Take, for example, TikTok. As of 2023, more than 150 million Americans were on the app—half of the country. According to the Pew Research Center, 59 percent of American adults under thirty use TikTok, and a slightly larger percentage (63 percent) of teenagers (thirteen to seventeen years old), "including 57% who use it daily and 16% who say they're on it 'almost constantly.'"

TikTok has become a major source of news. Some 52 percent of TikTok users over the age of eighteen say they regularly get news from the app, "up from 43% in 2023 and just 22% in 2020."[31] Among American adults who regularly get their news from the site, almost half (45 percent) are eighteen to twenty-nine years old.

Why does this matter?

A 2021 study, "TikTok's Spiral of Antisemitism," conducted by two

Israeli researchers, found that TikTok regularly failed to apply its Terms of Service to prohibit deliberately harassing or threatening content.[32] The Anti-Defamation League Center for Tech and Society likewise has found that "bad actors appear to be sidestepping TikTok's moderation policies to spread antisemitic content through slideshows (Photo Mode) and hashtags."[33]

Why has TikTok spiraled out of control? Part of it is the incredibly strong algorithm associated with the app, which supplies users with content akin to other content they have watched. Watch one "anti-Zionist" video and you're likely to get swamped by several more. Keep watching and they'll take over your feed.

But there's more at work than just technology. TikTok is controlled by ByteDance, a company intimately tied to the Chinese Communist Party, which has long shown an interest in undermining not only Israeli interests in the Middle East but also, more importantly, American interests worldwide. In September 2025, during a speech at Israel's Ministry of Foreign Affairs, Prime Minister Benjamin Netanyahu stressed the importance of countering China's subversive activities online: "Countries like Qatar and China invest huge sums to influence Western media with an anti-Israel agenda, using bots, AI, and publications. You open your phone, and you are bombarded with this, especially on TikTok. It is much more powerful than traditional media."[34]

So, a lot of what college students and other social media users are seeing on their phones is not "organic" social media activity, or real news being broadcast by trustworthy content creators. It is propaganda astroturfed by anti-American actors, from Islamist terrorist organizations to Chinese espionage agencies.

Or it is organic content exploited by those actors. In November 2023, TikTok users posted videos of themselves reading from or praising Osama bin Laden's 2002 "Letter to America," in which he cited U.S. support for Israel's "occupation" of Palestinian lands as part of the justification for the September 11, 2001, terrorist attacks and called for further violence against American civilians. Over the next few days, videos featuring the letter garnered tens of millions of views.

It wasn't only Americans who took notice. "The letter's spread online was celebrated by users on al Qaeda forums, according to SITE Intelligence Group, which tracks online extremism," *The Washington Post* wrote. "One user wrote that Islamist militants should capitalize on the opportunity, saying, 'I hope you all are seeing ongoing storm on Social Media. . . . We should post more and more content.'"[35]

Unfortunately, it turns out that "digital natives"—people who have never known a world without the Internet—have no exceptional ability to distinguish truth from falsehood online. Stanford University researchers Sam Wineburg and Joel Breakstone "tested the ability of high schoolers to identify misinformation on social media," CBS News reports. They showed more than three thousand high school students a video purporting to show voter fraud in the United States. In fact, the video showed voter fraud in Russia—as a quick Internet search revealed. "However, out of those more than 3,000 students, how many students actually discovered the link to Russia? Three. That's less than one-tenth of 1%."[36]

It's not just grandmas and grandpas falling for scams, propaganda, and fake news. It's everyone.

That's bad news when "social media pogroms" have only multiplied since October 7, 2023.

That's what music writer Eve Barlow has called the disparate and discriminatory treatment of pro-Israel voices online. In May 2021, following an outbreak of Palestinian-Israeli violence, Barlow observed that, on social media, pro-Israel Jews were regularly locked out of basic social media services, such as direct messaging or commenting, or found themselves being threatened with suspension or expulsion from platforms, simply because of their pro-Israel advocacy.[37]

The discriminatory treatment of pro-Israel social media users jibes with the transformation of social media platforms into openly antisemitic spaces—a reality that has only gotten worse post–October 7th.

The Anti-Defamation League, which tracks antisemitic incidents on-

and offline, conducted a study of nearly 163,000 X posts from September 30 to October 13, 2023—one week before to one week after the Hamas attacks. ADL discovered a staggering 919 percent week-over-week increase in antisemitic content on the platform.[38]

In 2024, again according to the ADL, 41 percent of Jewish adults "changed their online behavior to avoid being recognized as Jewish. Nearly two-thirds (63%) felt less safe than they did last year."[39]

As our look at campus antisemitism shows, what happens online doesn't stay online.

The American Jewish Committee's annual *State of Antisemitism in America* report for 2024 found that "in all, 33% of American Jews say they were a target of an antisemitic incident—a physical attack, a remark in person, antisemitic vandalism or messaging, antisemitic remark or post online or through social media, or any other form of antisemitism—in 2024."[40] That was up from 25 percent in 2023. The 2023 report found that 62 percent of Jews had witnessed at least one antisemitic episode on social media.[41]

Similarly, a recent study of more than seven thousand Jewish young adults (eighteen to mid-thirties) across the U.S., led by Leonard Saxe, Klutznick Professor of Contemporary Jewish Studies and Social Policy at Brandeis University, found that "overall rates of perceived hostility toward Jews" had doubled since 2016.[42]

Social media has been one of the most powerful vectors spreading the toxin of antisemitism far and wide.

....

And, of course, there's the problem of Students for Justice in Palestine, known as SJP. Since October 7th, no organization has been more integral to the rise of campus antisemitism than Students for Justice in Palestine. It is, says watchdog outfit NGO Monitor, "the campus organization most directly responsible for creating a hostile campus environment saturated with anti-Israel events, BDS initiatives, and speakers."

National SJP, founded in 1993, claims to support more than four hundred "Palestine solidarity organizations across occupied Turtle Island"—i.e., North America. More than two hundred are campus chapters.[43] According to a December 2024 "year-in-review" report, SJP claimed credit for starting "127 student encampments, the passing of 56 divestment resolutions, over 3,000 students and faculty being arrested and over 1,000,000 students mobilized for Gaza."[44]

As we've seen throughout this book, university SJP chapters have been hotbeds of antisemitism and sources of disorder on campus. In addition to the violations we've already recorded, SJP chapters have been suspended all over the country for violating university demonstration policies (Rutgers), for calling for violence against Jews (Brandeis), and for perpetrating violence (UCLA). The SJP chapter at George Mason University was suspended in November 2024 following a police raid on the home of SJP student leaders. The pair were suspected of leading a riot at George Mason in August of that year that resulted in thousands of dollars in property damage. When law enforcement entered the students' home, they found firearms, ammunition, foreign passports, Hamas and Hezbollah flags, and signs reading "Death to America" and "Death to Jews."[45] Not exactly traditional school supplies.

SJP chapters operate independently—on paper. But post–October 7th, there is strong reason to suspect a high degree of coordination. If you're wondering who is calling the shots (and footing the bills) for these organizations, you're not alone. Both the House Oversight Committee and the Senate HELP Committee have opened investigations into National SJP.

According to congressional testimony delivered by Foundation for the Defense of Democracies Executive Director Jonathan Schanzer in 2023, at least nine people associated with American Muslims for Palestine (AMP), which founded and controls National SJP, or AMP's partner organization, Americans for Justice in Palestine Educational Foundation (AJP), have past or present ties to Hamas. Several were fundraisers for the now-defunct Holy Land Foundation, a "charity" founded by Hamas Deputy Director Mousa Abu Marzook, which was shut down by the federal government for smuggling more than $12 million to Hamas.[46] Dr. Osama Abuirshaid, the current executive director of AMP, has "published interviews that highlight his communications with Hamas leader Abu Marzook and other Hamas leaders in Gaza . . . [and] in 2014 . . . was featured on the website of Hamas's self-declared military wing, the al-Qassam Brigades," according to Schanzer.[47] AJP is under investigation by the State of Virginia for "benefitting or providing support to terrorist organizations."[48]

Since 2010, AMP, the umbrella organization overseeing SJP, has been directly involved in training campus activists. In 2016, AMP claimed on its website that it dedicates "a large portion of its budget to support student activism on college campuses" and provides "free materials, information, speakers, infrastructure like the apartheid wall, and grants to help ensure [campus chapters have] the best chance possible of achieving [their] goals." As recently as 2023, AMP organized a National SJP conference at UCLA that gathered "hundreds" of students, according to AMP's website, including students from elite schools such as Harvard and Berkeley. Just since October 7th, AMP leaders have spoken at Columbia, the University of Pennsylvania, Berkeley, and George Washington University.[49]

So, just to put it plainly: I believe that Students for Justice in Palestine—the organization primarily responsible for the explosion of antisemitism on American campuses since October 7th—is financed, at least in part, by Hamas or Hamas-linked individuals or organizations. This is a scandal of monumental proportions.

Unfortunately, there's just too much here that we don't know. A report from the National Association of Scholars suggests that American universities have underreported foreign donations by as much as half—or what adds up to *billions* of dollars. So there is undoubtedly a massive amount of money flowing into these schools from unknown sources, which the universities would prefer to keep quiet.[50] Both universities and foreign donors have an interest in keeping names and amounts off the books. This is likely happening at universities across the country.

With my urging from Congress, the Trump administration has begun to take this problem seriously, though. An April 2025 executive order enjoins the secretary of education to enforce the reporting provisions of Section 117 of the Higher Education Act of 1965, which governs foreign gifts to universities and disclosures. To help advance the cause of financial transparency, Congress could reform Section 117, which governs financial disclosures to universities. We'll take a closer look at this in our final chapter.

....

Finally, there's the challenge of university governance.

Throughout this book, sometimes at the center of the action, sometimes hovering at the edges, have been university boards. Above the faculty, above the staff, above the administrators, are the boards of trustees, regents, fellows, etc., tasked with ultimate oversight responsibilities for these universities. It's their job to tend to the overall, long-term well-being of their institutions. It's their job to be the ultimate stewards of these universities, helping sustain them for generations of students to come.

These boards failed publicly and spectacularly after the Hamas attacks against Israel on October 7th. Instead of stepping up and taking responsibility for the crises their campuses faced, the boards closed ranks around corrupt presidents and administrators, enabling and perpetuating mismanagement, systemic lawbreaking, and pervasive antisemitism. The boards should have been proactively and decisively reorienting their institutions toward transparency and accountability. Instead, they rubber-stamped university presidents' worst impulses. As we saw above, in several cases members of the boards were part and parcel of the abysmal decision-making that made bad situations worse. It was Harvard's Corporation that backed Claudine Gay even after her shocking performance in front of our committee and her alleged habitual plagiarism. It was Columbia board member—and future Columbia president—Claire Shipman who privately attacked the board's sole Jewish trustee for her pro-Israel advocacy.

University boards are typically composed of prominent members of the university community, especially alumni. They generally have big jobs, deep pockets, and a genuine love for the institution. But they don't always want to make hard decisions. But that's exactly what they're there to do!

Think of it this way: A corporate board has a fiduciary duty to shareholders. They aren't there to serve themselves. When a corporate board fails in its fiduciary duty—when it acts in its own interests, rather than the interests of beneficiaries—it can be held to account, charged, even punished.

University boards are responsible for institutions that employ thousands of people and, in the case of the Ivy League, control billions of dollars in assets. If Harvard, which controls more than $55 billion in assets, were traded on the New York Stock Exchange, it would sit somewhere between FedEx Corporation and Ford Motor Company. What sort of duty do the thirteen handpicked members of the Harvard Corporation have to Harvard University—its students, faculty, staff, alumni, and other community members?

University boards today exhibit many of the same pathologies as the rest of the universities: cowardice, herd-mindedness, ideological mimicry, and self-protectiveness. That's a critical problem, because boards should be defining the institutional mission and charting a forward course. Breaking them out of this dysfunction will not be easy. There aren't many levers available to pull. But post–October 7th, it's clear that boards aren't impervious to outside influence.

Alumni, alumni institutions, and donors can play an important part. First, malpractice can be exposed. When boards fall down on their job to protect their institutions from inept administrators, alumni can expose it. Shine a light on bad decisions that compromise institutional integrity.

Similarly, outside actors can impose accountability. Marc Rowan at Penn helped push out a bad president. Bill Ackman helped expose the arguable malpractice of the Harvard Corporation. Alumni voices matter.

Third, more transparent board processes can and should be implemented. As Bill Ackman wrote, discussing the Harvard Corporation's absurd defense of Claudine Gay: "In a normal corporate context with the above set of facts [about Gay], the full board would resign immediately to be replaced by a group nominated by shareholders. In the case of Harvard, however, the board nominates itself and its new members. There is no shareholder vote mechanism to replace them."[51] Board selection processes should be transparent so that university stakeholders know that boards are composed of individuals with integrity and true viewpoint diversity.

Finally, Ivy League institutions might consider fundamental constitutional changes. That's the proposal of a group of Penn faculty who, in light of Penn's post–October 7th crisis, drafted "a summary of a vision for Penn based on a set of common principles," including "intellectual diversity and openness of thought," "civil discourse," and "institutional neutrality." More than 2,500 prominent signers had endorsed the outline as of November 2025.[52]

....

Hundreds of billions of hard-earned U.S. taxpayer dollars go to American higher education institutions every year. *Billions*. Many elite universities depend on federal funding for significant parts of their budget. The Urban Institute reports that during the 2022–23 academic year, Johns Hopkins University alone received more than $4 billion from the federal government, which worked out to 42 percent of its total annual revenue. MIT received $1.7 billion, or 48 percent of its total revenue. Federal dollars accounted for 29 percent of Northwestern's revenue ($726 million) and 22 percent at Columbia ($1.2 billion), Yale ($777 million), and Princeton ($223 million). For many schools, government dollars, in the form of research grants and government contracts, are a significantly bigger slice of revenue than student aid.[53]

And that's just the federal level. Add to it state and local government funding for higher education, which totaled $129 billion in FY2025, according to the National Education Association.[54]

Universities, especially private universities, are not entitled to taxpayer dollars. The long, winding road by which the government and the universities became entangled this way was a matter of historical accident. The relationship can be unwound, if it's no longer beneficial.

The obvious problem is that most universities no longer act as if they have obligations and responsibilities attached to their acceptance of taxpayer dollars. Instead, they treat them as entitlements.

Taxpayers don't see it that way. When I speak with constituents and fellow Americans about the craziness that takes place on our elite university campuses, I am always told, in no uncertain terms: *Defund them!* Why should taxpayer dollars support institutions that breezily break the law, that refuse to uphold their civil rights obligations, that deliver mediocre educations, and that frequently allow—or even enable—vicious anti-Americanism?

The post–October 7th explosion of antisemitism didn't just feature demonstrators shouting "Death to Israel!" At many places, that was paired with a refrain of "Death to America!" Why should patriotic Americans be paying the tuition of elite college students—many of whom are foreign—who express contempt and hatred for America and American citizens? If that's what universities want to teach, then they can foot the bill themselves.

For students, parents, and institutions that want better, though, there are alternatives to the madness that has swamped our most "elite" higher education institutions. Although few and far between, there are some bright spots—schools, new and old, that have not lost their way and that represent the very best of American ideals.

CHAPTER 8

How We Fix It

"Bigotry is the disease of ignorance, of morbid minds; enthusiasm of the free and buoyant; education & free discussion are the antidotes of both."

—Thomas Jefferson to John Adams, August 1, 1816[1]

In nearly every private and public event, whether I am speaking with my constituents or Americans across the country who are deeply worried and awakened to the need for significant higher education reform, I am always asked the obvious question: "So how do we fix it?" I always take a deep breath first and clarify that there is no one easy answer and there is also no immediate quick fix. Instead, I point out, our congressional oversight lit the initial match that will require decades of intensely consistent focus and action to dig us out of the decades of backsliding to get to this point. The pervasive moral and academic rot in our schools did not happen overnight, and it will not be immediately fixed overnight. However, I also add that I am confident that my questions and the university presidents' morally repugnant and tone-deaf answers did more to ignite the education reform movement than multiple previous decades of hard-fought advocacy.

Until now, this book has been mainly a catalogue of horrors. Honestly, I believe strongly that these stories have to be told for history to remember this particular chapter that the mainstream media may try to sweep under the rug in the years to come. This moment in time in higher education is the expression of a deep and systemic rot that is affecting our best and brightest. We have a dire need—and a responsibility—to confront this fact. For far too long, university leaders, administrators, faculty, and donors have turned a blind eye to the moral and academic failures of their institutions. But that's no longer possible. The evidence of this blight is overwhelming. And Americans know it's time to get to work.

And let me be clear, it's not just our American Jewish communities that are at stake in this debate. How we respond to this threat against Jewish students, faculty, and staff matters to every American. It shapes our campus cultures, establishes norms, sets precedents, and determines whether we strive for academic excellence or political indoctrination at our most esteemed colleges. Universities that fail to cut this problem out at the root are already watching it grow into something larger and even uglier in the future. Antisemitism is a sickness, and it can't go untreated.

So, what can we do?

In the previous chapter we attempted a diagnosis. In this chapter, we look at some potential remedies—some long-term, some short-term.

But first, it is important to recognize the exceptions to the rule, the *few* schools that didn't fall into the familiar pattern set by the poisoned Ivies. Which institutions responded to the rise of campus antisemitism correctly? What did they do? How did they buck the trend? No one handled things perfectly. No one got every decision right. But a few leaders and institutions showed that a different route was available to universities than the one that the presidents of Harvard, Columbia, Penn, and so many other schools chose.

Second, we'll look at what role government can play in reforming higher education. Many institutions need a push. There are ways that federal and state governments can nudge colleges and universities onto healthier paths and better hold them accountable when they go astray.

Finally, we'll look at hopeful developments in higher education. Despite the dire situation at most of our elite campuses, there are encouraging innovations happening elsewhere. Some of these developments are at traditional colleges and universities. Some are radical alternatives to the normal college path. Parents and students, especially, should be aware of these developments.

....

Nestled in snowy Hanover, New Hampshire, and known today as the "outdoorsy" Ivy, Dartmouth was one of the original pre–Revolutionary War colonial colleges. Dartmouth was initially founded with the mission of educating Native Americans in Christian ideology; however, it went on to primarily train Congregationalist ministers.

Nearly three hundred years later, Dartmouth proved to be the standout university in the Ivy League in terms of combatting the post–October 7th scourge of antisemitism on campus. Dartmouth administrators were swift to respond to antisemitic activity. Students who attempted to occupy common spaces or intimidate dissenting students were suspended, arrested, and expelled. University leaders also consistently reached out to the campus Jewish community in a way that was not true at any other Ivy League school. Jewish students felt welcomed on campus and supported by its leaders.

Dartmouth's current president, Sian Leah Beilock, writing in *The Atlantic* in September 2024, cogently argued for a depoliticized university where a variety of ideas and opinions can jostle, leading to breakthroughs and discoveries. "But when a group of students takes over a building or establishes an encampment on shared campus grounds and declares that this shared educational space belongs to only one ideological view, the power and potential of the university dies," she wrote.[2]

Dartmouth faculty have also modeled how universities can address sensitive or controversial topics. On October 10, 2023, just three days after Hamas's attacks, Susannah Heschel, chair of Dartmouth's Jewish studies program, and Tarek El-Ariss, chair of Middle Eastern studies, organized "A Discussion on the Horrific Events Unfolding in Israel and Gaza." Including online viewers, nearly two thousand people showed up or tuned in for the event.

It was an exemplary instance of the thoughtful, respectful dialogue that can happen on a university campus. Less than two months later,

Heschel and El-Ariss were being invited by other schools to come speak and to demonstrate how to hold constructive conversations about hot-button issues. The liberal Jewish outlet *Forward* published an article titled: "Dartmouth Got It Right." The House Antisemitism Task Force has used Dartmouth as a model for "best practices in handling discussions on antisemitism and the Middle East."[3]

Some colleges and universities outside the Ivies also responded to October 7th with the moral clarity to prevent a crisis.

At the University of Florida—one of the largest flagship universities in the U.S., with more than sixty thousand students—then President Ben Sasse, a former colleague who previously served in the U.S. Senate, chose a completely different path from the Ivy League presidents. He was a rare university leader who ably navigated this tumultuous chapter. In a letter on October 9, 2023, Sasse addressed Jewish students and alumni directly. He named Hamas's evil directly and condemned "people in elite academia" whose moral relativism had made them incapable of identifying vicious, antisemitic bigotry when it reared its head. Sasse likewise communicated a commitment both to the First Amendment rights of protesters and to vigorous enforcement of violations of UF's Student Honor and Conduct Codes, especially violations that threatened UF's Jewish community. He promised to protect both students' civil rights to a safe campus and students' free speech rights. Speech, he observed, is protected, but violence is not.

The following spring, Sasse made good on his commitment. When antisemitic activists repeatedly flouted university demands to remove an encampment, Sasse had nine demonstrators—seven students, one alumnus, and one outside agitator—arrested and banned from campus.

In July 2024, UF suspended all seven arrested students for up to four years. All have to reapply to UF for admission if they wish to continue studies there. The demonstrators were also charged with resisting arrest without violence, a misdemeanor, except for one student who spit on police officers during his detention. He was charged with felony battery on a police officer.[4] (Most of the students accepted plea agreements.)[5]

In June, the Anti-Defamation League awarded UF a commendation "for its swift action to address campus encampments."[6]

Nothing prevented the presidents of America's elite universities from acting with the same decisiveness. They chose not to.

Sasse also implemented major reforms to reverse the University of Florida system's stagnation. Under his leadership, the school followed Florida law and implemented five-year post-tenure review, which was designed to help ensure that faculty were meeting their teaching and research expectations. Some UF faculty revolted. How dare their leaders hold them accountable![7]

As we've seen, faculty unions often conscript unwilling professors into organizations that are openly hostile to their interests and concerns. As we've seen, Jewish professors across the country are often chained to unions that endorse BDS and characterize Israel as a "genocidal" "settler-colonial" state. Meanwhile, because many faculty unions often hold sway over faculty termination, and many unions are often resolutely anti-Israel, antisemitic faculty are protected from serious consequences.

In 2023, Governor Ron DeSantis and the Florida legislature weakened the grip of unions on university professors by forbidding automatic deduction of union dues from paychecks and requiring greater transparency about union leadership, including salaries. Stronger measures are under consideration. Other states should take note.[8]

Florida's reform-minded approach to higher education is a reminder that schools with major problems are not likely to reform from the inside. They're too broken for that. They need a push. Florida has shown how that can happen at the state level. But it can also happen at the federal level, as we'll explore below.

Another example of outstanding commonsense leadership was Vanderbilt's chancellor, Daniel Diermeier. Appointed in 2020, Diermeier launched his chancellorship by breaking from the herd on matters of academic freedom and free speech. While other university presidents issued statements on everything from abortion to Ukraine, Diermeier reiterated Vanderbilt's commitment to "institutional neutrality," according to which university leaders "refrain from taking public positions on controversial issues unless the issue is materially related to the core mission and functioning of the university."

Vanderbilt officially holds to three "pillars" of free expression: (1) open forums, or "spaces in which issues can be thoroughly explored and discussed without the threat of censorship"; (2) institutional neutrality; and (3) civil discourse, the "practice of engaging in conversation and debate in a constructive manner that demonstrates respect for those on the other side of an issue."[9]

As other campuses descended into chaos, Vanderbilt remained calm and allowed students to express themselves while also protecting students from lawlessness. They held firm to their principles and refused to bow down to student and faculty mobs.[10] When pro-BDS demonstrators broke into an administrative building, the students and participants faced consequences. University leaders spent the next twenty-one hours warning students that their occupation was in violation of Vanderbilt's demonstration policies. The following morning, all twenty-seven demonstrators were handed interim suspensions, pending further investigation. Three were arrested and charged with assault. A student who was protesting outside was charged with vandalism for breaking a window.[11]

"In these difficult times, each university will be tested," Chancellor Diermeier wrote in *The Wall Street Journal*, defending Vanderbilt's approach to the occupation. "And each university will follow its own path. Our approach is clear: We clearly state the principles and rules that support our mission as a university. Then we enforce them."

Chancellor Diermeier wasn't content with securing Vanderbilt's campus. He has offered a blueprint to university presidents across the country to do the same. In fall 2024, Vanderbilt's Board of Trustees, along with the board of Washington University in St. Louis, adopted a shared "Statement of Principles," affirming each university's commitment to pursuing excellence, to protecting academic freedom, and to supporting expanded access for disadvantaged students.[12] In an op-ed to the *Chronicle of Higher Education*, Diermeier and Washington University President Andrew Martin called on other universities to make a similar commitment. "In a polarized era in which every American institution has become a political Rorschach test, the Israel-Gaza conflict, in particular, has divided college campuses and public opinion to a degree unseen since the 1960s," they wrote. "With so much at stake, universities must return to their foundational purpose and recommit to the core principles that sustain them."[13]

But order on campus doesn't always come from presidents, administrators, and faculty. Sometimes the students themselves need to step up to the plate when everyone else fails. That is what the entire country saw happen at the University of North Carolina at Chapel Hill.

In late April 2024, students set up an antisemitic encampment on UNC's Polk Place. Within forty-eight hours, they had broken the rules surrounding campus demonstrations. Police began to clear the encampment, detaining thirty-six protesters who refused to leave, among them ten students. Six protesters, including three students, were arrested and criminally prosecuted.

Later that day, several hundred protesters broke through the barricade cordoning off Polk Place, relaunching protests. They pulled down the American flag and hoisted a Palestinian flag in its place.[14]

Interim Chancellor Lee Roberts took action—personally. Accompanied by police officers, Roberts crossed the campus and returned the American flag to its rightful place. From the steps of UNC's South Building, Roberts said: "That flag represents all of us. To take down that flag, and put up another flag no matter what other flag it is, that's antithetical to who we are, what this university stands for, and what we have done for 229 years," he said. "That flag will stand here as long as I'm chancellor."

Shortly after, protesters removed the flag again. This time, students rose to the occasion. Brothers of the Pi Kappa Phi fraternity raised the American flag again while standing guard around the flagpole. These patriotic frat boys became American legends.

It was a stirring reminder of the patriotism and civic-mindedness to which American universities were long committed. It was also a reminder that most students are not interested in radical ideology and being terrorized by their fanatical peers. They want to get on with their educations. It's a horrible injustice when bad administrators and broken institutions make it impossible for them to do that.

....

Government has an important role to play in cleaning up our higher education mess, too. It was crystal clear throughout our congressional investigation that while given ample opportunity and time after withering public scrutiny, the elite colleges failed to fix themselves. Instead they doubled down, proving that they are institutionally incapable of fixing themselves. So state and federal governments must help hold colleges and universities accountable when they stray from their core purpose and cross legal lines. In fact, it is our responsibility in federal elected office, as stewards of hardworking U.S. taxpayers, to see that universities that receive federal funds abide by the Civil Rights Act of 1964 (Title VI), which requires them to prevent and address hostile environments based on race, color, or national origin, including a hostile environment against religious groups based on shared ancestry or ethnic characteristics. America's elite universities failed to fulfill these legal obligations.

Since returning to office in 2025, President Trump has delivered nothing less than a massive dose of shock therapy to higher education. As I mentioned earlier, throughout his historic presidential campaign he paid close attention to the university presidents' hearings and the subsequent earthquake in higher education. His opponents are quick to level absurd charges: that President Trump is recklessly endangering elite institutions' achievements; that he is simply trying to tear down elite academia out of envy or resentment; that he does not understand all the good that our most prestigious schools do for the country and the world—all of this despite the fact that the president is a graduate of Penn's prestigious Wharton School!

The truth is that President Trump understands clearly how those institutions work—and how they *should* work. What he has done is correctly respond to our hearings and apply the levers of federal power to diseased institutions in order to give them a dose of medicine they've otherwise refused to take. President Trump isn't wrecking the Ivy League; the Ivy League wrecked itself. And since the Ivy League has refused to fix itself, it needs to be fixed for them.

On December 11, 2019, halfway through his first term, with our support, President Trump made a bold stroke against antisemitism as he saw it creeping into major institutions of American life. Executive Order 13899, "Combating Anti-Semitism," directed federal agencies to employ the International Holocaust Remembrance Alliance's (IHRA) working definition of antisemitism when enforcing civil rights laws. The order made clear that Jewish people are protected under Title VI of the Civil Rights Act of 1964, which prohibits discrimination on the basis of race, color, or national origin.

In January 2025, just days after his second inauguration, President Trump expanded his original 2019 order, in Executive Order 14188, "Additional Measures to Combat Anti-Semitism." In the order, President Trump stated the facts clearly:

> *[The October 7th attacks] unleashed an unprecedented wave of vile anti-Semitic discrimination, vandalism, and violence against our citizens, especially in our schools and on our campuses. Jewish students have faced an unrelenting barrage of discrimination; denial of access to campus common areas and facilities, including libraries and classrooms; and intimidation, harassment, and physical threats and assault.*

The new order directed federal agencies to make use of "all available and appropriate legal tools, to prosecute, remove, or otherwise hold to account the perpetrators of unlawful anti-Semitic harassment and violence." The order also specifically called for federal agencies to look into what authority they might have to further combat antisemitism on campus.

In short, no longer would the federal government turn a blind eye to antisemitic discrimination at our colleges and universities.

The result of President Trump's January order has been a full-bore executive effort to bring institutional antisemitism to heel, using the legal authority of a variety of federal agencies. Elite colleges and universities have been put on notice: their abuses—their discrimination, harassment, and neglect—will not be tolerated any longer. The federal government has the ability, and the responsibility, to intervene when federal contractors are violating the terms of their contract. And that is exactly what is happening in the case of elite schools. These schools took millions upon millions of dollars in taxpayer money, and in exchange they promised that they would abide by the law. They have broken their promise, and the bill is finally coming due.

None of this would have happened without my questions at our congressional hearing drawing the American people's riveted attention to the crisis in higher education.

Almost every university in the United States takes federal money to support its work. That money is not unconditional, though, nor should it be. In order to receive federal dollars, an institution has to be in compliance with federal law—including federal civil rights laws.

Under the Biden administration, this requirement went unenforced. Universities, especially elite universities, discriminated against Jewish students and faculty again and again—and nothing happened. The Biden administration ignored Jewish students and faculty, even as they were being assaulted on American campuses, and continued shoveling taxpayer dollars into the coffers of schools already worth billions of dollars. In fact, the Biden administration went so far as not to open up a single Department of Education investigation into any college regarding antisemitism, using ongoing litigation as the lame excuse for cowardly leadership.

With Congress's encouragement, the Trump administration has put a stop to that. In 2025, the Trump administration threatened to withhold and freeze billions in funding, including research funding, from universities, unless they could demonstrate compliance with federal civil rights laws.

In its March 2025 announcement canceling grants and contracts to Columbia, the Joint Task Force to Combat Anti-Semitism was crystal clear about its reasons. "Since October 7, Jewish students have faced relentless violence, intimidation, and anti-Semitic harassment on their campuses—only to be ignored by those who are supposed to protect them," said Secretary of Education Linda McMahon. "Universities must comply with all federal antidiscrimination laws if they are going to receive federal funding. For too long, Columbia has abandoned that obligation to Jewish students studying on its campus. Today, we demonstrate to Columbia and other universities that we will not tolerate their appalling inaction any longer." She cited our hearing.[15]

Other universities quickly followed. The numbers are staggering, and a reminder of just how much these universities depend on federal funding—your hard-earned taxpayer dollars—to function. Columbia saw $400 million vanish overnight. UCLA: $584 million. Northwestern: $790 million. Cornell: $1 billion. Harvard: $2.6 billion.

Unsurprisingly, university leaders went into full-blown panic mode. Those numbers took massive bites out of their budgets. That was the point. They were finally experiencing consequences for their gross mismanagement.

In an April 2025 letter to Harvard outlining terms of a potential settlement, Secretary Linda McMahon wrote: "The United States has invested in Harvard University's operations because of the value to the country of scholarly discovery and academic excellence. But an investment is not an entitlement. It depends on Harvard upholding federal civil rights laws, and it only makes sense if Harvard fosters the kind of environment that produces intellectual creativity and scholarly rigor, both of which are antithetical to ideological capture. Harvard has in recent years failed to live up to both the intellectual and civil rights conditions that justify federal investment. But we appreciate your expression of commitment to repairing those failures and welcome your collaboration in restoring the University to its promise."[16] The letter goes on to outline key reforms such as governance and leadership, merit-based hiring, merit-based admissions, international admissions, viewpoint diversity in admission and hiring, reforming programs with egregious records of antisemitism or other bias, discontinuation of DEI, student discipline, whistleblower protections, and transparency and monitoring. Each of these requirements is incredibly straightforward and strongly supported by the American people. Harvard's response was to viciously attack the Trump administration and double down on its downward spiral away from academic excellence and rigor.

Since then, several universities have reached landmark agreements or settlements with the Trump administration to restore funding. Columbia was the first to strike a deal after threatening to walk away. Brown University also struck a deal, agreeing to pay $50 million in return for $510 million in unfrozen funding. Other negotiations are still ongoing.[17]

But there is no question that more needs to be done. These agreements will need to be watched carefully for compliance. We know that schools will try to weasel their way out of their commitments. For example, in the last chapter, we saw that many schools have not eliminated their DEI programs, despite new federal regulations, but simply continued them under new names. Aggressive monitoring will be crucial to enforcing these agreements.

In early October 2025, the Trump administration unveiled the "Compact for Academic Excellence in Higher Education." The "Compact," sent to nine handpicked universities, sets out eight core commitments. Universities will: (1) establish equality in admissions; (2) foster a vibrant marketplace of ideas; (3) return to merit-based hiring; (4) maintain institutional neutrality; (5) end grade inflation; (6) treat students equally; (7) control costs; and (8) reduce foreign influence by capping foreign-student admissions at 15 percent and fully disclosing foreign funding. The administration has suggested that institutions that adopt the compact will have privileged access to federal dollars.

On the other hand, universities "are free to develop models and values other than" these—provided they are willing to go without federal benefits. If a university wants to hold on to its DEI programs, for example, it can do that. But it cannot also receive federal monies. That's the deal, and it's their choice.[18]

Apollo Global Management Chief Marc Rowan, who played a key role in the ouster of Penn President Liz Magill, as described earlier in the book, helped formulate the compact. In *The New York Times*, he defended its central purpose: "How do colleges and universities demonstrate that they are making decisions and carrying out policies that serve the public good by promoting excellence in their teaching and research? By agreeing to a few common-sense policies laid out in the compact."[19]

Despite the hostile reaction from university leaders—seven of the nine schools to which the Trump administration sent the compact proposal had rejected it as of mid-October 2025—there has been a positive reaction from surprising quarters. Harvard Professor Danielle Allen, a vocal critic of the Trump administration, wrote that "the compact introduces a chance to establish a much-needed fresh relationship between America and higher education." She disagreed with certain aspects of the compact as written, but she nonetheless hoped that university presidents might see it as "an opening to forge a national coalition of higher education institutions to secure a good, mission-aligned agreement with the federal government."[20]

That's an encouraging sign. As Boston University Professor E. Thomas Finan, writing in *The Atlantic* in September 2025, noted, "Since its inception, American higher education has been bound by political compacts," but today colleges and universities desperately need "to rebuild trust among not just prospective students, parents, and donors, but also voters and elected officials across party lines." America's institutions of higher learning do not exist outside our national social compact; they are part of our democracy, so they have democratic responsibilities. The Trump administration's compact is an important attempt to reset the relationship between higher education and the American public.

The federal government also has critical national security responsibilities in higher education. We saw in the previous chapter that foreign students make up a significant, in some cases shocking, percentage of elite university student bodies. Are those students upholding the obligations required of them to keep their visas in good standing? The federal government has a duty to investigate.

In August 2025, with my strong support and advocacy in Congress, Secretary of State Marco Rubio announced that the Department of State had revoked more than six thousand student visas. About two-thirds were because of violations of U.S. law, mainly assault, burglary, and driving under the influence (DUI). Some students overstayed their visas. And hundreds of others were deemed to have offered "support for terrorism" or have committed acts of "terrorism" as defined by the U.S. Immigration and Nationality Act.

The State Department also recently announced that it would require international students applying for visas to make available their social media. "Any indications of hostility toward the citizens, culture, government, institutions, or founding principles of the United States" could be grounds for denying a visa.[21]

And rightly so. Why should we be inviting onto our campuses students who have expressed hostility toward, or contempt for, America? A student visa is a privilege, not a right.

Finally, Congress must take action, too. The Article I branch has a significant role to play in making sure that colleges and universities are holding to their legal obligations. We have the power of the purse, and the only way to truly get these universities to respond is through the withholding of billions of dollars of U.S. taxpayer funds. Congress also can use the power of the purse to remind schools of their civic responsibilities. The One Big Beautiful Bill Act, which became law in 2025, imposed a new tiered federal tax on private university endowments, reaching 8 percent for the wealthiest schools, such as Harvard. For far too long universities have enjoyed a privileged tax status, all the while growing rich off inflated tuition and fees and collecting taxpayer dollars in the form of research grants and contracts. Some of that money should be moving in the other direction.

We must have stronger accountability and oversight measures. For example, in 2025, I helped pass the Defending Education Transparency and Ending Rogue Regimes Engaging in Nefarious Transactions, or DETERRENT Act, through the House. The bill closes loopholes and significantly toughens disclosure requirements related to foreign donations and partnerships with foreign countries, especially with China, Russia, and other geopolitical adversaries. I would go a step further and consider completely barring foreign dollars from funding U.S. higher education institutions at all.

We need to further scrutinize these schools' tax-exempt status. I'm one of the top leaders pushing the Universal Accountability Act, which would impose meaningful financial penalties against schools that are found to have violated their Title VI civil rights obligations. After three violations, the IRS could revoke their tax-exempt status. Schools should not be able to simply shrug off gross violations of students' rights.

Congress must pass the Stop Higher Education Espionage and Theft Act to enable the FBI, the Department of State, the Department of Homeland Security, and the Department of Defense to act aggressively against foreign agents working against American higher education institutions.

My Fairness in Higher Education Accreditation Act aims to rein in out-of-control higher education accreditation agencies. Accreditation agencies exist to make sure that colleges and universities are meeting basic standards. They're not supposed to be shielding them from accountability.

Congress should also modernize the Clery Act, which dictates how campus crimes are reported. Schools currently tend to significantly underreport antisemitic acts by lumping them in with more generic crimes, such as assault. Specifying reporting requirements for antisemitic crimes would enable greater transparency.

Fundamentally, the United States must prioritize American students first. Our colleges should strive to be American institutions and not obsess about being global institutions that put American students, values, and scholars last. We should cap foreign students at no more than 15 percent. Visas should be heavily scrutinized and, if necessary, revoked. So many of the pro-Hamas ring leaders were non-Americans who created a dangerous environment for American students. Foreign dollars from our nation's adversaries flowing into our universities by the billions must be halted. Full stop. Many university presidents cited foreign influence and funding as one of the sparks that led to the highly organized pro-Hamas encampments. This will also mean placing antisemitic Middle Eastern studies departments who have become hotbeds of anti-Americanism and terror into genuine receiverships, a legal process where a neutral third party is appointed to take control of the assets, finances, and organization.

We must completely dismantle DEI, which is by definition antisemitic and racist. Instead, schools must double their efforts to achieve true viewpoint diversity. A return to merit-based hiring and admissions, including mandatory standardized testing, will refocus higher education institutions on academic excellence and rigor rather than political correctness.

The tenured faculty system must be reformed and revamped. What was initially founded on the commitment to freedom of speech and protection of free inquiry to foster creative, challenging thought has turned into intellectually lazy and radically left-wing groupthink laced with a pervasive cancel culture invoked if one so much as questions the accepted Far Left liberal orthodoxy. Moreover, when students, faculty, or administrators break university rules or policies such as the time, place, and manner of protests, there needs to be a consistent disciplinary process with across-the-board accountability.

As I said, not an easy or short-term fix, but a worthy, long-term, and important one that must be multifaceted and aggressive to save American higher education from itself.

....

Ultimately, higher education will change only if American citizens continue to pressure it to do so. The government can and should look at whatever is in their constitutional authority to encourage change.

But Americans can also turn to what we know best: innovation, creativity, and using our free choice to send a message.

Take a look at the welcoming environment being cultivated at universities beyond the traditional elites. Recent trends have seen students of all sorts looking southward, but in August 2025 *The Atlantic* reported that Jewish students, in particular, are moving toward friendlier (and sunnier) institutions:

> *Jewish-student interest in Emory, as well as in Vanderbilt, has more than doubled since October 7, 2023. . . . Vanderbilt's Hillel had to hire new staff to host all the prospective students who wanted tours; the university's undergraduate Jewish population has grown by 20 percent in the past two years. The University of Florida's Hillel chapter experienced a 50 percent increase in student participation from 2021 to 2025. Clemson University . . . saw its Hillel grow fourfold over the same period. Southern Methodist University, near Dallas, now appears to have more Jewish students than Harvard, Hillel data show.*

The growth of American Jewish populations at these schools is not only a reflection of the "atmosphere of fear" that Jewish students and parents are subject to on elite northeastern campuses. It's also the result of being welcomed and wanted at other institutions. As we saw above, Washington University and Vanderbilt handled their antisemitic protests decisively and have made efforts to attract students away from Ivy League enclaves. "We want to create a place where there's thriving Jewish life, just like we do for all the other students," Vanderbilt Chancellor Daniel

Diermeier told *The Atlantic*. "But again, it's particularly salient right now because of the contrast with other universities."[22] While elite universities are wringing their hands about ties to Israel, in March 2025 Clemson established a partnership with two Israeli universities to help revitalize agricultural communities devastated by Hamas.[23] These universities are making it clear that Jewish students are welcome on their campuses and will have their rights protected.

A new red state movement in civic education also offers hope. At state flagship universities, as well as other public institutions, centers and institutes devoted to civic education, civil dialogue, and liberal education have sprung up.

The School of Civic and Economic Thought and Leadership at Arizona State University, founded in 2017, led the way. But it has since been joined by the Hamilton School (formerly the Hamilton Center for Classical and Civic Education) at the University of Florida and the Institute of American Civics at the University of Tennessee (Knoxville), founded in 2022; the School of Civic Leadership at the University of Texas, the School of Civic Life and Leadership at the University of North Carolina at Chapel Hill, and the Institute of American Constitutional Thought and Leadership at the University of Toledo, founded in 2023; the Center for Civics, Culture and Society at the University of Ohio (Miami), founded in 2025; and more still to come.

These schools, centers, and institutes offer opportunities for students to escape the suffocating left-wing atmosphere of most university departments. The centers have provided new hiring avenues for academics who are doing work that breaks from left-wing groupthink, so students can find dynamic scholars committed to open inquiry, free expression, and an education in the Western tradition. They will also be able to pursue studies not ruled by left-wing dogma—for example, the philosophy, politics, economics and law, and great books and ideas diplomas available at the Hamilton School.

Many new institutes reflect the influence of two major initiatives in elite higher education: the one at the Hoover Institution at Stanford and the James Madison Program in American Ideals and Institutions at Princeton.

Hoover was founded in 1919 by Herbert Hoover—a Stanford alumnus and not yet president—as an archival library, but within a few decades it had morphed into a major research institution and center for conservative thought. The list of luminaries who have called Stanford home is long and illustrious: economists such as Nobel laureate Friedrich Hayek and Thomas Sowell; historians such as Robert Conquest, the great anti-communist, and Niall Ferguson; and political leaders such as British Prime Minister Margaret Thatcher and former U.S. Secretary of State Condoleezza Rice, who is also Hoover's current director. She is as well a friend and a wise advisor on higher education issues.[24]

The James Madison Program is a more recent innovation. Founded in 2000 by Princeton political scientist Robert P. George, the Madison Program has been an oasis for liberal education and conservative politics at Princeton. The program hosts visiting fellows and postdoctoral fellows, who are invited to spend a sabbatical year at Princeton to advance their research. But it also sponsors events and supports undergraduates. In recent years, the Madison Program has been able to claim more than two hundred undergraduates involved in its programming.[25]

Professor George, one of Princeton's most recognizable presences, has also been one of American academia's most vigorous advocates for academic freedom and free speech, and an exemplar of its best traditions of open dialogue. He is well known for co-teaching courses with left-wing thinker and activist Cornel West. George and West have toured campuses together, modeling robust intellectual engagement and civil dialogue. In early 2025 they co-published *Truth Matters: A Dialogue on Fruitful Disagreement in an Age of Division*. Generations of students have been influenced by Professor George.

And many of them have been instrumental in the foundation of the new public university centers. It's an important lesson in how influence spreads, and a reminder that renewing the American university is a generational project.

These centers are examples of the institutional building that will be necessary to begin to restore and renew higher education. Other new projects offer even more radical innovations.

The University of Austin, in Texas, which was announced in 2021 and admitted its first class in the fall of 2024, was founded to be an alternative to the sclerotic institutions of elite higher education. UATX "is dedicated to the preservation and transmission of humanity's rich intellectual, scientific, artistic, and cultural inheritance . . . [and to] the discovery, creation, and communication of new knowledge." In order to achieve these ends, it is committed to "intellectual freedom and pluralism" and "the lively clash of ideas and opinions."[26]

UATX's three-day "Forbidden Courses" program, for high school seniors and college freshmen, is designed to facilitate conversation and dialogue about controversial questions that are often sidelined at traditional universities, because they fall afoul of the lines drawn by left-wing ideology and DEI.[27]

Supporting UATX are dozens of powerhouse intellectuals. On UATX's Board of Trustees are major public voices such as historian Niall Ferguson and fearless *The Free Press* founder Bari Weiss. On its Board of Advisors are transformative figures such as activist Ayaan Hirsi Ali. Psychologist and author Jordan Peterson has been known to drop by to visit with students.

UATX is new, vibrant, and its future is astonishingly bright. It aims to offer a boldly alternative vision of the future of higher education, completely different from what's on offer from the conventional elite colleges and universities. When it succeeds, it will no doubt help loosen their death grip on American higher education.

Beyond academia, programs such as the Thiel Fellowship, founded by entrepreneur Peter Thiel in 2011, pays students not to attend college. Thiel Fellow recipients receive $200,000 to "build new things instead of sitting in a classroom." For students with big ideas who are not interested in pursuing the typical political brainwashing through a four-year undergraduate degree, the Thiel Fellowship offers an opportunity to skip or drop out of college with support to become an entrepreneur or innovator.

The Thiel Fellowship now boasts more than three hundred alumni, who have together "founded companies or projects collectively worth hundreds of billions of dollars."[28] Fellows are responsible for, among many other things, new cryptocurrencies, defense tech and AI companies, and biomedical breakthroughs. As a member of Congress, I have met with many former and current Thiel Fellows who have built or are building incredible companies that are unapologetically asserting American dynamism on the world stage.

Not every college dropout will go on to launch a billion-dollar company. But the Thiel Fellowship has laid a foundation that other donors and institutions could follow. The traditional four-year undergraduate degree is more and more a dubious prospect. There are lots of students, including elite students, who are sitting in mandatory 101 courses, listening to stale lectures, who could be out there creating and building and inventing. Employers already know this. When grade inflation is rampant and GPAs and degrees are no longer useful signals to employers, they will start to look for other indications of who is worth hiring. Silicon Valley is already implementing alternative vetting processes, circumventing the conventional routes. Innovators should embrace this trend. There should be many more conduits for getting bright, ambitious students who don't want to pursue the traditional four-year degree into the workforce, where they can apply their knowledge and skills and enthusiasm.

Another growing sector in the higher education apparatus that is booming rather than combusting is workforce development, technical, and vocational programs. Rather than elite colleges saddling their graduates under the yoke of unaffordable student loan debt, these targeted workforce education programs are growing exponentially in popularity. Often known as the "trades," these alternative educational routes lead to successful and lucrative careers that are sorely needed in the American economy.

In my congressional district, my office has worked to deliver expanded access to welding, plumbing, culinary arts, and HVAC educational programs, as well as expanded shop classes that have waitlists at local public schools. College should never be one-size-fits-all for American students.

....

The explosion of antisemitism on campus in the wake of October 7th was not a coincidence. It was the result of years of rot deep within our most prestigious institutions of higher learning. Our elite universities chose ideological fanaticism over intellectual diversity. They chose groupthink over independence. They chose spineless moral bankruptcy instead of strong, principled leadership.

But we can choose differently. Other institutions are doing exactly that, right this minute: making different choices, charting a different future. Our country is far too dynamic, interesting, intellectually curious, and hopeful to limit ourselves to brainless indoctrination and moral stupidity. Americans are the world's innovators and entrepreneurs, its founders and creators. We're also proud believers in the equal dignity of all people. Once upon a time, our elite institutions embodied the best of America.

They can again. Elite academia and higher education writ large is in the midst of a generational upheaval. That's the time to begin to build anew. We have the incredible opportunity to reform and refashion our elite colleges and universities into institutions that can once again educate and elevate American leaders who will serve and promote the good of all citizens, not just a small elite. We can renew the compact between our elite institutions and the American people. And we must.

EPILOGUE

When I first ran for Congress over a decade ago, it would have been difficult to imagine the significant challenges facing our great country today. I started my first campaign at twenty-eight years old, turned twenty-nine before officially launching my candidacy, and turned thirty after my first primary win. I went on to flip a district from Democrat to Republican, consistently earning the highest number of votes in history for my district. I didn't know it when I started this journey, but I would make history as the youngest woman ever elected to Congress in U.S. history at the time. And I would go on to be elected by my peers to serve in top congressional leadership as the highest-ranking New York Republican in Congress in over one hundred years, the highest-ranking woman in the House, and the youngest woman from either party to achieve that standing. I ran for Congress on a platform of bringing fresh energy, new ideas, and a new generation of leadership to Washington on behalf of my constituents in Upstate New York. I am deeply humbled by the overwhelming support of voters across party lines who gave me the opportunity to work my hardest for them.

While I am extremely proud of the significant legislative and constituent services results that I delivered directly to the hardworking families and communities in my district, I believe that among the work of greatest long-term impact during my time in Congress will be this hearing heard around the world. It cut through the firestorm of day-to-day political chaos and shined a light on moral depravity when Americans were yearning for a strong moral compass and a beacon of hope amid darkness.

I will never forget one moment in particular. On the Saturday evening after the hearing, my husband and I had just put our precious, happy, healthy then-two-year-old son, Sam, to bed, when I received a text from a dear friend I hadn't heard from in a long time.

This was a friend whom I worked with in my early professional years at the White House, right out of college. I introduced her to her now husband at a get-together I hosted in Washington, D.C., when we were in our early twenties. Her husband is a close college friend. They are Jewish and have four beautiful children. Because of how busy life can get amid kids and work, we hadn't seen each other in a few years.

She texted me: "Over the past 7 weeks, like a lot of Jews, I've started to mentally note 'who would hide me.' It's an insane and maybe hysterical exercise, maybe not. But you, Elise, would do more than hide us. You are fighting for us, and what is True and what is Right."

Her words caught me short. I turned to my husband and started to cry. How was it possible that in modern-day America, my joyful, funny, creative, artistic, kind friend and her husband, whom I have so many wonderful memories from college with, were being forced to consider these horrifying possibilities? I knew my questions at the hearing had resonated, but I had not truly understood, until that moment, just what they might mean to so many.

I will keep fighting, shoulder to shoulder with many others. Truth and light will win. It does not depend on the context.

ACKNOWLEDGMENTS

I am incredibly grateful for the opportunity to share my insights and experiences related to a profoundly important issue impacting Americans and the world. My hope is that this book will be a deep dive, detailed historical account of a snapshot in time at a critical turning point in American higher education, public policy, and culture. I also hope that this book continues the long-overdue earthquake in higher education and the demands for a return to American academia's founding ideals and principles of academic excellence, critical thinking, and intellectual rigor guided by a strong moral compass.

During this particular chapter of my service in Congress, my office on Capitol Hill became the de facto repository of tens of thousands of documents, firsthand student accounts, and powerful personal impact statements, and the policy clearinghouse for combatting antisemitism in higher education and broader higher education reform. Many letters my office received would make fellow Americans weep with despair, but we also received inspiring correspondence and outreach that were incredibly hopeful and determined, particularly from extraordinarily brave students. I tried to weave some of these amazing young leaders into this book.

Thank you to my friend and book agent Keith Urbahn from Javelin. Keith, it has been a long road over the past two decades since we became friends the year after we graduated college and started our young professional lives in Washington. What an incredible journey for both of us. I will never forget you telling me after I was first elected that I had a book in me—and then ten years later, emailing me saying that the time had come for my first book. I appreciate the entire Javelin team for shepherding this first-time author and busy mom congresswoman through the book publishing process. I already have ideas for the next one!

Thank you to Simon & Schuster for your immediate interest—and then your continued commitment to this book over the span of a few years. Thank you to Natasha Simons for your initial interest in this project, and Jen Long for your continued support over three years. To Paul Choix, it has been a real highlight working with you as my editor. You answered all my novice author questions and had a deft and extremely helpful touch that vastly improved the book. Your comments were spot-on and insightful. I greatly enjoyed our phone conversations, especially during crunch time to get the manuscript done. I will always treasure the frantic emails about the cover that we both love.

The stars of this book are the brave students who shared their stories under extremely harrowing circumstances. I got to know so many courageous young American leaders throughout the course of our congressional investigation, and they inspire me every day. Many have become friends and professional colleagues as we work together to save higher education.

Over the last decade in Congress, I have been surrounded by an extremely dedicated and hardworking staff in my district and in Washington. My legislative team handling my education and national security portfolio were absolute superstars in compiling tomes of research material and brainstorming questions. Thank you to Marek Laco, Zach Deatherage, Jake Vreeburg, Jim Robertson, and Sarah Salas for ensuring our office consistently leads on this issue. To the chief investigator on the Education Committee, Ari Wisch, you are the best of the best and can distill 100,000-plus documents better than anyone I've ever worked with. You are a true friend, and I look forward to working together again someday. To Anderson Briggs, thank you for being a stellar teammate always keeping our operations afloat.

I have the best-in-the-business comms shop on Capitol Hill, led ably by Ali Black (thank you for coming back!) with an incredible team including Bernadette Breslin and over the years Karoline Leavitt, Francis Brennan, Anna Pusey, and Charyssa Parent. My entire leadership and personal office staff consistently hit home runs.

My longtime district staff are simply world class at delivering A+ constituent services to the hardworking families I represent. Thank you for your daily service to the people in our communities. Each of you always embodies my laser focus on delivering real results.

To my longtime friends and allies on this issue outside the office: Betsy, Chris, Tevi, Matt, Michael, Miriam, Mort, Mark, Noah, Cliff, Laurel, David, Mike, Dana, Trudy, Lini, Stanley, Adam, Arie, Eliana, Dan, Annie, Megan, Irit, Gena, Paul, Terrie, Ronald, Howard, Allison, Hailey, and Stephen. The late-night phone calls before and after hearings, real-time feedback, and tremendous advice throughout made this meaningful work possible.

I have been blessed by many professional mentors whom I've worked for and with, starting with Karl Zinsmeister and Joel Kaplan—I couldn't have started my career with two better examples of how to think, work, and lead with rigor, compassion, and intellectual curiosity. During my time in Congress, I am grateful for the speakers of the House who lifted up members to help them shine to the best of their abilities and make a difference in our country—thank you to John Boehner, Paul Ryan, and Kevin McCarthy for encouraging me to strive to be the best member that I could be for my constituents and the country.

Jim Jordan, Trey Gowdy, Patrick McHenry, Steve Scalise, Tom Emmer, Virginia Foxx, Cathy McMorris Rodgers, Susan Brooks, Tom Cole, Mac Thornberry, Peter Roskam, Jamie Comer, Bruce Westerman, Jason Smith, Ann Wagner, the EPAC women, too many members to name, and of course my favorites in the rowdy New York Republican Delegation both past and present, especially my fellow Upstaters John Katko and Nick Langworthy, it is a joy to serve and work with you.

Thank you to President Trump and Secretary of Education Linda McMahon for caring so deeply about this issue and for taking decisive action on Day One.

Everyone on Capitol Hill and in Republican politics knows that there are two mainstays on Team Elise who have been with me on this journey: my longtime trusted Chief of Staff Patrick Hester and my senior political advisor Alex DeGrasse. They have both been on this decade-long journey over hundreds of thousands of miles traveled, on many rocket ships, and experienced the highs and lows, and there are more to come. Words cannot express how you both have been steady professional rocks in an extremely tumultuous, complex, and personally and professionally challenging environment over the past decade. Just think, this is only the first book. Buckle up!

Thank you to the hardworking families of New York's 21st District for your overwhelming support for over a decade and giving me the opportunity of a lifetime to work my hardest to serve you and give a voice to our district at the highest levels of government. I have been so honored and humbled to work and fight for you.

I would not have been able to write a book or serve in Congress without my many exceptional teachers growing up. I am profoundly appreciative of your encouragement and guidance throughout my childhood. It is because of my experiences in your classrooms that I am so dedicated to ensuring Americans have the best educational opportunities in the world.

By far, my greatest blessing in life is my family. Being born to my parents is the greatest gift and most impactful lodestar of my life. They are truly my guardian angels, and I would not have had any of these opportunities were it not for their hard work and unconditional love and support. My brother Matty has been an extraordinary source of strength and encouragement from childhood to adulthood. I am so proud to be your sister.

To my husband Matt for his endless encouragement, patience, deep partnership, and love. We also discovered your tremendous talent as the world's greatest and most detailed proofreader and editor. It is Matt who always provides profoundly wise and heartfelt counsel.

And above all, there is no question that our North Star in life is our infinite love for our most treasured gift, our beautiful son Samuel.

Sam, you are and will always be our light. We love you more than anything. This book is for you.

APPENDIX

House Committee on Education and the Workforce Hearing
"Holding Campus Leaders Accountable and Confronting Antisemitism"
Witness List:
Claudine Gay, President of Harvard
Liz Magill, President of University of Pennsylvania
Sally Kornbluth, President of Massachusetts Institute of Technology
December 5, 2023
Washington, D.C.

Congresswoman Stefanik: Dr. Gay, a Harvard student calling for the mass murder of African Americans is not protected free speech at Harvard, correct?

President Gay: Our commitment to free speech—

Congresswoman Stefanik: It's a yes or no question. Is that correct? Is that okay for students to call for the mass murder of African Americans at Harvard? Is this protected free speech?

President Gay: Our commitment to free speech—

Congresswoman Stefanik: It's a yes or no question. Let me ask you this: you are president of Harvard so I assume you are familiar with the term "intifada," correct?

President Gay: I have heard that term, yes.

Congresswoman Stefanik: And you understand that the use of the term "intifada" in the context of the Israeli-Arab conflict is indeed a call for violent armed resistance against the State of Israel, including violence against civilians and the genocide of Jews. Are you aware of that?

President Gay: That type of hateful speech is personally abhorrent to me.

Congresswoman Stefanik: And there have been multiple marches at Harvard with students chanting "There is only one solution. Intifada revolution" and "Globalize the Intifada," is that correct?

President Gay: I've heard that thoughtless, reckless, and hateful language on our campus, yes.

Congresswoman Stefanik: So based upon your testimony, you understand that this call for intifada is to commit genocide against the Jewish people in Israel and globally, correct?

President Gay: I will say again, that type of hateful speech is personally abhorrent to me.

Congresswoman Stefanik: Do you believe that type of hateful speech is contrary to Harvard's Code of Conduct or is it allowed at Harvard?

President Gay: It is at odds with the values of Harvard.

Congresswoman Stefanik: Can you not say here that it is against the Code of Conduct at Harvard?

President Gay: We embrace a commitment to free expression even of views that are objectionable, offensive, hateful—it's when that speech crosses into conduct that violates our policies against bullying, harassment, intimidation . . .

Congresswoman Stefanik: Does that speech not cross that barrier? Does that speech not call for the genocide of Jews and the elimination of Israel? You testified that you understand that that is the definition of "intifada." Is that speech according to the Code of Conduct or not?

President Gay: We embrace a commitment to free expression and give a wide berth to free expression even of views that are objectionable, outrageous and offensive.

Congresswoman Stefanik: You and I both know that that is not the case. You are aware that Harvard ranked dead last when it came to free speech, are you not aware of that report?

President Gay: As I've observed earlier, I reject that characterization of our campus.

Congresswoman Stefanik: The data shows it's true. And isn't it true that Harvard previously rescinded multiple offers of admissions for applicants and accepted freshmen for sharing offensive memes, racist statements, sometimes as young as 16-years-old? Did Harvard not rescind those offers of admission?

President Gay: That long predates my time as president so I can't speak—

Congresswoman Stefanik: But you understand that Harvard made that decision to rescind those offers of admission.

President Gay: I have no reason to contradict the facts as you present them to me.

Congresswoman Stefanik: Correct, because it's a fact. You're also aware that a Winthrop House faculty dean was let go over who he chose to legally represent. Correct? That was while you were dean.

President Gay: That is an incorrect characterization of what transpired.

Congresswoman Stefanik: What's the characterization?

President Gay: I'm not going to get into details about a personnel matter.

Congresswoman Stefanik: Well let me ask you this: Will admission offers be rescinded or any disciplinary action be taken against students or applicants who say, "from the river to the sea" or "intifada," advocating for the murder of Jews?

President Gay: As I've said, that type of hateful, reckless, offensive speech is personally abhorrent to me.

Congresswoman Stefanik: No action will be taken? What action will be taken?

President Gay: When speech crosses into conduct that violates our policies, including policies against bullying, harassment and intimidation, we take action. We have robust disciplinary processes that allow us to hold individuals accountable.

Congresswoman Stefanik: What action has been taken against students who are harassing and calling for the genocide of Jews on Harvard's campus?

President Gay: I can assure you, we have robust disciplinary actions.

Congresswoman Stefanik: What actions have been taken? I'm not asking . . . I'm asking what actions have been taken against those students.

President Gay: Given students' rights to privacy and our obligations under FERPA, I will not say more about any specific cases other than to reiterate that processes are ongoing.

Congresswoman Stefanik: Do you know what the number one hate crime in America is?

President Gay: I know that over the last couple of months there has been an alarming rise of antisemitism which I understand is the critical topic that we are here to discuss.

Congresswoman Stefanik: That's correct. It is anti-Jewish hate crimes. And Harvard ranks the lowest when it comes to protecting Jewish students. This is why I have called for your resignation and your testimony today and not being able to answer with moral clarity speaks volumes.

....

Congresswoman Stefanik: Harvard receives funding from foreign entities and governments which support its Middle East Studies Department. Correct?

President Gay: We receive funding from a variety of sources because we have alumni from all over the world.

Congresswoman Stefanik: But that is correct, right? The Middle Eastern Studies Department.

President Gay: We receive funding from various sources.

Congresswoman Stefanik: It's a yes or no. Are you not aware where the Middle Eastern Studies Department receives funding?

President Gay: We receive funding from various sources.

Congresswoman Stefanik: I am asking you a yes or no question. You are under oath in front of the United States Congress. You are giving lip service provided by your attorneys. It's a yes or no question. Harvard receives funding from foreign entities and governments which support its Middle Eastern Studies Department. Correct?

President Gay: We have alumni all over the world, and we benefit from their philanthropy.

Congresswoman Stefanik: So the answer's correct, yes, yes, the answer is correct?

President Gay: We receive support from alumni all over the world, from individuals.

Congresswoman Stefanik: And what amount of support is that reported to the federal government?

President Gay: I'd have to actually look at our filings.

Congresswoman Stefanik: You don't know? As the President of the University, you don't know?

President Gay: Not that particular number.

Congresswoman Stefanik: It's 1.5 billion dollars over the past three years. Are you aware of that?

President Gay: I don't know if that is the correct number, but that's the number you've shared.

....

Congresswoman Stefanik: Thank you, Dr. Gay. According to the Hillel college guide, the Crimson freshman survey and even Harvard's own *Education Next* journal, the population of Jewish undergrads at Harvard has plummeted from roughly 25% in the 1980s to between five and 10%. Now, why is that?

President Gay: That is not data that we collect as part of the admissions process. So I can't speak to those numbers or to the trajectory.

Congresswoman Stefanik: So what is the percentage of students who are Jewish at Harvard in undergraduate now?

President Gay: We do not collect religious affiliation as part of the admissions process.

Congresswoman Stefanik: Do you not rely on data collected by Harvard Hillel, which you visited for the first time after October 7? I'll just be honest with you. When I was a freshman, I enjoyed going to Harvard Hillel and had the opportunity to celebrate Shabbat dinners with my fellow undergrads. The fact that it took you until after October 7 to go to Harvard Hillel is unacceptable. Yield back.

....

Congresswoman Stefanik: Dr. Gay, did anyone contact you about flying the Israeli flag over Harvard Yard?

President Gay: Yes.

Congresswoman Stefanik: And the decision was made not to allow the flag to be flown over Harvard Yard.

President Gay: It's been standard protocol at the university for years to only fly the American flag unless we have a visiting dignitary.

Congresswoman Stefanik: So the decision was made to allow the Ukraine flag to be flown over Harvard Yard.

President Gay: That was a decision that was made by my predecessor, as an exception to a long-standing rule.

Congresswoman Stefanik: So it was an exception. So you made an exception for the Ukrainian flag, but not the, the university made an exception for the Ukrainian flag, but not the Israeli flag.

President Gay: That was a choice made by my predecessor.

Congresswoman Stefanik: Are you aware that there are stickers that are placed on Harvard University dining services food calling for Israeli apartheid? It says "Warning. Sabra funds Israeli apartheid and the murder of Palestinians." Is that acceptable?

President Gay: I can assure you that we have strong disciplinary processes when there are violations of our rules.

Congresswoman Stefanik*:* And this is a violation of the rules.

President Gay: I can't see that very clearly but.

Congresswoman Stefanik: Are you not aware of the stickers being placed on the food items provided to Harvard students?

President Gay: I do recall an episode like that.

Congresswoman Stefanik: And there are disciplinary actions ongoing?

President Gay: Given students' privacy and FERPA which I'm sure you know, well. I will not say more about these particular cases other than to say that disciplinary processes are underway.

....

Congresswoman Stefanik: Dr. Gay, does calling for the genocide of Jews violate Harvard's rules on bullying and harassment?

President Gay: The rules around bullying and harassment are quite specific. And if the context in which that language is used amounts to bullying and harassment then we take, we take action against it.

Congresswoman Stefanik: Can you say yes to that question of: does calling for the genocide of Jews violate Harvard's rules on bullying and harassment?

President Gay: Calling for the genocide of Jews is antisemitic.

Congresswoman Stefanik: So yes?

President Gay: And that is antisemitic speech, and as I've said.

Congresswoman Stefanik: And it's a yes?

President Gay: When speech crosses into conduct, we take action.

Congresswoman Stefanik: So is that a yes? Is that a yes? The witness hasn't answered, Madam Chair. Is that a yes? You cannot answer the question.

President Gay: When speech crosses into conduct, we take action.

....

Congresswoman Stefanik: Dr. Kornbluth, at MIT, does calling for the genocide of Jews violate MIT's code of conduct or rules regarding bullying and harassment? Yes or no?

President Kornbluth: If targeted at individuals not making public statements.

Congresswoman Stefanik: Yes or no, calling for the genocide of Jews does not constitute bullying and harassment?

President Kornbluth: I have not heard calling for the genocide for Jews on our campus.

Congresswoman Stefanik: But you've heard chants for Intifada.

President Kornbluth: I've heard chants which can be antisemitic depending on the context when calling for the elimination of the Jewish people.

Congresswoman Stefanik: So those would not be, according to the MIT's code of conduct or rules.

President Kornbluth: That would be investigated as harassment if pervasive and severe.

Congresswoman Stefanik: Ms. Magill at Penn, does calling for the genocide of Jews violate Penn's rules or code of conduct? Yes or no?

President Magill: If the speech turns into conduct, it can be harassment. Yes.

Congresswoman Stefanik: I am asking, specifically calling for the genocide of Jews, does that constitute bullying or harassment?

President Magill: If it is directed, and severe, pervasive, it is harassment.

Congresswoman Stefanik: So the answer is yes.

President Magill: It is a context dependent decision, Congresswoman.

Congresswoman Stefanik: It's a context dependent decision. That's your testimony today, calling for the genocide of Jews is depending upon the context, that is not bullying or harassment. This is the easiest question to answer "yes," Ms. Magill. So is your testimony that you will not answer yes? Yes or no?

President Magill: If the speech becomes conduct. It can be harassment, yes.

Congresswoman Stefanik: Conduct meaning committing the act of genocide? The speech is not harassment? This is unacceptable. Ms. Magill, I'm gong to give you one more opportunity for the world to see your answer. Does calling for the genocide of Jews violate Penn's Code of Conduct when it comes to bullying and harassment? Yes or no?

President Magill: It can be harassment.

Congresswoman Stefanik: The answer is yes. And Dr. Gay at Harvard? Does calling for the genocide of Jews violate Harvard's rules of bullying and harassment? Yes or no?

President Gay: It can be depending on the context.

Congresswoman Stefanik: What's the context?

President Gay: Targeted at an individual targeted, as at an individual.

Congresswoman Stefanik: It's targeted at Jewish students, Jewish individuals. Do you understand your testimony is dehumanizing them? Do you understand that dehumanization is part of antisemitism? I will ask you one more time. Does calling for the genocide of Jews violate Harvard's rules of bullying and harassment? Yes or no?

President Gay: Antisemitic rhetoric when it crosses into conduct, that amounts to bullying, harassment, intimidation, that is actionable conduct, and we do take action.

Congresswoman Stefanik: So the answer is yes. That calling for the genocide of Jews violates Harvard Code of Conduct, correct?

President Gay: Again, it depends on the context.

Congresswoman Stefanik: It does not depend on the context, the answer is yes, and this is why you should resign. These are unacceptable answers across the board.

....

House Education and the Workforce Committee
Columbia in Crisis: Columbia University's Response to Antisemitism
Witness List:
Minouche Shafik, President of Columbia University
David Schizer, Harvey R. Miller, Professor of Law and Economics and Dean Emeritus, Columbia Law School

Claire Shipman, Co-Chair, Board of Trustees, Columbia University
David Greenwald, Co-Chair, Board of Trustees, Columbia University
April 17, 2024
Washington, D.C.

Congresswoman Stefanik: I want to follow up on my colleague Rep. Walberg's question regarding Professor Joseph Massad. So let me be clear, President, that he was spoken to. Who spoke with him?

President Shafik: He was spoken to by his Head of Department and his Dean.

Congresswoman Stefanik: And what was he told?

President Shafik: I was not in those conversations. I think he was told that that language was unacceptable.

Congresswoman Stefanik: But you're not aware of what he was told? What was he told?

President Shafik: That that language was unacceptable.

Congresswoman Stefanik: And were there any other enforcement actions taken? Any other disciplinary actions taken?

President Shafik: In his case, he has not repeated anything like that ever since.

Congresswoman Stefanik: Does he need to repeat stating that the massacre of Israeli civilians was "awesome"? Does he need to repeat his participation in an unauthorized, pro-Hamas demonstration on April 4th? You know, Professor David Schizer talked about the lack of enforcement. Do you agree that this is an issue with a lack of enforcement when the policy of Columbia specifically stated on April 5th said, "I want to make clear that it is absolutely unacceptable for any member of this community to promote the use of terror or violence," and yet you have no action? No disciplinary action. Do you agree with how the university has handled this?

President Shafik: Yeah, we have 4,700 faculty at Columbia, most of whom spend all of their time dedicated to teaching their students.

Congresswoman Stefanik: But I'm talking about the faculty members who are supporting terror and it's not just that case. Let me bring your attention to Mohamed Abdou who was hired after the October 7th terrorist attack against Israel. He, on October 11th, posted: "Yes, I'm with Hamas and Hezbollah and Islamic Jihad." He also decried false reports accusing Arabs and Muslims of decapitating the heads of children and being rapists. We know that there were decapitations of babies, of innocent Israeli citizens, of seniors, of women, there were rapes and yet Columbia hired this individual as a professor. How did that hiring process work? Were you aware of those statements before the hiring?

President Shafik: I share with you your repugnance at those remarks. I completely understand that. On my watch, faculty who make remarks that cross the line in terms of antisemitism, there will be consequences for them.

Congresswoman Stefanik: What are the consequences in this case?

President Shafik: I have five cases at the moment who have either been either taken out of the classroom or dismissed.

Congresswoman Stefanik: And is he one of those?

President Shafik: He will never work at Columbia again.

Congresswoman Stefanik: So he has been terminated?

President Shafik: He has been terminated and not just terminated, but his files will show that he will never work at Columbia again.

Congresswoman Stefanik: So he is currently not employed by Columbia?

President Shafik: He is grading his students' papers and will never teach at Columbia again and that will be on his permanent record.

Congresswoman Stefanik: How are you changing the hiring processes? Because on your watch, he was hired after he made these statements publicly? How are you ensuring this does not happen with your hiring process going forward?

President Shafik: So when we hire people, obviously they have to meet the academic qualifications, but we do an employment check and a criminal record check. We also ask everyone to do an attestation that they have never been accused of discrimination or part of an investigation around harassment or discrimination. And that attestation has to be signed by all new employees.

Congresswoman Stefanik: And it didn't work in this case.

President Shafik: I think in this case, while he may not have been subject to an investigation on discrimination or found guilty, it has to be found guilty.

Congresswoman Stefanik: But don't you think it's a problem when the hiring process of Columbia is hiring someone who makes those statements, and is hiring them after making those statements?

President Shafik: I agree with you that I think we need to look at how to toughen up those requirements. We do have a requirement, but I agree with you. I think we need to look at how we can make it more effective.

Congresswoman Stefanik: Let me ask about Professor Katherine Frank from the Columbia Law School who said that "all Israeli students who have served in the IDF are dangerous and shouldn't be on campus." What disciplinary action has been taken against that professor?

President Shafik: I agree with you that those comments are completely unacceptable and discriminatory.

Congresswoman Stefanik: But I'm asking you what disciplinary action has been taken?

President Shafik: She has been spoken to by very senior person in the administration and she has said that that was not what she intended to say.

Congresswoman Stefanik: And has she publicly apologized?

President Shafik: I have suggested that. I think she will be finding a way to clarify her position.

Congresswoman Stefanik: You see the concern here though, with the lack of enforcement. You see the concern that speaking to these professors is not enough and it's sending a message across the university that this is tolerated. These antisemitic statements from a position of authority in professors in the classroom is tolerated. My time has expired, but I will have multiple rounds with questions.

....

Congresswoman Stefanik: Just to follow up, you should know this, President Shafik, but Massad is still in fact listed on the Columbia website as Chair of the Academic Review Committee. Are you aware of that?

President Shafik: I would need to check that.

Congresswoman Stefanik: The website's right here. So he hasn't been removed as Chair? Do you have my commitment that he'll be removed as Chair today?

President Shafik: I have my commitment that I will come back to you and give you the facts.

Congresswoman Stefanik: So he hasn't been removed. So you said in front of Congress, under oath, that he was removed.

President Shafik: No, I said I am not sure. I need to check.

Congresswoman Stefanik: Well, I'll tell you what he's still listed as chair. Let me ask the Board of Trustees. Is that acceptable that he's chair of this committee? Should he be removed today, Ms. Shipman?

Board of Trustees Co-Chair Shipman: Congresswoman, you've put your finger on one of the hardest issues we as board chairs face right now. I think you can see our systems from the videos you played, everything you're talking about, our systems of rules and enforcement . . .

Congresswoman Stefanik: Are broken, they're broken. My question to you, Ms. Shipman, and I'm the one asking the questions here as the United States Member of Congress, is: Do you believe that he should be removed as chair because currently he's listed as chair on Columbia University's website?

Co-Chair Shipman: I don't believe any professor at Columbia should say anything like, our professors have to be held to a higher standard than our students. And I can tell you that our board—

Congresswoman Stefanik: But you can't say at this hearing that he should be removed as chair even though he violates university rules?

Co-Chair Shipman: I personally don't want him as chair and we are looking at the issue of faculty and what we expect from our faculty.

Congresswoman Stefanik: Mr. Greenwald, do you think he should be removed as chair?

Board of Trustees Co-Chair Greenwald: His comments are abhorrent and I believe that one of the steps that we could take in terms of discipline is to remove him from that leadership position.

Congresswoman Stefanik: Thank you for that direct answer. And just to let you know, Mr. Abdou is not grading papers right now. He's on campus at the unsanctioned anti-Israel, antisemitic event that is being supported by pro-Hamas activists on campus. So that's what Professor Abdou is doing at this very moment.

....

House Committee on Education and the Workforce
Calling for Accountability: Stopping Antisemitic College Chaos
Witness List:
Michael Schill, President of Northwestern University
May 23, 2024
Washington, D.C.

Congresswoman Stefanik: President Schill, the ADL released its report card for universities' responses to antisemitism and you're aware that Northwestern was the only university whose grade was downgraded, correct?

President Schill: Yes, I am aware of that.

Congresswoman Stefanik: And isn't it also true that Northwestern earned an "F" for your failure to respond and combat antisemitism and they called for your resignation? Is that correct?

President Schill: I have great respect for the ADL.

Congresswoman Stefanik: I'm not asking about your respect for the ADL, I'm asking is it a fact that you earned an "F" and they called for your resignation?

President Schill: I have great respect for the ADL. I am sad that they gave Northwestern an "F."

Congresswoman Stefanik: But it's true you got an "F." Yes. Moving on. Let me tell you why you earned an "F." I want to discuss what has been referred to as the Deering Meadows Agreement, your unilateral capitulation to the pro-Hamas, anti-Israel, antisemitic encampment. But let's talk about what has occurred on this encampment. Isn't it true that a Jewish Northwestern student was assaulted?

President Schill: So, I want to question the premise of your question.

Congresswoman Stefanik: No, no, no, no. I'm asking the questions. You're answering. Wasn't it true . . .

President Schill*:* Well my answer is not a capitulation.

Congresswoman Stefanik: I'm asking the question. You're required to answer. Isn't it true that a Jewish Northwestern student was assaulted?

President Schill: There are allegations that a Jewish student was assaulted. We are investigating those allegations.

Congresswoman Stefanik: Isn't it true that a Jewish student was verbally harassed and stalked to Hillel?

President Schill: There are allegations of that sort and we are investigating them.

Congresswoman Stefanik: Isn't it true that a Jewish student wearing a yarmulke was spat on?

President Schill: All of these are allegations that are being investigated.

Congresswoman Stefanik: How long are these investigations going to occur?

President Schill: Well, if you remember the encampment was up just a few weeks ago so we believe at Northwestern in due process. We believe in investigations.

Congresswoman Stefanik: So, when are the investigations going to be finalized?

President Schill: I'm not going to be able to tell you that, they'll be finalized when the Conduct Office and the Title VI Office, which are well on this issue—

Congresswoman Stefanik: This is why you've earned an "F." Isn't it true that a Jewish student was told to "go back to Germany and get gassed"?

President Schill: I've heard that alleged. Again, it is being investigated. We will investigate any claim of discrimination.

Congresswoman Stefanik: But it is a fact you said that there have been zero suspensions, zero expulsions.

President Schill: Thus far. With lots of investigations on their way.

Congresswoman Stefanik: You said something that was very important. You said we did not give into demands but the commitments we made as part of the Deering Meadows Agreement, you said the word "commitments." Let me talk about those commitments. One of those commitments was funding two visiting Palestinian faculty for two years. Is that true?

President Schill: This is part of a program that we have had. We have used it with Afghanistan, Ukraine, it's for war-torn countries.

Congresswoman Stefanik: But isn't it true? I'm asking you. Okay. The other one is you will fund the full cost for five Palestinian undergrads.

President Schill: That is also part of the programs sponsored by our Buffett Institute. It is not a new program. It exists for people whose education and research has been interrupted.

Congresswoman Stefanik: But it was announced as part of the Deering Meadows Agreement, is that correct?

President Schill: It was part of it. It was a goal set forth in the Deering Meadows Agreement. It will also include people from Israel.

Congresswoman Stefanik: Who was consulted when you embarked on the Deering Meadows Agreement? Was the President's Advisory Committee on Preventing Antisemitism and Hate consulted?

President Schill: That was not within the purview of the antisemitism and other forms of hate committee.

Congresswoman Stefanik: So, they were not consulted. Was Northwestern's Board of Trustees consulted?

President Schill: The Chair of our Board was consulted.

Congresswoman Stefanik: But not the entire Board of Trustees?

President Schill: Our Board of Trustees has over 120 members.

Congresswoman Stefanik: And isn't it a fact that members of the Board of Trustees expressed dissatisfaction with your failure to consult them?

President Schill: There's been some members of our Board of Trustees who have expressed dissatisfaction that they were not part of the decision making.

Congresswoman Stefanik: Did you consult with the General Counsel of Northwestern or an outside counsel on the Deering Meadows Agreement before it was agreed to?

President Schill: Yes.

Congresswoman Stefanik: Are you aware that board members asked you this question and you said that you had not consulted?

President Schill: Not the outside counsel. The General Counsel of the university was part of my team managing this problem.

Congresswoman Stefanik: Did you consult with two members of the advisory committee that I referenced previously, the anti-Israel professor, Jessica Winegar, and the Kellogg Professor, Nour Kteily. Were they consulted on the Deering Meadows Agreement?

President Schill: I consulted with several members, including them, but also including the Hillel Director and also including the Chair of the Committee.

Congresswoman Stefanik: Let's talk about the Hillel Director consultation. Isn't it true that you asked the Hillel Director whether it was possible to hire an anti-Zionist, head of Hillel, Rabbi?

President Schill: I did not. I absolutely did not. I would never hire anyone based upon their views of being Zionist or anti-Zionist. That is not what I do. That's not what a great university does.

Congresswoman Stefanik: That's not according to the whistleblowers that have come forward to this committee.

President Schill: I can't say who has talked to you or not talked to you but I can tell you the truth.

Congresswoman Stefanik: I can assure you many people have spoken to this committee.

....

Congresswoman Stefanik: President Schill, you talked about, you said there's been a wide range of discipline after testifying there have been zero suspensions, zero expulsions, and you said "discipline has been meted out." How has discipline been meted out?

President Schill: Discipline has run the gambit. That is the discipline that's already completed, run the gambit from meetings with student affairs staff at the very lowest level of severity up to disciplinary probation, which means there is another offense students will be expelled or suspended.

Congresswoman Stefanik: And you testified when I asked about the Deering Meadows Agreement with the visiting Palestinian faculty members, isn't it true that the university committed to fundraise above and beyond its current commitment as part of the Deering Meadows Agreement?

President Schill: I did not commit. I don't know who told you that.

Congresswoman Stefanik: I'm reading it from the statement put out by the university that says, "The university commits to fundraise to sustain this program beyond this current commitment." I'm reading your words put out by your office.

President Schill: That is a program that is not just about the Middle East. That is a program that is about war, war-torn areas all across this world. Ukraine for example.

Congresswoman Stefanik: But isn't it a fact that that was part of the agreement to increase the commitment to that.

President Schill: I don't think the agreement increased the commitment.

Congresswoman Stefanik: It did. I'm reading it for you. You put this out from your office, "The University commits to fundraise to sustain this program beyond this current commitment." Is that no longer part of the Deering Meadow Agreement?

President Schill: When I hear beyond this commitment . . .

Congresswoman Stefanik: I'm reading what your office put out.

President Schill: Are you asking me to interpret what my office put out? Or are you just reading it?

Congresswoman Stefanik: No, I'm asking you, isn't that the fact? What does "beyond this current commitment" mean?

President Schill: What I read that to be is beyond this current commitment, the rest of the world, and over time.

Congresswoman Stefanik: That's not . . . it's specifically focused on the Palestinian faculty members. Let me ask you this . . .

President Schill: But we're also going to be including Israeli faculty members.

Congresswoman Stefanik: It doesn't say that in commitment. Why didn't you include Israeli faculty members when you put out the Deering Meadows Agreement?

President Schill: Because the Deering Meadows Agreement, which I actually never called it that, but the Deering Meadows Agreement was just a framework of an agreement that was reached with students at 4 o'clock in the morning.

Congresswoman Stefanik: At the pro-Hamas encampment.

President Schill: If you would like to see the entire program, go on our website and that will explain it to you and you will see it doesn't violate Title XI.

Congresswoman Stefanik: No, I'm asking you about what the university put out. There is no mention of Israeli students or Israeli faculty, isn't that the case?

President Schill: In the agreement that we reached, there wasn't Israeli students there or Jewish students there.

Congresswoman Stefanik: Because they weren't consulted. Isn't that the fact? Jewish students were not consulted.

President Schill: Jewish and Israel students were not consulted with respect to the agreement.

Congresswoman Stefanik: Exactly.

NOTES

INTRODUCTION

1. Lydia Saad, "Perceived Importance of College Hits New Low," Gallup, September 11, 2025, https://news.gallup.com/poll/695003/perceived-importance-college-hits-new-low.aspx.
2. Kevin Wallsten, "Why Do So Many Young Americans Justify Political Violence?," *Wall Street Journal*, September 12, 2025, https://www.wsj.com/opinion/why-do-so-many-young-americans-justify-political-violence-ee8d2e2d?mod=mhp.
3. Michael Brickman, "Breaking the College Remediation Cycle," AEI, February 21, 2024, https://www.aei.org/education/breaking-the-college-remediation-cycle/.
4. Jane Nam, "Grade Inflation in College: Trends and Why It Happens," BestColleges, May 23, 2024, https://www.bestcolleges.com/research/grade-inflation-trends-and-causes/.
5. "Facts and Statistics," International Center for Academic Integrity, https://academicintegrity.org/aws/ICAI/pt/sp/facts.
6. Jessica Dickler, "Incoming College Freshmen Are Set to Rack Up $40,000 in Student Debt by Graduation, Report Finds," CNBC, April 23, 2025, https://www.cnbc.com/2025/04/23/incoming-college-freshmen-may-owe-40k-in-student-debt-by-graduation.html.
7. "The Missing Link: Accountability in Career Readiness," Cengage Group, September 9, 2025, https://cengage.widen.net/s/c2cxf76fcr/cg-employability-survey-report-2025.

CHAPTER 1: THE HEARING HEARD AROUND THE WORLD

1. Melissa Koenig, "George Washington University Students Project Messages in Support of Hamas on School Library," *New York Post*, October 25, 2023, https://nypost.com/2023/10/25/news/gwu-students-project-messages-in-support-of-hamas/.
2. Jonathan Stempel, "NYU Is Sued by Jewish Students Who Allege Antisemitism on Campus," Reuters, November 14, 2023, https://www.reuters.com/legal/nyu-is-sued-by-jewish-students-who-allege-antisemitism-campus-2023-11-14/.
3. Talia Khan, "Testimony Before U.S. House Committee on Education and the Workforce," March 4, 2024, https://www.congress.gov/118/meeting/house/116625/documents/HHRG-118-ED00-20231205-SD003.pdf.

4. Joshua Rhett Miller, "Jewish Students Reveal What Really Happened at Cooper Union Protest," *New York Post*, October 26, 2023, https://nypost.com/2023/10/26/metro/jewish-students-reveal-what-happened-at-cooper-union-protest/.
5. Crimson News Staff, "Joint Statement by Harvard Palestine Solidarity Groups on the Situation in Palestine," *Harvard Crimson*, October 10, 2023, https://www.thecrimson.com/widget/2023/10/10/psc-statement/.
6. Germania Rodriguez Poleo, "Inside UC Berkeley's Secretive Bears for Palestine Student Group That Supports Hamas Terrorists While Hiding Their Identities," *Daily Mail*, October 15, 2023, https://www.dailymail.co.uk/news/article-12625035/UC-berkeley-Bears-Palestine-SJP-Isreal-hamas-professor-history.html.
7. Ryan Quinn, "Cornell Professor 'Exhilarated' by Hamas Attack Is Back Teaching," *Inside Higher Ed*, September 17, 2024, https://www.insidehighered.com/news/quick-takes/2024/09/17/cornell-prof-exhilarated-hamas-attack-back-teaching.
8. Joseph Massad, "Just Another Battle or the Palestinian War of Liberation?," *Electronic Intifada*, October 8, 2023, https://electronicintifada.net/content/just-another-battle-or-palestinian-war-liberation/38661.
9. Snejana Farberov, "'Radical' Yale Professor Faces Calls to Be Fired Over Comments on Hamas Attacks," *New York Post*, October 12, 2023, https://nypost.com/2023/10/12/radical-yale-professor-faces-calls-to-be-fired-over-comments-on-hamas-attacks/.
10. Maggie Hicks, "Pro-Palestinian Student Groups' Use of This Image Is Drawing Outrage. Here's Where It Came From," *Chronicle of Higher Education*, October 11, 2023, https://www.chronicle.com/article/pro-palestinian-student-groups-use-of-this-image-is-drawing-outrage-heres-where-it-came-from?sra=true.
11. *Yakoby v. University of Pennsylvania*, Civil Action No. 2:23-cv-04789 (E.D. Pa.), filed December 5, 2023 (Complaint, ¶ 166), https://www.kasowitz.com/media/focjlca0/university-of-pennsylvania-complaint.pdf.
12. *Ingber v. New York University*, Civil Action No. 1:23-cv-10023-PAC (S.D.N.Y.), filed January 31, 2024 (Amended Complaint, ¶ 1), https://www.kasowitz.com/media/ezklq4ya/amended-complaint-against-nyu.pdf.
13. Sylvia Burwell, "Dear AU Community," American University, October 20, 2023, https://www.american.edu/president/announcements/october-20-2023.cfm.
14. M. Elizabeth Magill, "Responding to Antisemitic Threat to Our Campus," *Penn Today*, November 6, 2023, https://penntoday.upenn.edu/announcements/responding-antisemitic-threat-our-campus.
15. "Frankel v. Regents of the University of California," The Becket Fund for Religious Liberty, https://becketfund.org/case/frankel-v-regents-of-the-university-of-california/.

16. Sahar Tartak, "I Was Stabbed in the Eye at Yale," *Free Press*, April 21, 2024, https://www.thefp.com/p/i-was-stabbed-in-the-eye-at-yale.
17. Virginia Foxx, "Letter to Dr. Michael V. Drake," U.S. House Committee on Education and the Workforce, May 15, 2024, https://edworkforce.house.gov/uploadedfiles/ucla_final.pdf.
18. Eleanor Muller and Bianca Quilantan, "'She's Just a Bull': Meet the Woman Leading the GOP's Charge on Schools and Work," *Politico*, August 18, 2023, https://www.politico.com/news/2023/08/18/virginia-foxx-gop-labor-education-00109716.
19. Stephanie Saul and Anemona Hartocollis, "College Presidents Under Fire After Dodging Questions About Antisemitism," *New York Times*, December 6, 2023, https://www.nytimes.com/2023/12/06/us/harvard-mit-penn-presidents-antisemitism.html.
20. Dave Portnoy (@stoolpresidente), "Just to reiterate I will never hire a Harvard Grad again," X, December 12, 2023, 11:00 a.m., https://x.com/stoolpresidente/status/1734604259117916506?s=20.
21. @_schwim_, "These morally bankrupt Presidents of @Harvard, uofpenn and @mit testify before congress," Instagram, December 7, 2023, https://www.instagram.com/reel/C0kibLoL450/?hl=en.
22. Elise Stefanik (@RepStefanik), "One down. Two to go," X, December 9, 2023, 5:03 p.m., https://x.com/RepStefanik/status/1733608373990343015?s=20.
23. "Justice Department Announces Formation of Task Force to Combat Anti-Semitism," U.S. Department of Justice, February 3, 2025, https://www.justice.gov/opa/pr/justice-department-announces-formation-task-force-combat-anti-semitism.

CHAPTER 2: HARVARD

1. Harvey C. Mansfield, "Who's Holding Up the Ivory Tower?," *Wall Street Journal*, January 11, 2024, https://www.wsj.com/opinion/whos-holding-up-the-ivory-tower-academia-harvard-pursuit-of-truth-or-societal-progress-6ab173da.
2. "Full Transcript: President Summers' Remarks at the National Bureau of Economic Research, Jan. 14, 2005," *Harvard Crimson*, February 18, 2005, https://www.thecrimson.com/article/2005/2/18/full-transcript-president-summers-remarks-at/.

CHAPTER 3: HARVARD EXPOSED

1. Meimei Xu, "More Than 80 Percent of Surveyed Harvard Faculty Identify as Liberal," *Harvard Crimson*, July 13, 2022, https://www.thecrimson.com/article/2022/7/13/faculty-survey-political-leaning/.
2. Samuel A. Church and Cam N. Srivastava, "Most Harvard Students Do Not Feel Comfortable Sharing Controversial Opinions in Class, Survey Finds," *Harvard Crimson*, February 10, 2025, https://www.thecrimson.com/article/2025/2/10/survey-results-controversial-opinions/.

3. https://spectrumlocalnews.com/us/snplus/education/2023/10/11/harvard-president-faces-backlash-over-response-to-hamas-attacks-on-israel/.
4. Press Release, Washington D.C., October 31, 2024, U.S. House Committee on Education and the Workforce, *Antisemitism on College Campuses Exposed*, https://edworkforce.house.gov/uploadedfiles/10.30.24_committee_on_education_and_the_workforce_republican_staff_report_-antisemitism_on_college_campuses_exposed.pdf.
5. Washington Free Beacon Editors, "The Harvard Scandal Is Bigger Than Claudine Gay," *Washington Free Beacon*, December 22, 2023, https://freebeacon.com/columns/the-harvard-scandal-is-bigger-than-claudine-gay/.
6. "Harvard's Detailed Description of Its Review Process," Harvard University, March 1, 2024, https://www.harvard.edu/media-relations/wp-content/uploads/sites/3/2024/01/Harvards-Detailed-Description-of-its-Review-Process.pdf.
7. Maureen Farrell and Rob Copeland, "How Harvard's Board Broke Up with Claudine Gay," *New York Times*, January 6, 2024, https://www.nytimes.com/2024/01/06/business/claudine-gay-harvard-corporation-board.html.
8. Ibid.
9. U.S. House Committee on Education and the Workforce, *Antisemitism*.
10. U.S. Department of Education, "Letter to Dr. Alan M. Garber," April 11, 2025, https://www.harvard.edu/research-funding/wp-content/uploads/sites/16/2025/04/Letter-Sent-to-Harvard-2025-04-11.pdf.
11. Alan M. Garber, "The Promise of American Higher Education," Harvard University, April 14, 2025, https://www.harvard.edu/president/news/2025/the-promise-of-american-higher-education/.
12. *Kestenbaum v. President and Fellows of Harvard College*, Civil Action No. 1:24-cv-10092 (D. Mass.), filed January 10, 2024, https://www.kasowitz.com/media/unxcnvpo/harvard-complaint.pdf.
13. Shabbos Kestenbaum, "Testimony Before the U.S. House Committee on Education and the Workforce," May 15, 2024, https://www.congress.gov/118/meeting/house/117305/witnesses/HHRG-118-JU10-Bio-KestenbaumS-20240515-U3.pdf.

CHAPTER 4: UNIVERSITY OF PENNSYLVANIA

1. *Yakoby v. University of Pennsylvania* (Complaint, ¶ 56).
2. Ibid.
3. Ibid. (Amended Complaint, ¶ 99), https://www.saainc.org/media/1ovphvcs/amended-complaint-against-penn.pdf.
4. U.S. House Permanent Select Committee on Intelligence, "Letter to The Honorable Pamela Jo Bondi," April 6, 2025, https://drive.google.com/file/d/1Ah1mgVhVjD8Evl30W9_JHH1dOFo6rjMu/view.

5. Ramishah Maruf, “UPenn Donors Were Furious About the Palestine Writes Literature Festival. What About It Made Them Pull Their Funds?,” CNN, October 25, 2023, https://www.cnn.com/2023/10/25/business/palestine-writes-literature-festival-what-happened/index.html.
6. “Palestine Writes Exposed,” https://www.palestinewritesexposed.com/.
7. *Yakoby v. University of Pennsylvania* (Amended Complaint, ¶ 101).
8. Susan Abulhawa, “Israel Is on Its Colonial Deathbed,” *Electronic Intifada*, October 12, 2023, https://electronicintifada.net/content/israel-its-colonial-deathbed/38746.
9. Susan Abulhawa (@susanabulhawa), “Jewish supremacist vampires can buy up all the airways,” X, September 26, 2025, 4:40 p.m., https://x.com/susanabulhawa/status/1971676379206111735.
10. Susan Abulhawa (@susanabulhawa), “If someone so much as hinted that Hamas did what had to be done,” X, September 25, 2025, 9:28 p.m., https://x.com/susanabulhawa/status/1971386429155512768.
11. Susan Abulhawa (@susanabulhawa), “through their Zionist proxy owners,” X, September 26, 2025, 2:27 p.m., https://x.com/susanabulhawa/status/1971642676270584185.
12. *Yakoby v. University of Pennsylvania* (Amended Complaint, ¶ 152).
13. Isabel Keane, “UPenn Library Staffer Caught Taking Down Posters of Kidnapped Israelis,” *New York Post*, October 18, 2023, https://nypost.com/2023/10/18/upenn-student-removing-posters-of-kidnapped-israelis/.
14. U.S. House Committee on Education and the Workforce, *Antisemitism*.
15. Alan Yu, “Penn Police Called FBI to Help Investigate Threatening Antisemitic Emails,” WHYY, November 7, 2023, https://whyy.org/articles/university-of-pennsylvania-fbi-antisemitic-threats-emails-israel-hamas-war/.
16. Sophia Liu, “Penn Denounces Projections of Pro-Palestinian Messages onto Campus Buildings as ‘Antisemitic,’” *Daily Pennsylvanian*, November 9, 2023, https://www.thedp.com/article/2023/11/penn-pro-palestinian-projections-huntsman-hall-penn-commons.
17. Marc Rowan, “Marc Rowan to Funders: Show UPenn That Words Matter,” eJewishPhilanthropy, October 11, 2023, https://ejewishphilanthropy.com/marc-rowan-to-funders-show-upenn-that-words-matter/.
18. Evan Mandery, “The First Casualty in the War Against Elite Universities,” *Politico Magazine*, June 2, 2025, https://www.politico.com/news/magazine/2025/06/02/liz-magill-college-antisemitism-university-pennsylvania-00338864.
19. Bianca Quilantan, “Democrats Slam Harvard, MIT, UPenn Presidents After Stefanik Grilling,” *Politico*, December 6, 2023, https://www.politico.com/news/2023/12/06/democrats-harvard-mit-upenn-stefanik-00130471.
20. Saul and Hartocollis, “College Presidents Under Fire.”

21. Emily Scolnick, "Pro-Palestinian Supporters Rally Against War in Gaza as Penn Investigates Graffiti Along March Route," *Daily Pennsylvanian*, December 4, 2023, https://www.thedp.com/article/2023/12/penn-protest-rally-palestine-gaza-uc-townhomes.
22. "Video Message from President Magill on Congressional Hearing," University of Pennsylvania, https://magill-archived.www.upenn.edu/content/video-message-president-magill-congressional-hearing.
23. Eyal Yakoby, "Testimony Before the House Judiciary Subcommittee on Constitution and Limited Government," May 15, 2024, https://judiciary.house.gov/sites/evo-subsites/republicans-judiciary.house.gov/files/evo-media-document/Yakoby%20Testimony.pdf.

CHAPTER 5: COLUMBIA

1. David M. Friedman (@DavidM_Friedman), "To the stewards of @Columbia—a once great institution founded by Alexander Hamilton in 1754," X, April 18, 2024, 6:26 p.m., https://x.com/DavidM_Friedman/status/1781087044908855425?s=20.
2. Carl Campanile, "Jewish Alumni Rip Columbia University Over Antisemitic Incidents, Tell Administration to 'Do Their Job,'" *New York Post*, April 8, 2024, https://nypost.com/2024/04/08/us-news/jewish-alumni-rip-columbia-university-over-antisemitic-incidents-and-tell-administration-to-do-their-job/.
3. Katherine Knott, Jessica Blake, Josh Moody, and Johanna Alonso, "Live Analysis: Columbia President Testifies on Capitol Hill," *Inside Higher Ed*, April 17, 2024, https://www.insidehighered.com/news/government/politics-elections/2024/04/17/live-analysis-columbia-president-testifies-congress.
4. Jason Cohn, "How Much Federal Funding Do Colleges and Universities Receive?," Urban Institute, May 8, 2025, https://www.urban.org/urban-wire/how-much-federal-funding-do-colleges-and-universities-receive.
5. Abigail Anthony, "Suspect in Assault on Israeli Columbia Student Charged with Hate Crime," *National Review*, October 17, 2023, https://www.nationalreview.com/news/suspect-in-assault-on-israeli-columbia-student-charged-with-hate-crime/.
6. U.S. House Committee on Education and the Workforce, "Letter to Dr. Minouche Shafik, President, Columbia University," February 12, 2024, https://edworkforce.house.gov/uploadedfiles/2-12-24_foxx_letter_to_columbia_university.pdf.
7. U.S. House Committee on Education and the Workforce, *Antisemitism*.
8. U.S. House Committee on Education and the Workforce, "Letter to Dr. Minouche Shafik."
9. "Columbia's Jewish Problem," *New Criterion*, March 2005, https://newcriterion.com/article/columbias-jewish-problem/.

10. U.S. House Committee on Education and the Workforce, "Letter to Dr. Minouche Shafik."
11. "Columbia's Jewish Problem."
12. Joseph Massad, "Just Another Battle or the Palestinian War of Liberation?," *Electronic Intifada*, October 8, 2023, https://electronicintifada.net/content/just-another-battle-or-palestinian-war-liberation/38661.
13. Emily Forgash and Amanda Chapa, "Hundreds of Faculty Sign Open Letters in Debate Around Free Speech, Student Safety Following Palestinian Solidarity Statement," *Columbia Spectator*, November 1, 2023, https://www.columbiaspectator.com/news/2023/11/01/hundreds-of-faculty-sign-open-letters-in-debate-around-free-speech-student-safety-following-palestinian-solidarity-statement/.
14. Franklin Foer, "The Golden Age of American Jews Is Ending," *Atlantic*, March 4, 2024, https://www.theatlantic.com/magazine/archive/2024/04/us-anti-semitism-jewish-american-safety/677469/.
15. U.S. House Committee on Education and the Workforce, "Letter to Dr. Minouche Shafik."
16. Rebecca Massel, "'I Am a Target': Dozens of Jewish Students Report Feeling Unsafe on Campus," *Columbia Spectator*, November 2, 2023, https://www.columbiaspectator.com/news/2023/11/02/i-am-a-target-dozens-of-jewish-students-report-feeling-unsafe-on-campus/.
17. Mahmood Mamdani, *Good Muslim, Bad Muslim: America, the Cold War, and the Roots of Terror* (New York: Three Leaves Press, 2005), 222.
18. Mahmood Mamdani, *Neither Settler nor Native: The Making and Unmaking of Permanent Minorities* (Cambridge, MA: Harvard, 2020), 252.
19. Alec Schemmel, "NYC Mayoral Frontrunner Zohran Mamdani's Professor Father Claimed Hitler Inspired by Abraham Lincoln," Fox News, July 6, 2025, https://www.foxnews.com/politics/zohran-mamdanis-college-professor-dad-said-hitler-drew-inspiration-from-abe-lincoln-during-2022-panel-talk.
20. Isabel Vincent, "Mamdani's Dad Sits with Hamas-Linked Financier on Gaza Tribunal Pushing for US, Israel to Face War Charges," *New York Post*, October 29, 2025, https://nypost.com/2025/10/29/world-news/mamdanis-dad-sits-with-hamas-linked-financier-on-gaza-tribunal/.
21. MAZE (@mazemoore), "September, 2023. Zohran Mamdani: 'We have to make clear that when the boot of the NYPD is on your neck, it's been laced by the IDF,'" X, October 27, 2025, 8:56 p.m., https://x.com/mazemoore/status/1982974662175752646.
22. Shai Davidai (@ShaiDavidai-xz1cw), "An Open Letter to Every Parent in America," YouTube, October 18, 2023, https://www.youtube.com/watch?v=uo7fdxrjMlc.
23. Shai Davidai and Yardenne Greenspan, "What Happens When You Teach at Columbia and Reject Hamas," *Tablet*, February 13, 2024, https://www.tabletmag

.com/sections/arts-letters/articles/what-happens-when-you-teach-at-columbia-and-reject-hamas.

24. "October 17, 2024 University Statement," Columbia University, October 17, 2024, https://communications.news.columbia.edu/news/october-17-2024-university-statement.
25. Shai Davidai, "Why I'm Leaving Columbia," *Tablet*, July 15, 2025, https://www.tabletmag.com/sections/news/articles/leaving-columbia-shai-davidai.
26. Eden Yadegar, "Written Testimony Before the United States House of Representatives Committee on Education and the Workforce, 'Roundtable with Jewish Students Impacted by Antisemitism,'" February 29, 2024, https://edworkforce.house.gov/uploadedfiles/yadegar_updated_written_statement.pdf.
27. Canary Mission, "Khaled Barakat," June 23, 2025, https://canarymission.org/individual/Khaled_Barakat.
28. Isabel Vincent and Dana Kennedy, "Pro-Terror Radical Launched 2-Hour Anti-Israel Tirade at Columbia University Event Weeks Before Protests Exploded: 'Nothing Wrong with Being a Hamas Fighter,'" *New York Post*, April 24, 2024, https://nypost.com/2024/04/24/us-news/palestinian-radical-at-columbia-nothing-wrong-with-hamas/.
29. U.S. House Committee on Education and the Workforce, *Antisemitism*.
30. Tim Walberg, "Walberg Grills Columbia President over Lack of Repercussions for Antisemitism," April 17, 2024, https://walberg.house.gov/media/press-releases/walberg-grills-columbia-president-over-lack-repercussions-antisemitism.
31. Elise Stefanik, "ICYMI: Stefanik Demands Columbia University President Commit to Fighting Antisemitism on Campus," April 17, 2024, https://stefanik.house.gov/press-releases?ID=DA524C1F-4A2B-46ED-A3CD-24979768EBB8.
32. https://x.com/DavidM_Friedman/status/1781087044908855425.
33. Canary Mission, "Mahmoud Khalil," March 12, 2025, https://canarymission.org/individual/Mahmoud_Khalil.
34. David Zimmerman, "Mahmoud Khalil Omitted Past UNRWA Work from Green Card Application, DOJ Alleges," *National Review*, March 24, 2025, https://www.nationalreview.com/news/mahmoud-khalil-omitted-past-unrwa-work-from-green-card-application-doj-alleges/.
35. "Withdrawing the United States from and Ending Funding to Certain United Nations Organizations and Reviewing United States Support to All International Organizations," The White House, February 4, 2025, https://www.whitehouse.gov/presidential-actions/2025/02/withdrawing-the-united-states-from-and-ending-funding-to-certain-united-nations-organizations-and-reviewing-united-states-support-to-all-international-organizations/.
36. "INVESTIGATIVE SUMMARY: USAID OIG's Investigative Work to Prevent UNRWA Staff Associated with Hamas from Circulating to Other Government-

Funded Aid Organizations," U.S. Agency for International Development, April 14, 2025, https://oig.usaid.gov/node/7597.

37. Associated Press, "Mahmoud Khalil Vows to Continue Protests After Release from Detention," *Politico*, June 21, 2025, https://www.politico.com/news/2025/06/21/mahmoud-khalil-vows-to-continue-protests-after-release-from-detention-00416402.
38. Meghan Blonder, "'Socialism Is Not a Dirty Word Anymore': Zohran Mamdani's Victory Emboldens the Far Left," *Washington Free Beacon*, November 5, 2025, https://freebeacon.com/democrats/socialism-is-not-a-dirty-word-anymore-zohran-mamdanis-victory-emboldens-the-far-left/.
39. Frannie Block, "'I Could Have Been Killed in There,'" *Free Press*, May 7, 2024, https://www.thefp.com/p/columbia-custodian-invasion-traumatized.
40. Frannie Block, "'Reminiscent of the KKK': Columbia Janitors Sue Protesters Who Took Over Hamilton Hall," *Free Press*, April 26, 2025, https://www.thefp.com/p/exclusive-columbia-janitors-sue-protesters.
41. Chelsea Rose Marcius, "Why Bragg Dropped Charges Against Most Columbia Student Protesters," *New York Times*, June 23, 2024, https://www.nytimes.com/2024/06/23/nyregion/columbia-protest-charges-bragg.html.
42. Eliana Johnson, "What Columbia University President Katrina Armstrong Really Told Faculty Members About Changes the School Is Making," *Washington Free Beacon*, March 26, 2025, https://freebeacon.com/campus/what-columbia-university-president-really-told-faculty-members/.
43. Elise Stefanik, "Stefanik Leads Letter Exposing Columbia University's Leadership for Potential Title VI Violations and Betrayal of Jewish Students and Board Members," July 1, 2025, https://stefanik.house.gov/2025/7/stefanik-leads-letter-exposing-columbia-university-s-leadership-for-potential-title-vi-violations-and-betrayal-of-jewish-students-and-board-members.
44. Columbia University Task Force on Antisemitism, "Report #2: Columbia University Student Experiences of Antisemitism and Recommendations for Promoting Shared Values and Inclusion," August, 2024, https://www.columbia.edu/content/report-2-task-force-antisemitism.
45. "DOJ, HHS, and GSA Announce Initial Cancelation of Grants and Contracts to Columbia University Worth $400 Million," U.S. Department of Education, March 7, 2025, https://www.ed.gov/about/news/press-release/doj-hhs-ed-and-gsa-announce-initial-cancelation-of-grants-and-contracts-columbia-university-worth-400-million.
46. "Our Resolution with the Federal Government," Columbia University, https://president.columbia.edu/content/our-resolution-federal-government.
47. Grace Hamilton and Spencer Davis, "Jonathon Kahn, GSAS '03, Appointed Inaugural Columbia Senior Associate Dean of Community and Culture," *Columbia*

Spectator, September 17, 2025, https://www.columbiaspectator.com/news/2025/09/17/jonathon-kahn-gsas-03-appointed-inaugural-columbia-senior-associate-dean-of-community-and-culture/.

48. Columbia Jewish & Israeli Students (@CUJewsIsraelis), "Yesterday, @Columbia announced that it had hired Jonathon Kahn," X, September 3, 2025, 11:24 a.m., https://x.com/CUJewsIsraelis/status/1963261719007936823?s=20.
49. Aaron Sibarium and Eliana Johnson, "Columbia's Armstrong to Return from Sabbatical as CEO of Medical Center," *Washington Free Beacon*, May 12, 2025, https://freebeacon.com/campus/columbias-armstrong-to-return-as-ceo-of-medical-center/.

CHAPTER 6: THE OTHER IVIES AND BEYOND

1. Michael Starr, "Jewish Student Jabbed in Eye with Flag Pole by Anti-Israel Protesters—Exclusive," *Jerusalem Post*, April 21, 2024, https://www.jpost.com/diaspora/antisemitism/article-798092.
2. Netanel Crispe, personal communication.
3. Sahar Tartak, personal communication.
4. Sahar Tartak and Netanel Crispe, "CRISPE & TARTAK: Yale Graduate Students Deny Hamas' Responsibility for October 7 and Compare Jews to Nazis—and It's Yale's Fault," *Yale Daily News*, March 7, 2024, https://yaledailynews.com/blog/2024/03/08/crispe-tartak-yale-graduate-students-deny-hamas-responsibility-for-october-7-and-compare-jews-to-nazis-and-its-yales-fault/.
5. U.S. House Committee on Education and the Workforce, *Antisemitism*.
6. Noam Barenholtz, "BARENHOLTZ: Welcome to Beinecke Plaza," *Yale Daily News*, May 2, 2024, https://yaledailynews.com/blog/2024/05/02/barenholtz-welcome-to-beinecke-plaza/.
7. Ibid.
8. Bret Stephens, "To Be (Visibly) Jewish in the Ivy League," *New York Times*, April 23, 2024, https://www.nytimes.com/2024/04/23/opinion/university-jewish-antisemitism-ivy.html.
9. U.S. House Committee on Education and the Workforce, *Antisemitism*.
10. @ampalestinect, "BREAKING: YALE STUDENTS RELAUNCH THEIR ENCAMPMENT," Instagram, April 22, 2025, https://www.instagram.com/p/DIxSevWMarG/?hl=enm.
11. Jamie Joseph, "Yale Drops Alleged Hamas-Tied Student Group's Status After 'Disturbing Antisemitic Conduct,'" Fox News, April 24, 2025, https://www.foxnews.com/politics/yale-drops-alleged-hamas-tied-student-group-status-after-disturbing-antisemitic-conduct; and Mark Zaretsky, "Yale Pro-Palestinian Group Stripped of Status After Protesters Pitch Tents to Oppose Appearance by Israeli Security Minister," *New Haven Register*, April 23, 2025, https://www.nhregister.com/news/article/yale-palestine-protest-ben-gvir-israel-ct-20290559.php.

12. Christopher L. Eisgruber, "Class of 2023 Commencement Address by President Eisgruber: 'Let Your Voices Rise,'" May 30, 2023, https://www.princeton.edu/news/2023/05/30/class-2023-commencement-address-president-eisgruber-let-your-voices-rise.
13. Matthew Wilson, "On Eisgruber's Commencement Sermon," *Daily Princetonian*, May 31, 2023, https://www.dailyprincetonian.com/article/2023/06/princeton-opinion-eisgruber-commencement-remarks-free-speech-divisive.
14. Elaine Huang and Charlie Roth, eds., "Senior Survey," *Daily Princetonian*, 2023, https://projects.dailyprincetonian.com/senior-survey-2023/views.html#PoliticsNav; and Princetonians for Free Speech, "Princeton's Free Speech Campus Culture: A Princetonians for Free Speech Study," May 2023, https://infogram.com/princetons-free-speech-campus-culture-1h7g6k0dyry7o2o?live.
15. "Princeton Students for Justice in Palestine: Statement on Recent Events in Palestine," https://acrobat.adobe.com/link/track?uri=urn%3Aaaid%3Ascds%3AUS%3A90e1b2a1-6894-31ae-8d70-278439115f78&viewer%21megaVerb=group-discover.
16. Zach Kessel, "Princeton Students for Justice in Palestine Escape Consequences After Using University Listserv to Defend Hamas," *National Review*, February 1, 2024, https://www.nationalreview.com/news/princeton-students-for-justice-in-palestine-escape-consequences-after-using-university-listserv-to-defend-hamas/.
17. Zach Kessel, "Princeton University Group Scheduled Pro-Hamas 'Teach-In' for Same Time as Vigil for Slain Israelis," *National Review*, October 17, 2023, https://www.nationalreview.com/news/princeton-university-palestinian-group-scheduled-pro-hamas-teach-in-for-same-time-as-vigil-for-slain-israelis/.
18. Danielle Shapiro and Yonah Berenson, "How Campus Politicization Fed Today's Hatred," *Wall Street Journal*, October 23, 2023, https://www.wsj.com/opinion/how-campus-politicization-fed-todays-hatred-israel-hamas-protest-58bbc002.
19. Danielle Shapiro, "I Committed Journalism, and Princeton Told Me Not to Communicate," *Wall Street Journal*, September 23, 2022, https://www.wsj.com/articles/i-committed-journalism-and-princeton-told-me-not-to-communicate-nco-title-ix-regulations-campus-israel-misconduct-chicago-principles-11663945517.
20. FIRE (@TheFIREorg), "JUST SENT: FIRE and the @ADL are challenging @Princeton's ongoing improper use of no-contact orders," X, January 25, 2024, 2:56 p.m., https://x.com/TheFIREorg/status/1750608587024453774?s=20.
21. Princeton University, "No Communication Orders and No Contact Orders: Frequently Asked Questions," November 2024, https://odus.princeton.edu/sites/g/files/toruqf896/files/documents/FAQs%20re%20NCOs%20%28ODUS%2C%20GS%2C%20HR.%20DOF%29.pdf.

22. Lawrence Richard, "Hezbollah Terror Flag Found at Princeton's Anti-Israel Encampment, Cruz Torches the Protesters," Fox News, April 26, 2024, https://www.foxnews.com/politics/hezbollah-terror-flag-found-princeton-anti-israel-campus-cruz-torches-protesters.
23. Zack Dulberg (@pianozack), "A wildcard from the @Princeton encampment—allying with North Korea!," X, April 28, 2024, 4:22 p.m., https://x.com/pianozack/status/1784679530365341711.
24. Abigail Anthony, "Princeton Professors Lead Chants, Hold Classes at Pro-Palestinian Sit-In," *National Review*, April 26, 2024, https://www.nationalreview.com/news/princeton-professors-lead-chants-hold-classes-at-pro-palestinian-sit-in/.
25. Mark F. Bernstein, "What Really Happened When Protesters Occupied Clio Hall?," *Princeton Alumni Weekly*, May 23, 2024, https://paw.princeton.edu/article/what-really-happened-when-protesters-occupied-clio-hall.
26. Ibid.
27. Julie Bonette, "Judge Dismisses Charges Against Clio Hall Protesters, Asks for Apology," *Princeton Alumni Weekly*, June 27, 2025, https://paw.princeton.edu/article/judge-dismisses-charges-against-clio-hall-protesters-asks-apology.
28. Danielle Shapiro, "I Was Called an 'Inbred Swine' at Princeton Last Night," *Free Press*, April 8, 2025, https://www.thefp.com/p/anti-israel-princeton-protest.
29. @netanel_crispe, "A powerful moment from Princeton," Instagram, April 8, 2025, https://www.instagram.com/reel/DIMiVkNRS4B/.
30. Hope Perry, "Princeton Opens Investigation After Protesters Disrupt Event with Former Israeli Prime Minister," *Princeton Alumni Weekly*, April 8, 2025, https://paw.princeton.edu/article/princeton-opens-investigation-after-protesters-disrupt-event-former-israeli-prime-minister.
31. Danielle Shapiro, "Princeton Fails to Enforce Its Rules on Free Speech, Antisemitism," *Real Clear Politics*, June 4, 2025, https://www.realclearpolitics.com/articles/2025/06/04/princeton_fails_to_enforce_its_rules_free_speech_antisemitism_152870.html.
32. Representatives of Brown University, Brown Divest Coalition, "Final Agreement," April 30, 2024, https://www.brown.edu/sites/default/files/encampment-agreement-04-30-24.pdf.
33. "Brown Becomes First US University to Consider Divesting from Israel," *Times of Israel*, May 1, 2024, https://www.timesofisrael.com/brown-becomes-first-us-university-to-consider-divesting-from-israel/.
34. American Jewish Committee, "BDS," 2025, https://www.ajc.org/issues/bds.
35. Collin Brinkley, "DeVos: Efforts to Boycott Israel Are a 'Pernicious Threat,'" Associated Press, July 15, 2029, https://apnews.com/parenting-united-states-government-98e9500a59d6436ab0a30a0d90dba3cd.

36. Joseph Edelman, "Why I Am Resigning as a Brown Trustee," *Wall Street Journal*, September 8, 2024, https://www.wsj.com/opinion/why-i-am-resigning-as-a-brown-trustee-gaza-antisemitism-protesters-1479f433?mod=article_inline.
37. Janet Lorin, "Brown Gets Warning from 24 States on Israel Divestment Vote," *Bloomberg*, August 26, 2024, https://www.bloomberg.com/news/articles/2024-08-26/brown-gets-warning-from-24-state-ags-on-israel-divestment-vote?embedded-checkout=true.
38. The Corporation of Brown University, "Brown Corporation Decision on Divestment," 2024, https://corporation.brown.edu/announcement/divestment-decision-2024.
39. Maysa Mustafa, "'The Only Liberated Place': Birzeit University and the Fight for the Future of Palestine," *Public Source*, September 22, 2025, https://thepublicsource.org/birzeit-palestinian-students-occupation; Aaron Boxerman, "Hamas Wins Landslide Victory in Student Elections at Flagship Birzeit University," *Times of Israel*, May 18, 2022, https://www.timesofisrael.com/hamas-wins-landslide-victory-in-student-elections-at-flagship-birzeit-university/; and "Palestinian Student Elections Provide Rare Test of Voter Mood," Reuters, May 24, 2023, https://www.reuters.com/world/middle-east/palestinian-student-elections-provide-rare-test-voter-mood-2023-05-24/.
40. Khaled Abu Toameh, "Bir Zeit University Bans 'Paramilitary' Rally, Sparking Student Protests," *Jerusalem Post*, December 11, 2019, https://www.jpost.com/israel-news/bir-zeit-university-bans-paramilitary-rally-sparking-student-protests-610643.
41. Abbie Cheeseman, Lior Soroka, and Gerry Shih, "Gunmen Kill 6 in Shooting Attack at Jerusalem Bus Stop, Police Say," *Washington Post*, September 8, 2025, https://www.washingtonpost.com/world/2025/09/08/jerusalem-bus-shooting-israel/.
42. Gino DeAngelis, "Supporters of Palestine, Israel Protest at Brown Commencement," ABC News, https://www.abc6.com/supporters-of-palestine-israel-protest-at-brown-commencement/.
43. The White House, "Fact Sheet: President Donald J. Trump Secures Major Settlement with Brown University," July 30, 2025, https://www.whitehouse.gov/fact-sheets/2025/07/fact-sheet-president-donald-j-trump-secures-major-settlement-with-brown-university/.
44. U.S. House Committee on Education and the Workforce, *Antisemitism*.
45. U.S. House Committee on Education and the Workforce, "Interview of: Michael Harry Schill," August 5, 2025, https://edworkforce.house.gov/uploadedfiles/edworkforce_final_transcript_aug_5_2025_redacted.pdf.
46. Northwestern University, "Agreement on Deering Meadow," 2024, https://www.northwestern.edu/leadership-notes/2024/agreement-on-deering-meadow.pdf.

47. "Live: Pro-Palestinian Demonstrators Continue to Push for Divestment on Deering Meadow Following Agreement," *Daily Northwestern*, May 3, 2024, https://dailynorthwestern.com/2024/04/25/campus/live-pro-palestinian-student-activists-set-up-encampment-on-deering-meadow/.
48. Jacob Wendler and Avani Kalra, "Administrators, Student Demonstrators Reach Agreement to End Encampment on Deering Meadow," *Daily Northwestern*, April 29, 2024, https://dailynorthwestern.com/2024/04/29/campus/breaking-administrators-student-demonstrators-reach-agreement-to-end-encampment/.
49. U.S. House Committee on Education and the Workforce, *Antisemitism*.
50. Nineth Kanieski Koso, "Q&A: Visiting Pro. Mkhaimar Abusada Talks Growing Up in Gaza, Teaching at Northwestern," *Daily Northwestern*, May 5, 2025, https://dailynorthwestern.com/2025/05/05/campus/qa-visiting-prof-mkhaimar-abusada-talks-growing-up-in-gaza-teaching-at-northwestern/.
51. NGO Monitor, "Palestinian Center for Human Rights (PCHR)," February 10, 2025, https://ngo-monitor.org/ngos/palestinian_center_for_human_rights_pchr_/.
52. Jessica Costescu, "Meet the Professor Northwestern Hired as Part of Deal with Student Radicals," *Washington Free Beacon*, May 27, 2025, https://freebeacon.com/campus/meet-the-professor-northwestern-hired-as-part-of-deal-with-student-radicals/.
53. Scott Hwang, "Highlights from The Daily's Spring 2025 Campus Poll: AI, Campus Antisemitism, Long-Distance Relationships," *Daily Northwestern*, May 7, 2025, https://dailynorthwestern.com/2025/05/07/campus/s25-poll/.
54. *Gartenberg v. The Cooper Union for the Advancement of Science and Art*, 24 Civ. 2669 (JPC) (S.D.N.Y.) (Opinion and Order, filed February 5, 2025), https://www.nysd.uscourts.gov/sites/default/files/2025-02/24cv2669%20Opinion%20and%20Order.pdf.
55. Jacob Khalili, "Testimony Before the U.S. House Committee on Education and the Workforce," February 29, 2024, https://edworkforce.house.gov/uploadedfiles/jacob_khalili_testimony.pdf.
56. MIT Coalition Against Apartheid, "Joint Statement on the Current Situation in Palestine," October 8, 2023, https://docs.google.com/document/d/1TYVBSuqOj_lAG0SSb21ff0ZoIrnQcsd2TNswIXpd7iI/edit?tab=t.0.
57. Matthew Handel, Yevgeniya Nusinovich, and Lori Ullman, "CAA Suspension Must Be Made Permanent," *The Tech*, March 21, 2024, https://thetech.com/2024/03/21/mit-jaa-suspend-caa.
58. "Update on the Events of November 9," Office of the President, MIT, November 14, 2023, https://president.mit.edu/updates/update-events-november-9.
59. Sally Kornbluth, "Dear members of the MIT community," November 10, 2023, https://inj9.mjt.lu/nl3/5guo3-ydhytxrZHgwY-Dvw?m=AWMAACqy5C0AAcrtEZAAAJDyfPsAAAAAGqoAJdFPAAiQzwBlTaRfOevmG8h2SBit3dw1DtYOyQAIIWc&b=5f368de0&e=7042b894&x=SdNG8TSOG-mah9nHncOGOg.

60. SZH (@StopZionistHate), "A Zionist extremist physically assaults a woman and multiple others during an anti-war protest at MIT," X, November 10, 2023, 7:30 p.m., https://x.com/StopZionistHate/status/1723136107905208681.
61. United States Holocaust Memorial Museum, "Kristallnacht," *Holocaust Encyclopedia*, https://encyclopedia.ushmm.org/content/en/article/kristallnacht.
62. Retsef Levi (@RetsefL), "Now on @MIT campus!," X, March 2, 2024, 4:54 p.m., https://x.com/RetsefL/status/1764046561640640518.
63. Talia Khan (@realtaliakhan), "Terrorist support on @MIT campus," X, March 20, 2024, 8:15 a.m., https://x.com/realtaliakhan/status/1770423993398427742.
64. Stu Smith (@thestustustudio), "BREAKING: Students at MIT, Emerson, and Tufts University have set up encampments," X, April 21, 2024, 11:52 p.m., https://x.com/thestustustudio/status/1782256107563446476.
65. Sally Kornbluth, "Rejecting Antisemitism," August 28, 2024, https://president.mit.edu/writing-speeches/rejecting-antisemitism.
66. Sally Kornbluth, "Actions Out of Bounds in Our Community," December 6, 2024, https://orgchart.mit.edu/letters/actions-out-bounds-our-community.
67. Ellie Montemayor, "NOTICE: Retraction of Vol. 144 Issue 18 Guest Opinion Piece," *The Tech*, December 12, 2024, https://thetech.com/2024/12/12/notice-vol-144-n18-retraction.
68. Steve McGuire (@sfmcguire79), "BREAKING: Direct Action Movement for Palestinian Liberation (DAMPL) vandalized an MIT professor's lab," X, July 6, 2025, 10:54 p.m., https://x.com/sfmcguire79/status/1942054531459613056.
69. Sally Kornbluth, "Deeply Troubling Campus Incident," July 8, 2025, https://president.mit.edu/writing-speeches/deeply-troubling-campus-incident.
70. Sera Congi, "Member of Pro-Palestinian Group Arrested After Massachusetts State House Gate, Steps Vandalized with Paint," WCVB5, August 11, 2025, https://www.wcvb.com/article/vandalism-paint-massachusetts-state-house-in-boston-arrest/65652381.
71. Sally Kornbluth, "Campus Incidents," September 12, 2025, https://president.mit.edu/writing-speeches/campus-incidents.
72. Ronney Reyes, "Cornell University Official Slammed for Disturbing Posts Calling Hamas Terror Attacks a 'Resistance,'" *New York Post*, October 10, 2023, https://nypost.com/2023/10/10/cornell-diversity-and-inclusion-director-slammed-for-tone-deaf-posts-on-israel-hamas-war/.
73. Quinn, "Cornell Professor 'Exhilarated' by Hamas Attack Is Back Teaching."
74. U.S. Department of Justice, "Former Cornell Student Sentenced for Posting Online Threats Against Jewish Students on Campus," August 12, 2024, https://www.justice.gov/archives/opa/pr/former-cornell-student-sentenced-posting-online-threats-against-jewish-students-campus.
75. Sofia Rubinson, Jonathan Mong, Gabriel Munoz, Kate Sanders, and Evan Liberman, "Pro-Palestinian Demonstrators Occupy Campus Buildings, Stage Mock Trial of

President Pollack," *Cornell Daily Sun*, December 1, 2023, https://www.cornellsun.com/article/2023/12/live-coalition-for-mutual-liberation-stages-mock-trial-of-president-pollack.

76. Benjamin Leynse, "Amid Encampment, Day Hall Occupation's 22 Arrested Student Protestors Navigate Potential Consequences of Re-Arrest," *Cornell Daily Sun*, April 27, 2024, https://www.cornellsun.com/article/2024/04/amid-encampment-day-hall-occupations-22-arrested-student-protestors-navigate-potential-consequences-of-re-arrest.
77. Matt Butler, "Cornell Encampment Protest Ends After 18 Days," *Ithaca Voice*, May 14, 2024, https://ithacavoice.org/2024/05/cornell-encampment-protest-ends-after-18-days/.
78. "Slope Day Concert," Cornell University, April 23, 2025, https://statements.cornell.edu/2025/20250423-slope-day-concert.cfm.
79. "Chairman Smith: Elite Universities Failing to Protect Jewish Students Calls into Question Their Tax-Exempt Status," U.S. House Committee on Ways & Means, January 10, 2024, https://waysandmeans.house.gov/2024/01/10/chairman-smith-elite-universities-failing-to-protect-jewish-students-calls-into-question-their-tax-exempt-status/.
80. Julia Senzon and Anushka Shorewala, "BREAKING: President Pollack to Retire After Seven Years of Leadership," *Cornell Daily Sun*, May 9, 2024, https://www.cornellsun.com/article/2024/05/breaking-president-pollack-to-retire-after-seven-years-of-leadership.
81. U.S. Department of Education, "U.S. Department of Education's Office for Civil Rights Sends Letters to 60 Universities Under Investigation for Antisemitic Discrimination and Harassment," March 10, 2025, https://www.ed.gov/about/news/press-release/us-department-of-educations-office-civil-rights-sends-letters-60-universities-under-investigation-antisemitic-discrimination-and-harassment.
82. "The United States Announces Agreement with Cornell University," U.S. Department of Justice, November 7, 2025, https://www.justice.gov/opa/pr/united-states-announces-agreement-cornell-university.

CHAPTER 7: WHAT WENT WRONG?

1. Eric Kaufmann, "Academic Freedom in Crisis: Punishment, Political Discrimination, and Self-Censorship," Center for the Study of Partisanship and Ideology, March 1, 2021, https://www.cspicenter.com/p/academic-freedom-in-crisis-punishment.
2. Nathan Honeycutt, "Silence in the Classroom: The 2024 FIRE Faculty Survey Report," Foundation for Individual Rights in Education, 2024, https://www.thefire.org/research-learn/silence-classroom-2024-fire-faculty-survey-report.

3. Douglas Belkin and Sara Randazzo, "Internal Harvard Report Criticizes School's Response to Antisemitism," *Wall Street Journal*, April 29, 2025, https://www.wsj.com/us-news/education/harvard-report-antisemitism-trump-3bfd4a2d.
4. Mathilda Heller, "UC Berkeley Advertises Lit Course Which Praises Hamas as a 'Revolutionary Resistance Force,'" *Jerusalem Post*, November 17, 2024, https://www.msn.com/en-in/news/Hindi-Lifestyle/uc-berkeley-advertises-lit-course-which-praises-hamas-as-a-revolutionary-resistance-force/ar-AA1ufdxJ.
5. Shiri Moshe, "Book Accusing Israel of Sparing Palestinian Lives 'In Order to Control Them' Wins Women's Studies Award," *Algemeiner*, September 12, 2018, https://www.algemeiner.com/2018/09/12/book-accusing-israel-of-sparing-palestinian-lives-in-order-to-control-them-wins-womens-studies-award/.
6. Adam Kissel, Rachel Alexander Cambre, and Madison Marino Doan, *Slacking: A Guide to Ivy League Miseducation* (New York: Encounter Books, 2025).
7. Office of the Registrar, Princeton University, "Black + Queer in Leather: Black Leather/BDSM Material Culture," 2022, https://registrar.princeton.edu/course-offerings/course-details?courseid=016732&term=1234.
8. Jenna A. Robinson, "A Win for Syllabus Transparency," James G. Martin Center for Academic Renewal, September 4, 2025, https://jamesgmartin.center/2025/09/a-win-for-syllabus-transparency/.
9. Mary Ellen Flannery, "The Union Boom in Higher Education!," National Education Association, September 18, 2024, https://www.nea.org/nea-today/all-news-articles/union-boom-higher-education.
10. George Leef, "CUNY Faculty Take On Their Union," January 19, 2024, https://jamesgmartin.center/2024/01/cuny-faculty-take-on-their-union/.
11. Avraham Goldstein, "I'm Stuck with an Anti-Semitic Labor Union," *Wall Street Journal*, January 20, 2022, https://www.wsj.com/opinion/im-stuck-anti-semitic-semitism-public-labor-union-intimidation-dues-cuny-city-university-new-york-janus-11642714137.
12. Wilfred Reilly, "What Is Critical Race Theory, Really?," *City Journal*, October 13, 2021, https://www.city-journal.org/article/what-is-critical-race-theory-really.
13. Ankita Jagdeep et al., "Instructing Animosity: How DEI Pedagogy Produces the Hostile Attribution Bias," Network Contagion Research Institute, November 13, 2024, https://networkcontagion.us/wp-content/uploads/Instructing-Animosity_11.13.24.pdf.
14. Timothy K. Minella, "The University of Michigan Went All In on DEI. The Results Were Disastrous," *National Review*, October 25, 2024, https://www.nationalreview.com/2024/10/the-university-of-michigan-went-all-in-on-dei-the-results-were-disastrous/.
15. Renu Mukherjee, "Are Universities Following the Supreme Court's Affirmative-Action Ban?," *City Journal*, March 10, 2025, https://www.city-journal.org/article/universities-supreme-court-affirmative-action-racial-preferences.

16. Robert VerBruggen, "Test Score Requirements Can Help Poor Students Most," *City Journal*, January 28, 2025, https://www.city-journal.org/article/test-optional-admissions-underprivileged-students-dartmouth.
17. Sarah Wood, "Some Colleges Are Requiring Test Scores Again: What It Means for Applicants," *U.S. News & World Report*, May 13, 2024, https://www.usnews.com/education/best-colleges/applying/articles/some-colleges-are-requiring-test-scores-again-what-it-means-for-applicants.
18. Abigail Anthony, "Dozens of Universities Rebranded DEI Offices After Trump Administration Crackdown," *National Review*, April 16, 2025, https://www.nationalreview.com/news/dozens-of-universities-rebranded-dei-offices-after-trump-administration-crackdown/.
19. Abigail Anthony, "'The Four I's of Oppression': Inside DEI Training for Princeton's Dorm Supervisors," *National Review*, August 29, 2025, https://www.nationalreview.com/news/the-four-is-of-oppression-inside-dei-training-for-princetons-dorm-supervisors/.
20. Haley Strack, "Northwestern University Anti-Discrimination Training Criticized as Biased," *National Review*, January 16, 2025, https://www.nationalreview.com/corner/northwestern-university-anti-discrimination-training-criticized-as-biased/.
21. Jeanne Batalova, "International Students in the United States," Migration Policy Institute, July 24, 2025, https://www.migrationpolicy.org/article/international-students-united-states.
22. Emily Badger et al., "These Are the U.S. Universities Most Dependent on International Students," *New York Times*, May 23, 2025, https://www.nytimes.com/2025/05/23/upshot/harvard-trump-international-students.html.
23. Shen Lu, Liyan Qi, and Ming Li, "Targeting Chinese Students Threatens the Bottom Line at American Universities," *Wall Street Journal*, May 29, 2025, https://www.wsj.com/us-news/education/targeting-chinese-students-threatens-the-bottom-line-at-american-universities-c64a89b5.
24. Frannie Block and Maya Sulkin, "Qatar and China Are Pouring Billions into Elite American Universities," *Free Press*, April 27, 2025, https://www.thefp.com/p/explosion-in-foreign-funding-for-american-universities.
25. U.S. Department of State, "'Confucius Institute U.S. Center' Designation as a Foreign Mission," August 13, 2020, https:/2017-2021.state.gov/confucius-institute-u-s-center-designation-as-a-foreign-mission/.
26. Lee Edwards, "Confucius Institutes: China's Trojan Horse," Heritage Foundation, May 27, 2021, https://www.heritage.org/homeland-security/commentary/confucius-institutes-chinas-trojan-horse.
27. "How Many Confucius Institutes Are in the United States?," National Association of Scholars, June 22, 2023, https://www.nas.org/blogs/article/how_many_confucius_institutes_are_in_the_united_states.

28. "Northwestern Qatar University: Qatar's Multimillion-Dollar Plan to Influence American Media," Canary Mission, February 2022, https://canarymission.org/campaign/Northwestern_Qatar_University.
29. Michael Bass et al., "The Corruption of the American Mind: How Foreign Funding in U.S. Higher Education by Authoritarian Regimes, Widely Undisclosed, Predicts Erosion of Democratic Norms and Antisemitic Incidents on Campus," Network Contagion Research Institute, November 6, 2023, https://networkcontagion.us/reports/11-6-23-the-corruption-of-the-american-mind/.
30. Jay Greene, Adam Kissel, and Lindsey Burke, "Protecting American Universities from Undue Foreign Influence," Heritage Foundation, February 13, 2024, https://www.heritage.org/education/report/protecting-american-universities-undue-foreign-influence.
31. Pew Research Center, "Social Media and News Fact Sheet," September 25, 2025, https://www.pewresearch.org/journalism/fact-sheet/social-media-and-news-fact-sheet/.
32. Gabriel Weimann and Natalie Masri, "TikTok's Spiral of Antisemitism," *Journalism and Media* 2, no. 4: 697–708, https://doi.org/10.3390/journalmedia2040041.
33. Anti-Defamation League Center for Technology and Society, "Sliding Through: Spreading Antisemitism on TikTok by Exploiting Moderation Gaps," November 20, 2023, https://www.adl.org/resources/article/sliding-through-spreading-antisemitism-tiktok-exploiting-moderation-gaps.
34. Israel Kasnett, "How China and Qatar Wage War on Israel's Legitimacy," Jewish News Syndicate, September 19, 2025, https://www.jns.org/how-china-and-qatar-wage-war-on-israels-legitimacy/.
35. Drew Harwell and Victoria Bisset, "How Osama bin Laden's 'Letter to America' Reached Millions Online," *Washington Post*, November 16, 2023, https://www.washingtonpost.com/style/2023/11/16/guardian-osama-bin-laden-letter-to-america/.
36. Tom Hanson et al., "Teens Struggle to Identify Misinformation about Israel-Hamas Conflict—the World's Second 'Social Media War,'" CBS News, December 19, 2023, https://www.cbsnews.com/news/israel-hamas-misinformation-social-media-war/.
37. Eve Barlow, "The Social Media Pogrom," *Tablet*, May 25, 2021, https://www.tabletmag.com/sections/news/articles/the-social-media-pogrom.
38. Anti-Defamation League Center for Technology and Society, "Online Antisemitism Increased After Hamas Attack," November 9, 2023, https://www.adl.org/resources/article/online-antisemitism-increased-after-hamas-attack.
39. Anti-Defamation League Center for Technology and Society, "Online Hate and Harassment: The American Experience 2024," https://www.adl.org/resources/report/online-hate-and-harassment-american-experience-2024.

40. American Jewish Committee, "The State of Antisemitism in America 2024," 2024, https://www.ajc.org/AntisemitismReport2024.
41. American Jewish Committee, "The State of Antisemitism in America 2023: AJC's Survey of American Jews," 2023, https://www.ajc.org/AntisemitismReport2023/AmericanJews.
42. Leonard Saxe, "Why Campus Antisemitism Matters," *Tablet*, February 5, 2024, https://www.tabletmag.com/sections/news/articles/why-campus-antisemitism-matters.
43. National SJP, "National Students for Justice in Palestine," https://www.nationalsjp.org/.
44. NGO Monitor, "Students for Justice in Palestine (SJP)," February 27, 2025, https://ngo-monitor.org/ngos/students-for-justice-in-palestine-sjp/.
45. Collin Anderson, "'Death to Jews': Inside the Home of 2 SJP Leaders at George Mason University, Police Find Guns, Ammo, and Terrorist Flags," *Washington Free Beacon*, December 9, 2024, https://freebeacon.com/campus/death-to-jews-inside-the-home-of-2-sjp-leaders-at-george-mason-university-police-find-guns-ammo-and-terrorist-flags/.
46. U.S. Senate Committee on Health, Education, Labor, and Pensions, "Letter to Dr. Hatem Bazian," March 26, 2025, https://www.help.senate.gov/imo/media/doc/2025-03-26_bc_to_hatem_bazian_003pdf.pdf.
47. U.S. House Committee on Oversight and Accountability, "Letter to National Students for Justice in Palestine," May 29, 2024, https://oversight.house.gov/wp-content/uploads/2024/05/Letter-to-National-SJP-5.29.24.pdf.
48. U.S. Senate Committee on Health, Education, Labor, and Pensions, "Letter to Dr. Hatem Bazian."
49. Neetu Arnold, "Shadows of Influence: Uncovering Hidden Foreign Funds to American Universities," September 29, 2024, https://www.nas.org/reports/shadows-of-influence/full-report.
50. The White House, "Transparency Regarding Foreign Influence at American Universities," April 23, 2025, https://www.whitehouse.gov/presidential-actions/2025/04/transparency-regarding-foreign-influence-at-american-universities/.
51. Bill Ackman, "Bill Ackman: How to Fix Harvard," *Free Press*, January 3, 2024, https://www.thefp.com/p/bill-ackman-how-to-fix-harvard.
52. "A Vision for a New Future of the University of Pennsylvania," December 2023, https://www.pennforward.com/.
53. Jason Cohn, "How Much Federal Funding Do Colleges and Universities Receive?," Urban Institute, May 8, 2025, https://www.urban.org/urban-wire/how-much-federal-funding-do-colleges-and-universities-receive.
54. National Education Association, "State Funding Update: The Fiscal and Political Crossroads Facing Public Higher Education," September 12, 2025, https://www.nea.org/resource-library/higher-ed-state-funding-report.

CHAPTER 8: HOW WE FIX IT

1. “Letter from Thomas Jefferson to John Adams,” August 1, 1816, Library of Congress, https://www.loc.gov/item/mtjbib022524/.
2. Sian Leah Beilock, “Saving the Idea of the University,” *Atlantic*, September 14, 2024, https://www.theatlantic.com/ideas/archive/2024/09/saving-idea-university-dartmouth/679790/.
3. Talia Elkin, “Jewish Professors Grapple with Shifting Roles on Campus,” *Tablet*, September 20, 2024, https://www.tabletmag.com/sections/community/articles/jewish-professors-grapple-shifts-campus-antisemitism.
4. Vivienne Serret, “UF Kicks Arrested Pro-Palestinian Protesters Out of School for Up to 4 Years,” WUFT, July 9, 2024, https://www.wuft.org/fresh-take-florida/2024-07-09/uf-kicks-arrested-pro-palestinian-protesters-out-of-school-for-up-to-4-years.
5. Vivienne Serret, “Three More Student Protesters Arrested at UF Accept Plea Deals in Criminal Cases,” WUFT, September 11, 2024, https://www.wuft.org/fresh-take-florida/2024-09-11/three-more-student-protesters-arrested-at-uf-accept-plea-deals-in-criminal-cases.
6. Anti-Defamation League, “University of Florida,” March 3, 2025, https://www.adl.org/campus-antisemitism-report-card/university-florida.
7. Kayla Bartsch, “Ben Sasse Made Enemies Within the University of Florida Because He Followed State Law,” *National Review*, February 17, 2025, https://www.nationalreview.com/2025/02/ben-sasse-made-enemies-within-the-university-of-florida-because-he-followed-state-law/.
8. Ryan Quinn, “Florida Law Threatens to Defund, Disband Higher Ed Unions,” *Inside Higher Ed*, March 21, 2024, https://www.insidehighered.com/news/faculty-issues/labor-unionization/2024/03/21/florida-law-threatens-defund-disband-higher-ed.
9. Vanderbilt University, “Vanderbilt’s Commitment to Free Expression,” https://www.vanderbilt.edu/dialogue-vanderbilt/free-expression/; and Lamar Alexander, “Vanderbilt’s Bold Stand for ‘Neutrality,’” *Wall Street Journal*, May 15, 2023, https://www.wsj.com/us-news/at-vandy-speech-is-dandy-principled-neutrality-roe-diermeier-discourse-college-university-e6a741f0.
10. Neetu Arnold, “Vanderbilt University’s Chancellor Sees the Problem—Can He Find a Solution?,” *City Journal*, October 2, 2025, https://www.city-journal.org/article/vanderbilt-university-chancellor-daniel-diermeier.
11. Tasfia Alam et al., “Kirkland Hall Sit-In and Encampment Influenced Last Semester’s Wave of Pro-Palestine Protests,” *Vanderbilt Hustler*, September 2, 2024, https://vanderbilthustler.com/2024/09/02/how-vanderbilts-kirkland-hall-sit-in-and-encampment-influenced-last-semesters-wave-of-pro-palestine-protests/#vandy-encampment.
12. Boards of Vanderbilt University and Washington University in St. Louis, “Statement of Principles,” 2024, https://higheredstatementofprinciples.com/.

13. Daniel Diermeier and Andrew D. Martin, "Universities Must Reject Creeping Politicization," *Chronicle of Higher Education*, February 18, 2025, https://www.chronicle.com/article/universities-must-reject-creeping-politicization.
14. Bryan Anderson, "Tensions Rise at U.N.C. Chapel Hill After Dozens of Pro-Palestinian Demonstrators Are Detained," *New York Times*, April 30, 2024, https://www.nytimes.com/2024/04/30/nyregion/unc-chapel-hill-protests.html.
15. "DOJ, HHS, and GSA Announce Initial Cancelation of Grants and Contracts to Columbia University Worth $400 Million," U.S. Department of Education, March 7, 2025, https://www.ed.gov/about/news/press-release/doj-hhs-ed-and-gsa-announce-initial-cancelation-of-grants-and-contracts-columbia-university-worth-400-million.
16. U.S. Department of Education, "Letter to Dr. Alan M. Garber."
17. Ira Porter, "Universities Are Paying the US Millions of Dollars. Where Will the Money Go?," *Christian Science Monitor*, September 23, 2025, https://www.csmonitor.com/USA/Education/2025/0923/universities-trump-administration-settlements.
18. Emily Hallas, "White House Offers Funding Advantage to Colleges that Sign 'Compact for Academic Excellence,'" *Washington Examiner*, October 2, 2025, https://www.washingtonexaminer.com/policy/education/3833857/white-house-funding-advantage-colleges-sign-compact-for-academic-excellence/.
19. Marc Rowan, "Academia Is Broken. Trump's University 'Compact' Can Help Fix It," *New York Times*, October 10, 2025, https://www.nytimes.com/2025/10/10/opinion/trump-compact-universities-rowan.html.
20. Danielle Allen, "Why I'm Excited About the White House's Proposal for a Higher Ed Compact," October 6, 2025, https://ash.harvard.edu/articles/why-im-excited-about-the-white-houses-proposal-for-a-higher-ed-compact/.
21. Ana Faguy, "US State Department Revokes 6,000 Student Visas," BBC News, August 18, 2025, https://www.bbc.com/news/articles/cz93vznxd07o.
22. Rose Horowitch, "College-Aged Jews Are Heading South," *Atlantic*, August 26, 2025, https://www.theatlantic.com/ideas/archive/2025/08/jewish-college-ivy-league-south/684006/.
23. Denise Attaway, "Clemson-Israeli Universities Partnership Will Advance Agriculture," Clemson News, March 16, 2025, https://news.clemson.edu/clemson-israeli-universities-partnership-will-advance-agriculture/.
24. Hoover Institution, https://www.hoover.org/.
25. James Madison Program in American Ideals and Institutions, https://jmp.princeton.edu/.
26. University of Austin, "Our Principles," https://www.uaustin.org/our-principles.
27. University of Austin, "Forbidden Courses," https://www.uaustin.org/forbidden-courses.

28. Muskaan Arshad, "These Gen Z and Millennial Founders Dropped Out of College, Took $200,000 from Peter Thiel, and Have Now Built Companies Worth Over $100 Billion," *Fortune*, August 16, 2025, https://fortune.com/2025/08/16/gen-z-millennial-founders-college-dropout-entrepreneurs-peter-thiel-fellowship/.